On a SINGLE
STACK
STEAMER

On a SINGLE STACK STEAMER

Plying Northwest Waters

Christian Parker

OLYMPIC DISPATCH PUBLISHING

Copyright ©2011, Christian Parker

2nd edition, revised.

Published by Olympic Dispatch
Chimacum, Washington.

ISBN-10: 0-9815838-5-7
ISBN-13: 978-0-9815838-5-3

Library of Congress Control Number: 2011919325

Printed in the United States of America

Photographs and illustrations are from the author's collection unless otherwise credited.

ACKNOWLEDGEMENTS

The majority of this work is taken from a family history compiled in the 1990s.

I owe a special debt of gratitude to my Norwegian letter translators, Barbro Carter of Chimacum, Washington, and her cousin and dear friend of the author Karin Nordström, way up in the north of Sweden at Piteå.

Bill Dennison provided editorial services.

A special thank you should be given to the helpful staffs over the years of the Puget Sound Maritime Historical Society, down in the basement of the Museum of History and Industry. Thank you to the staff of the Jefferson County Historical Society. The University of Washington Libraries were an invaluable asset in compiling this book. Thank you to Sandra at the Alaska State Archives for help with the Alaska Steam collection.

Lastly, and firstly, the author would like to acknowledge the Creator of all things, and He who makes all good things possible. Let this work be dedicated to His purpose.

PREFACE TO THE 2ND EDITION

I had become interested in genealogy in the 90s, and I wrote a family history. It had been more than a decade since a serious look had been given to revision. In 2009 I was embroiled in revising this history, when my father Charles Parker, jr. died. It was an untimely death and emotions ran the gamut.

I had been wanting for some time to extract a Pacific Northwest nautical story out of the history, for a commercial product. Having written the book *The Care and Maintenance of Heavy Jets* the previous year, I viewed this book as a prequel to that work, and thought it important.

In 2011, with a clearer head, I decided that I had not given enough attention to the story of the American Merchant Marine, and its lessons for us today. So, here I have endeavored to give a fuller story of that significance, while trying to achieve a pleasantly illustrated book to grace your coffee table.

Regards,

Christian Parker

CONTENTS

INTRODUCTION

In *The Story of the American Merchant Marine* (1910) by John R. Spears, we learn that America had grown a large and prosperous Merchant Marine by the decades preceding the American Civil War. This was in the age of sail, and it was the American Clipper Ships that figured so prominently, the American sailor being among the finest in the world in that era. The American Merchant Marine had achieved this by enterprise, daring, and grit—and little else. By contrast, the governments of Europe sought to help their merchant marines by subsidies, politics and military interventions. The War of 1812 had been started over the Merchant Marine.

The sail was giving way to the steam engine in this era, however, and America started out behind England in the trans-Atlantic steamship game...in these last decades before the Civil War. To promote the new American steamship lines, Congress adopted a policy of subsidies to give the industry a boost—and in so doing created *unhealthy* steamship lines that were doomed to fail...and did. Then came the ruinous Civil War...

The first white settlers to arrive on Puget Sound were the Denny party. They landed at Alki Beach, across from what is now downtown Seattle, in 1851. Members of this party were to be prominent in the founding, and raising, of Seattle over the next several decades. Though they labored much, Seattle and vicinity remained a small mill town like the other settlements on Puget Sound. The city of Seattle had the most vision conscious entrepreneurs however, and by the 1880s started to grow.

Among the many new immigrants to the state of Washington would be a large number of people from Scandinavia. There was a large migration of Scandinavians during the later part of the nineteenth century to the United States. This of course coincided with the rise of settlement in Washington State. The Scandinavians no doubt had heard how much the scenery of western Washington was like their own countryside. Washington is wooded, mountainous, and has many inland waterways and bays; making the state similar to the mountains and fjords of Norway. Consequently, many of the original homesteads in Washington were settled by Scandinavians, and Scandinavian names are very common in western

Washington; such as the city of Poulsbo, known as a Little Norway.

One of the reasons for people coming to the Northwest was the marine trades. Ships were the principle means of travel in the northwest in the early days. Many small steamers plied the waters of Puget Sound. Still larger steamers made regular trips to Alaskan waters, and up and down the west coast.

In addition to commercial traffic, the U.S. government was making its presence known in the North Pacific. The United States Revenue Cutter Service, forerunner of the Coast Guard, had established a base in Port Townsend and in 1892 sent out the first Bearing Sea Patrol. In addition, the government was charting all the U.S. waters in the Pacific, as well as the Atlantic. This fleet was called the Coast and Geodetic Survey Service. Many young mariners would get their sea legs in this service, others would make it a career.

In the 1890s a hardy Norwegian named Adolf Loken found his way to Puget Sound with the Revenue Cutter *Grant.*

In the late 1800s the railroads were looking to have a terminus at one of the Washington cities: Olympia, Tacoma, Seattle, one of the more northerly townsites, or maybe even Port Townsend. The Northern Pacific Railroad first went to Tacoma in 1873, but that year also brought a depression. Tacoma grew and seemed to be the favored city. But thanks to a more stable economy, Seattle grew anyway. Seattle was still a viable seaport, and it had many industries of its own. These things would be very useful to a railroad terminus, and so the incentive was there. The Great Northern Railroad reached Seattle in 1893, but that year also saw the beginning of a depression. Then in 1897 the Klondike gold rush up in Alaska did for Seattle what the California gold rush of '49 did for San Francisco. By 1905 the Great Northern Railroad had its terminal built on the Seattle waterfront, and was doing a thriving business.

For one reason or another, the mariners who had traveled to the new city of Seattle had found something they liked. The mild climate, the opportunities of the growing city, the cheap land. They were not alone. In 1900 the population of Seattle was 80,671, in 1910 in was 237,174. In 1880 it had been 3,553!

For one young Bostonian, Benjamin Parker, finding the woman that was to be his wife made Seattle seem a nice place to nest. These were the type of people that were our "founding fathers." They represented the first wave of settlers to the Northwest, making them truly founding fathers. Seattle is a product of the twentieth century. When Ben first came to the city it was little more than a lumber mill town, and scarcely a century later Seattle is a metropolis with sky scrapers, heavy industry, and a world recognized culture all it's own. Cities that have been famous for thousands of years are not half as large or affluent. Seattle is truly a renaissance city.

When Benjamin Poole Parker had graduated from his maritime school, Washington had only been a state for eight years. The Klondike gold rush had been just a year before, and Seattle was still in a league with Port Townsend, that small Victorian city which exists today much as it did then on the Olympic Peninsula. The new Naval Ship Yard at Bremerton, the present day city across the bay from Seattle, was just being built.

The business in the Pacific Northwest was lumber—lumber and ships. In the Northwest there were a few indomitable entrepreneurs who would found businesses to last for decades. One of these was a Scotch Canadian lumberman named Robert Dollar. Coming from a humble Scottish beginning, and after working hard all his life, in 1893 Dollar had purchased his first mill. In 1895 he purchased his first steamer to carry his lumber. Being an early promoter of the Asian market, in the following decades he would build America's largest steamer fleet, with service spanning the Pacific Ocean, and even around-the-world service…

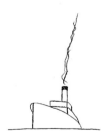

CHAPTER I

The Marine Engineer and the Golden Era of the Steamship

Ships and mariners from the most ancient times were of the greatest importance to the economic world. More than just haulers of cargo, they were also the means by which knowledge of other peoples and cultures were spread.

This great dependence on ships for communication and transport of people over long distances was going to greatly diminish in the later half of the twentieth century. Scores of centuries of tradition were about to change. The age of ships sailing by way of the wind was indeed passing as Benjamin Poole Parker[1] grew up in the eastern United States. The age of the steamship was beginning. The Industrial Revolution brought to the high seas; and the high seas would eventually be tamed as they had never been tamed before.

Before the end of the importance of ships as they had always been known, as we had always depended on them for communication and travel, we would have the golden era of the steamship. Three would-be Seattle men, Adolf Loken, Benjamin Parker, and Charles Parker would have a direct part in this shipping industry; right in the engine rooms that made these new ships different.

When the age of sail had passed, traditionalists lamented the extinction of "real" sailors, claiming that they had been replaced by a few mechanics. True, the job of the ship's master had gotten easier, the skipper could just point the ship in the direction he wanted to go and hold her there until they arrived. He had a steady source of power that didn't rely on the elements. There were no sails to operate and take care of. But replacing sailors up in rigging was a new breed of sailor, the "black gang" of the engine room, so named because of their sometimes "greasy," or "coal dusted" appearance. In charge of this group were the engineering officers, now in many ways the "real" masters of the ship, for they were in charge of the very heart and soul of the ship.

If a man came from a well-heeled family, he might go to a maritime academy to learn his trade. But if a lad was not as fortunate, he would have to work his way up, learn what he could, study the books, and might someday be able to pass the Board of Trade examinations to become a licensed marine officer. This latter process was referred to as "working your way up through the hawsepipe," meaning to climb your way up the anchor chain—a euphemism for doing it the hard way.

Ben Parker's school ship *U.S.S. Enterprise,* of the Massachusetts State Nautical School, was a type of ship first used at the time of the American Civil War. *Enterprise* was a steam sailing ship of 1375 tons. Being a former naval frigate, she first

---

[1] The story of Benjamin is found in Chapter VII, Out of New England.

U.S.S. Enterprise *of the Massachusetts State Nautical School.*

entered the service of the school in October 1892 and began making trans-Atlantic voyages regularly. She was a screw steamship, but in the early days they did not trust steam power much for reliability, so they built these ships as sailing ships with steam propulsion systems incorporated into the sailing ship design. So even though Ben Parker went to learn one of the newest fields at that day in age, marine engineering, he learned this on a sailing ship, and quite likely learned a bit about the lost art of sailing with the wind on a tall ship. *Enterprise* sailed by wind much of the time, winds and seas permitting.

At the heart of a steamship is a steam boiler. It creates steam for use in the engine at enormous pressures. In the early nineteenth century when steamships made their début, there were a number of accidents with steam boilers. Turns out a boiler could be an enormous bomb, with literally enough power to blow the ship up. Hence the phrase "if I give 'er any more,

she's gonna blow!" It was decided that a professional approach to marine engineering would be necessary.

Marine engineering was one of the most "high-technology" fields of the day. Ben would learn advanced mathematics, physics, the complete anatomy of a ship, ship design, mechanical engineering, thermodynamic properties of steam, triple-expansion reciprocating steam engines, advanced machining, AC and DC electric generation and use, refrigeration, the very important science of maintaining steam pressure vessels(boilers), seamanship, fire fighting and first aid. He might have been introduced to the then brand new technology of the steam turbine. The steamships would utilize almost every technology available at the time, and in giant sized doses.

Things like steam may sound simple, but there is a lot of science to controlling steam power plants. It is enough of a big deal, that, even today an engineer of a steam vessel must be government licensed

Benjamin Parker on board **Enterprise.** *Ben is on the left next to telemotor.*

The triple expansion steam engine had three unequally sized dual acting pistons that would extract the steam's energy one piston at a time, starting with the high-pressure piston and moving towards the low-pressure piston. The steam acted on the piston both on the down stroke, and also on the upstroke; thus dual acting. The steam piston engine turned at slow rpm's; from 50 rpm to a maximum of a few hundred rpm, less than the idle speed of a modern car engine. The engine shaft was usually directly connected to the propeller—there was no gearbox or transmission. The engine was reversed by a reversing gear contained within the engine itself. The mechanical connecting rods and crankshaft were exposed and presented a spectacular sight of wildly moving, reciprocating machinery.

An Oiler is an engine room attendant and mechanic. Oilers had to make sure the connecting rod bearings, which were flailing out in the open, did not get too hot(as a result of under lubrication). They checked

them by putting their hand on the moving rod bearings. There was automatic lubrication, but it didn't always keep up. They could squirt some oil on them from their squirt cans if the bearing needed some.

Also in the engine room were a myriad of pumps and various machinery, electricity generation sets, and of course the boilers.

Stokers kept the fire in the boilers "stoked" by shoveling coal into them almost constantly. Occasionally, the boilers had to be cleaned of "clinkers," or hardened chunks of coal residue. This was done with a steel crowbar-like pole. There were usually at least two boilers on a ship of any size, at least one on each side of the ship, forming a "fireroom" in the middle. On large ships, the fire room could be huge, with many stokers laboring away in the 110°+ heat. The stokers, keeping the originally coal fired boilers fed, had a miserable, hellish job. They had to pay the stokers more that the Able Bodied(AB) seamen that were up on the deck because the

Typical three-cylinder reciprocating triple-expansion marine steam engine. Such an engine could be sized anywhere from as tall as a man, to several stories high. This type had been replacing the old compound engines (two-cylinder and double-expansion) used in the mid-1800s.

From this time on, four-cylinder triple-expansion engines would be common also, utilizing two intermediate pistons, and even quadruple-expansion engines.

USS Enterprise had a compound engine that could drive her at five knots. After she was re-boiled in 1896, she could make eight knots.

4800 hp engines of the type used in the steamship **Minnesota,** built in 1903. Note the figure of the man in between, and the catwalk half way up the engine for access to the upper end of the connecting rods and valve gear.

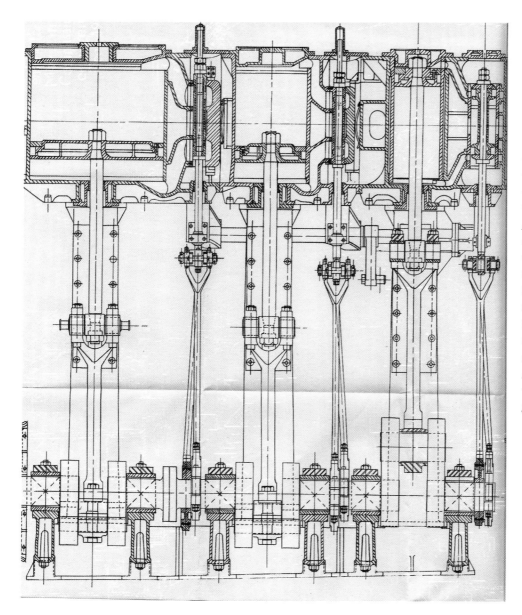

Side view of a marine triple-expansion steam engine. The crankshaft, very similar to an auto crankshaft, is at the bottom, with the main bearings and connecting rod bearings. The three connecting rods in the middle, pistons and cylinders at top. High pressure right, middle, low pressure left. These engines also had a series of valves, also running off the crankshaft, to allow the steam in and out. All these moving parts required vigilant attention by the Oilers. The Engineer had to be vigilant in monitoring the steam pressure.

job was so hard. Later when the ships turned to oil-fired boilers, the low job in the engine room was much better.

In 1896 *Enterprise* was based out of Charlestown Navy Yard. The master of *Enterprise* was Commander J. Giles Eaton and her Chief Engineer was W.P. Winchell, then in October S.H. Leonard. *Enterprise* could handle 110 cadets, in 1896 she had 92. Having begun school operations April 5, 1893, she had graduated her first class of cadets April 1895.

The winter was for classroom study at pier side. The 1896 summer cruise embarked May 23 across the great Atlantic, first dropping anchor at Horta in the Azores, followed by Queenstown in Ireland, Southampton in England, Lisbon in Portugal, Funchal at Madeira, and then back to Boston arriving September 29. On a summer cruise *Enterprise* would visit ports all over the mid-Atlantic islands, Europe and the West Indies.

Graduations took place in April. In 1896 20 cadets graduated from the seamanship class and 17 from the engineering class. Several cadets dropped out or were dismissed.

Wickes Vertical Water Tube Boiler

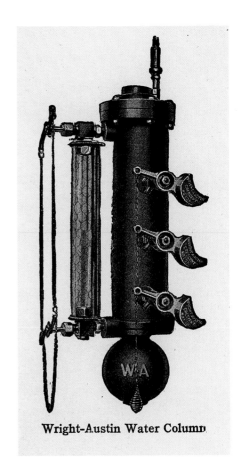

Wright-Austin Water Column

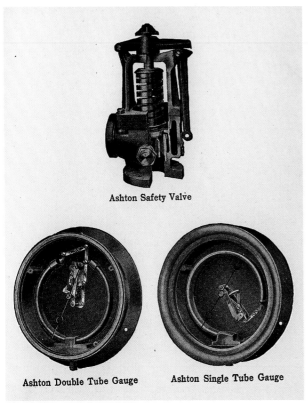

Ashton Safety Valve

Ashton Double Tube Gauge   Ashton Single Tube Gauge

FRONT VIEW—BABCOCK & WILCOX BOILER
Showing Drum Fittings—Patented

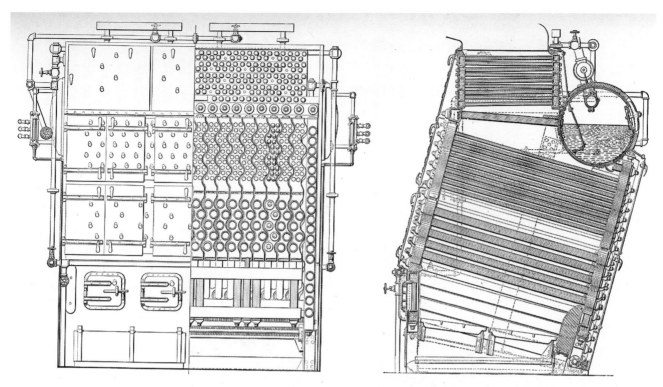

DESIGN OF BABCOCK & WILCOX WATER-TUBE BOILERS FOR LAKE FREIGHT STEAMER
"ZENITH-CITY," 1895—PATENTED

Internal workings of Babcock & Wilcox coal fired water-tube boiler. Coal is shoveled in doors at bottom. Coal fire heats water in angled tubes, which produces steam in vessel at top.

The boiler was the chief reason of the marine engineer's extensive scientific education. The boiler was a potential bomb of enormous proportions, and could literally blow the ship up. The engineer had to inspect and maintain the boiler, and make sure it was not run at too high a pressure.

Most steamships of any size had at least two boilers, and large ships could have ten or more.

The engineers would periodically inspect the boilers for corrosion and burned metal in the steam tubes, loose rivets, cracks in welds, etc. This was a very serious matter, a job for the most senior engineers. The inspection criteria were detailed and scientific.

The boilers and engines worked by the steam cycle. Boilers make the steam, engine uses the steam, spent steam is condensed into water again, and the cycle repeats.

The engineer could calculate fuel consumption of the coal by determining the amount burned on a given square footage of the grate at the bottom of the boiler per hour.

The engineer had to monitor various gauges to make sure everything kept working the way it was supposed to. The engineer was the professional and boss of the engine room, and was responsible for the mechanical functioning of the entire ship. They were responsible for everything, not just the engine itself. Other items they were responsible for were the steering gear and the anchor windlass, the plumbing and hot water, electricity, etc.

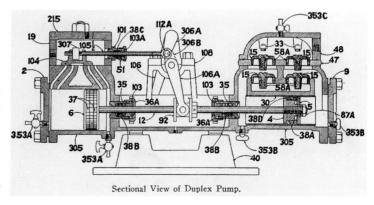

Sectional View of Duplex Pump.

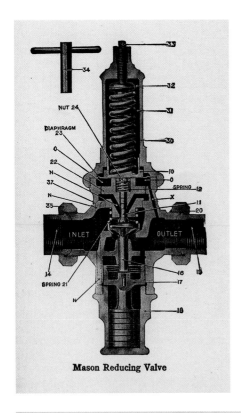

Mason Reducing Valve

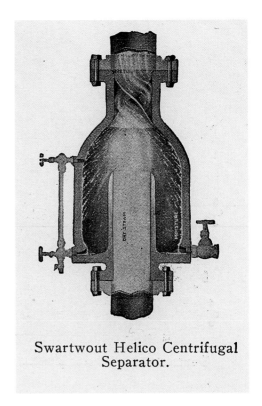

Swartwout Helico Centrifugal Separator.

Shaft Governor. Troy Horizontal Steam Engine

1890's Steamships were marvels of their day, and employed the latest in scientific technology. In the days when people still got around town by horse and buggy, steamships had electric lights, refrigeration to keep food fresh, hot and cold running water, full bathrooms, steam heating throughout, and steady power to speed to your destination without delay.

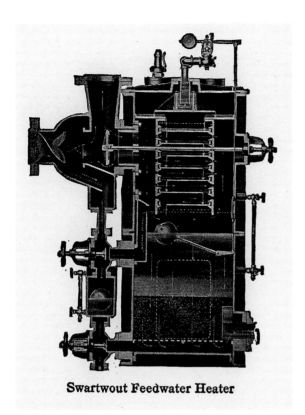

Swartwout Feedwater Heater

Wach's Type E Vertical Engine

FIG. 220.—FOUR-POLE DYNAMO AND ENGINE COMPLETE.

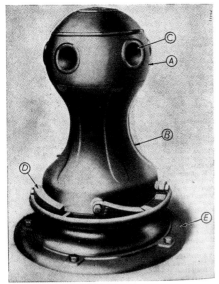

Fig. 39. Hand-powered capstan.

Fig. 38. Chain stoppers as installed.

Fig. 19. Electro-hydraulic gear transmitter unit.
20-30

Fig. 16. Quadrant type steering gear.

In addition to the ship's propulsion machinery, the engineers had to take care of all the ship's other machinery as well.

Facing page: *In the nineteenth century, and well into the twentieth, iron and steel ships were constructed of plates riveted to each other and the substructure. The construction was not unlike that of the metal fuselage of an aeroplane that was to come later. Though "electro-welding" was known in the late 1800s, welded hulls were not common until the 1930s.*

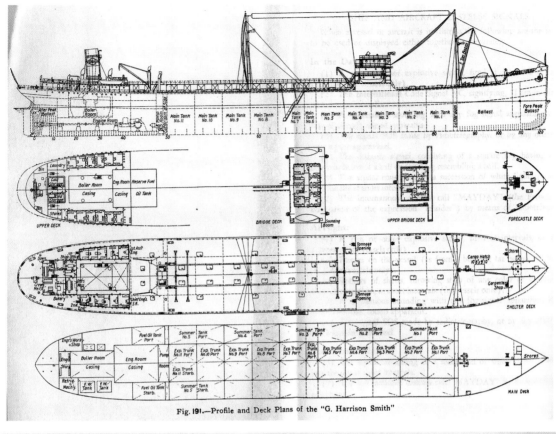

Fig. 191.—Profile and Deck Plans of the "G. Harrison Smith"

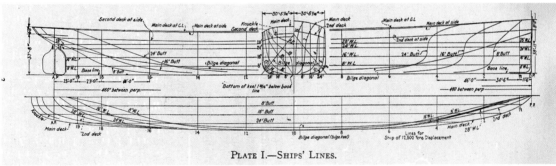

PLATE I.—SHIPS' LINES.

AMERICAN MERCHANT SEAMAN'S MANUAL

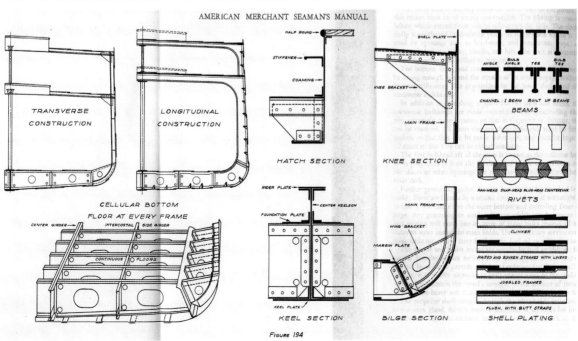

FIGURE 194

From The Steamship Conquest of the World, *1913:*

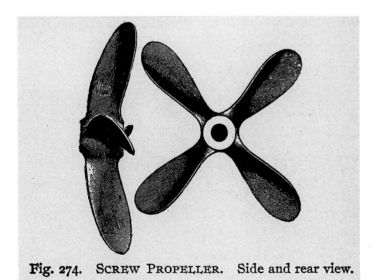

Fig. 274. SCREW PROPELLER. Side and rear view.

"Perhaps the navigator has been unable to catch a glimpse of the sun for days, in order to pick up his bearings, but has been compelled to rely upon "dead reckoning." In making this calculation the mileage indicated upon the patent log—the liner's speedometer—for the previous twelve or twenty-four hours, is compared with the number of revolutions which have been made by the screws during the selfsame period. The engineer knows how far forward his vessel moves with each revolution of the propellers, and then, by making certain allowances for drift by currents, and so on, the position of the ship may be determined fairly accurately."

The Chief Engineer answered only to the Captain, and was of a similar status and pay. The Captain and Chief Engineer were administrators; the Captain oversaw navigation, the disposition of the passengers and cargo, and the "deck gang," which

A young Ben Parker embarking on his career as a marine engineer.

consisted of the Able Bodied Seamen and the Ordinary Seamen, who were led by the First, Second, and Third Mates.

The Chief Engineer oversaw the fuel, engines, boilers, the engine room crew, and the very ship itself. The First Assistant Engineer was the actual dayshift supervisor, the Second and Third Assistants supervising on off shifts, and each with special duties. In this era it was recognized that the Chief Engineer was actually becoming the more important member of the crew, though still under the master.

An engineer could work on a government ship such as a Revenue Cutter or Survey boat, or in the Merchant Marine. The Merchant Marine had two general classes of ships: Ships on regular scheduled service referred to as "lines" of ships, i.e.

"steamship line," and tramp ships, which were typically individually owned. A tramp would get a cargo or passengers wherever it could, and take it wherever was needed.

Merchant Marine traffic was divided into two distinct categories: Coastwise and Foreign. At this time the coastwise traffic was thriving, but U.S. ships only carried 9% of the foreign trade.

Early on, Ben Parker was to show an aptitude for his new career, as in a letter to his aunt Fannie he writes, "I don't care about going ashore at all now, a ship feels like home." Ben assures his aunt that he is studying and learning a lot, and tells her "Once in a while we get together and have great disputes about engineering." Ben graduated from the Massachusetts State Nautical School in 1898.

CHAPTER II

From the Old Country

Our story begins in old Norway along the shores of the southern fjords.

Christian Loken was a corporal in the Royal Norwegian Regiment. He was likely born sometime between 1830-1850. It can be safe to say that his family had lived in Norway in one town or in one area for many centuries, as was usually the case from the Viking era all the way until the mid nineteenth century. Christian married Johanne Rud. Christian had a position at the military prison in the castle and fort of Akershus, next to Christiana on the Oslofjord. The family lived at the fort for ten years.

About the time his son, young Adolf, was graduating from middle school, things for Christian began to take a turn for the worse. Christian was at the military prison one day when he was apparently involved in an incident—which compromised his judgment. There was a certain officer there, interred for drunkenness. Out of compassion, Christian arranged for this officer's unauthorized release, and was then censured severely. He finally resigned after twenty-two years in the service of the army.

It is historically known that opportunities were meager in Norway at this time, and Christian no doubt faced a bleak situation trying to care for his family. Many a Norwegian would immigrate to the United States near the end of the nineteenth century. So, at some point after frustrated efforts to find suitable employment, Christian decided to try his luck in New York City. He went all by himself, leaving his son Adolf to care for the family, probably with the idea that his family would join him later after he had landed a good job. Christian got a job at the Steinway & Sons piano company in New York. His situation was not to improve very much though, as when he was working in one of the shops, he got his hand caught in some machine, which appears to have crippled him somewhat and impaired his ability to send for his entire family. It is not known when or where Christian died. But in a letter dated January 6, 1915, Christian explains how he will get a pension from Steinway for the rest of his life, of six dollars per week. He also mentions how his brother and sister had died in close succession the year before. On the letter his address is 932 Steinway Avenue, L. I. City, New York. This was an address in Steinway Village, a company town and factory built by Steinway & Sons in Queens at Astoria, New York. The company had a lot of immigrant workers and provided for them well. The Steinways had emigrated just before the Civil War from Germany. Also, the company found this arrangement to work well for the quality manufacturing of their pianos.

Johanne stayed in Christiana, Norway, even after the children had left for New York, or gone to sea. On October 29, 1895 Johanne died in a hospital of anemia. She didn't have a chance to make the voyage to New York. Christian lived more than twenty more years, but does not appear to have remarried.

Johanne Loken.   *Adolf as a military cadet in the 1880s.*

The children of Christian and Johanne were: Adolf Nils Loken, b. December 8, 1869, Harold O. Loken, b. October 24, 1877, Gustaf Loken, and Maria Loken.

Adolf had grown up with the military all around him. When he became of age, he entered the regiment that his father had served in at Akershus as an officer's aspirant. He received eight Kroner per month, his uniform, and quarters. Apparently the object was to train and study to one day enter the military academy. There were hurdles to overcome. Adolf's study had to be done privately and at his own expense. A friend helped him with another ten Kroner a month, but this was still not enough. So, after eighteen months of training, Adolf resigned as officer aspirant for the Norwegian Army, very discouraged.

He must have felt the need to work to help support the family, and he still thought he might be able to try for the Norwegian Naval Academy, but he needed some sea time for this. So Adolf went to sea for a while in Norwegian waters as a crewman. This he found very rough indeed, and in later life he did not have pleasant things to say about this time in his life.

Adolf's sister Marie also came over to New York. She was there by the early 1890s. She lived there for the rest of her life, never traveling again. She was the only family Christian had in New York, and they probably kept in touch a lot. However, when Johanne was dying, Marie did not write her mother who was so hoping to have a word from her. This greatly displeased her brothers.

These were times when Scandinavians and Europeans were emigrating to the U.S. by the shiploads. They mainly came from the poorer parts of Europe, where opportunity was scarce, and the rich owned all the land. The Loken ancestors can rightly be said to be European gentle folk, however. Struggling, but dignified. The U.S. was expanding by leaps and bounds. There were jobs to be had in the big cities, in factories, shipyards, and mills. And, there was even free land still to be had out west for those who wanted to farm or have a ranch. It was still the last days of the "Wild West;" cowboys, outlaws, and Indians. In the newest frontier, the Pacific Northwest, there were trees to cut, and ships to build and run—prime trades of the Northmen.

The Life at Sea in the Revenue Cutter Service

Adolf started out on sailing ships in Norway at a very young age, intending to get sea time so as to enter the Norwegian Naval Academy. Years later, when reflecting back, he said his first days on the sailing ships in Norway were so rough, that, at times he "wished he was dead."

A decade later, in the early 1890s, Adolf's younger brothers Harold and Gustaf would also ship out on the old windjammers as young teenage boys. This was a common practice in Norway. There were not many jobs to be had in Norway ashore.

Adolf's brothers Harold and Gustaf went to sea as teenage boys, 14 or 15 years old. The boys went to sea, it is rumored, to help support their mother. Apparently Christian did not make enough in New York to support himself and the household of his wife in Norway as well. Going to sea was a very popular occupation in the Scandinavian countries, especially in those days. Scandinavians were famed as mariners, and boat and ship builders. The sea was a natural choice for a Norseman.

In the mid 1890s Harold was sailing out of Bristol, Scotland, crossing the Atlantic. Harold would eventually return to Christiana and attend a maritime school and become an officer. One day he would be the Port Captain of Colon, Panama, the Caribbean entrance to the Panama Canal! Harold held that position for thirty years.

Sometime around the late 1880s Adolf's father sent him a ticket on a Norwegian ship to New York City. There was a lot of immigration from Norway, as well as from many other parts of Europe, to New York in this period. But when Adolf got to New York and all was said and done; he seems to have decided on having a life spent on the sea, and was in the Revenue Cutter Service in May of 1890 on the cutter *Chase*. He was twenty-one years old.

The Revenue Cutter Service was the forerunner of the modern Coast Guard. In the nineteenth century there was a huge amount of merchant shipping up and down the coasts. The early mandate of the service was to prevent illegal smuggling, and thus "evasion" of taxes and import duties. The Revenue Cutter Service was the general government presence on the seas where they supervised, policed smuggling, inspected ships, enforced the rules of navigation; and provided a life saving service, particularly in the winter. The ships were well armed for small-scale action.

The U.S.R.C. *Salmon P. Chase* was a small 115', 142 ton, three-masted bark used for training cadets of the Revenue Cutter Service School of Instruction. She was based at New Bedford, Massachusetts.

Chase was taken out of service that year and Adolf was next on the wooden 130', 350

ton, screw steamer U.S.R.C. *Levi Woodbury*, based out of Eastport, Maine. *Woodbury* was a veteran of the Civil War and had a long and distinguished service. She had a two-cylinder oscillating engine driving an 8' screw propeller, and was also equipped as a two-masted topsail schooner. She was a typically sized and equipped revenue cutter.

When Adolf first came into contact with the engine room of a ship, he knew this was the job for him. The engine was amazing, a mechanical symphony of whirring things: Great connecting rods, out in the open, beating up and down to their rhythm. Pipes running every which way in a maze, pumps and various mechanical apparatus everywhere. The gritty but extremely intelligent Chief Engineer seemed larger than life, a "hands on" kind of man, but one who knew many of the secrets of science—Adolf knew that this was his destiny. The steamship was one of the wonders of the day, and many enjoyed the advances of science like electricity.

The U.S.R.C. *Albert Gallatin* was a 137', 250 ton, iron-hulled two-masted topsail schooner with a two-cylinder compound steam engine. She made regular patrols on New England seas between Portsmouth, New Hampshire and Holmes Hole at Martha's Vinyard, Massachusetts. Adolf was among her crew.

Early on the sixth of January, 1892, *Gallatin* was heading south from her northern base towards Provincetown, Massachusetts under an overcast sky. Visibility at the start of the trip was good. *Gallatin* passed Cape Ann on the Massachusetts coast at nine in the morning. Within an hour the weather turned for the worse, visibility diminished and it began to snow. With the fading visibility, Captain Eric Gabrielson decided to turn back towards the nearby safe harbor of Gloucester, Massachusetts. Seeing land, a depth sounding was taken—twelve fathoms. Through the gloom, in the distance to the north he could see Kettle Island. He had to be careful, as there were numerous rocks and shoals in these coastal seas. As the ship was turned around and headed east, out to seaward of Kettle Island, Adolf was below in the engine space. He felt the ship change course. Suddenly, a shudder through the ship and the sickening groan of the iron hull impaling itself on Boo Hoo Ledge! With a *start* Captain Gabrielson realized that that was not Kettle Island he saw in the distance, but Great Egg Rock! She was stuck hard and fast, there was no getting her off the rocky ledge. The North Atlantic seas were pounding her, sweeping away her deck structures and skylights. The ship began to take on water. She wallowed in the pounding seas. On the listing and rolling ship the funnel broke loose and fell on the ship's carpenter, J. Jacobsen, killing him.

Captain Gabrielson ordered the men to the boats. The lifeboat that Adolf was in had just got away as they watched their ship go down. She had broken in two. They all made it to shore, landing in a cove of the rocky promontory of Eagle Head, near Manchester.

Adolf had only a pair of coveralls on, no shoes or socks. Snow was falling and it was freezing. When the crew reached the shore in their boats, they had to walk for two miles before reaching anyone who could help. When they finally

Above: U.S.R.C. *Woodbury*   U.S.R.C. *Gallatin*

U.S. Revenue Cutter **Grant.** *She truly had the beautiful lines of a late nineteenth century ship. The* **Grant** *was the ship that Adolf sailed from the east coast to Puget Sound on.* Puget Sound Maritime Historical Society

reached some people, one of the boys there gave Adolf an oilskin coat which he quickly tore into separate pieces and wrapped them around his feet, thus saving him from severe frostbite. Oh, the romantic life at sea. Adolf left the service February 1892.

On May 13, 1893 Adolf reentered the Revenue Service. He was stationed on the Revenue Cutter *Grant,* as an oiler. The *Grant* was a 163', 350 ton, iron hulled steam propeller, and carried enough sail for backup. It was the *Grant* that was ordered to take up patrols on Puget Sound. Since there was no Panama Canal in those days, Adolf and the *Grant* had to come around the Horn of South America, through the Strait of Magellan. On the trip around the Horn, Adolf noted the strange islanders, then still cannibals. He was intrigued by their strange dances at night by the light of the fires.

The business in Puget Sound was lumber—lumber and ships. Beginning in the early 1850s, timber was being cut as fast as it could be, and shipped around the world. There were several lumber boomtowns around the West Sound. Sea Beck down Hood's Canal had already gone boom and bust by the time Adolf arrived. Many ships had been built at Sea Beck. Further up Hood's Canal there was Port Gamble with the Pope and Talbot operation, churning out Northwest Fir lumber as fast as it could. There was Port Ludlow, producing lumber and ships. And then there was the prominent seaport at the entrance to Puget Sound on the Strait of Juan de Fuca, Port Townsend. Port Townsend was the Port

Port Townsend, c 1890. Revenue cutter on right.   Jefferson County Historical Society photo

of Entry to Puget Sound, and therefore had the Customs House, and for that reason was stationed the base of the local contingent of the Revenue Cutter Service.

After arriving on Puget Sound in the *Grant*, Adolf found himself doing regular patrols out of Port Townsend. Port Townsend was a "Wild West" Victorian era seaport, with saloons, cathouses, and drunken sailors, where a man might have a whiskey bottle smashed over his head in a bar fight. The flourishing of a knife or pistol was commonplace, and their deadly employment far from unknown. The waterfront saloons were the haunt of rum-runners, opium smugglers, and those employed in trafficking illegal aliens of Chinese nationality.

The harbor was always filled with ships from all over the world, mostly windjammers, which were typically individually owned cargo ships, tramping across the ocean and down the coast. Agents in town would find crews and cargos for them.

There were also steamers such as the Revenue Cutters, and passenger liners such as those of the Pacific Coast Steamship Company of San Francisco, whose schedules were regularly advertised in the local papers. The Pacific Coast Steamship Co. steamers regularly called at Union Wharf bound for ports in California and Alaska. Smaller steamers of the Mosquito Fleet also called at Port Townsend piers, bound for local ports as close as Irondale, Hadlock, and Whidby Island.

In the days of sail, the masters and mates, that is the officers of the ship, lived in the after compartments on the stern of the ship. The ordinary seamen, as they were called,

Downtown and Union Wharf.   Jefferson County Historical Society photo

lived in the forecastle on the bow of the ship, or in sailor's terms, in the foc'sle. Life spent between the foc'sle and up in the rigging was difficult at best.

On some of the ships—known as "hell-ships," the masters and mates were known for vicious brutality—even murder. For these reasons, it was often difficult to get crews for the windjammers.

West coast ports did a steady trade with the distant ports of Asia like Shanghai, China. By the 1890s, Port Townsend had been a busy seaport for many years. Schooners carrying Northwest timber were traveling in and out continually, mostly in the coastwise trade to places like San Francisco. Port Townsend Bay was normally full of barks and schooners at anchor. A majority of the sailors on these were Scandinavians.

Port Townsend was the Port of Entry into Puget Sound, and most of these ships would unload their sailors here, save for a few hands for the tow to the mill, elsewhere on the Sound.

The waterfront was a rough place. This was the red light district and the haunt of sailors, whiskey, loggers, gamblers, and women of the evening. There were many saloons—lively saloons. Crimps, prowling marauders looking for men to hand over to ship's masters to be impressed into work on the windjammers, kept an ever watchful eye out for a feller they could "Shanghai." Looking for easy prey like drunks in the saloons, the crimps were known for dirty tricks to get their prey. Knock-out drugs in the whiskey, trap doors in the floor of saloons that were built on pilings over the water, and other devious methods were the normal vice of this trade. The unfortunate fellers woke up on a sailing bark or schooner, having been kidnapped, the result of their foggy night of drunken debauchery.

It was a lucrative employment for a man of low moral character, a crimp might make more than a doctor or lawyer. It was a business like that of the pimp, or the madam of a cathouse; part of the local economy, but none too respectable. This was the "Downtown" of Port Townsend.

In addition to the fact that working on the sail ships was hard work, the root cause of the Shanghai was simple greed. The practice derived out of a sense to squeeze a profit at men's expense. Some of the hell-ships treated their sailors miserably so that the sailors would bail out on them when they got to their destination, and they wouldn't have to pay them. The ship's master would then buy another "Shanghai" crew, which was cheaper.

A law passed in 1895 in the United States tried to put the practice of Shanghaiing to an end, but the practice continued. Shanghaiing continued on the west coast of the United States until the days of the windjammers were gone, well into the twentieth century.

But Port Townsend was also home to a community of respectable Victorian folks. The respectable citizens lived up on the "bluff" in the "Uptown" district. Here there were quaint Victorian houses, churches and schools; ladies and gentlemen. A Sunday ride on a horse and buggy, a stroll through flowered gardens, or a dinner in one of the grand houses; the lady of the house sitting at the piano, the guests gathered around. These were the pastimes of the Uptown district.

The town was trying to woo business interests, and had built many impressive buildings, which thankfully stand to this very day. It was going to be the first city of Washington, they thought. However, the truth was that Port Townsend had already gone boom and bust. People were leaving town for elsewhere on the Sound. The later 1880s had been the boom years, and 1893 saw depression. The railroad terminus that had been so hoped for in Port Townsend didn't come, and the Great Northern railroad went to Seattle.

The *Grant* was stationed on Puget Sound for nine months of the year, and made seasonal trips to Alaska. Adolf first saw Ketchican, Alaska in 1893 while on a patrol to the Bering Sea in the *Grant*. For a couple of years he was stationed back and forth from Port Townsend to Bellingham and served on the little 65' cutters *Scout* and *Guard*, hunting down Chinese smugglers trafficking in opium and Chinese laborers, and other ships smuggling liquor and cigars from Canada. These clandestine activities were carried out all over north Puget Sound, and even in the quiet beaches and bays around the general area of Port Townsend. Places like North Beach, Hadlock, Discovery Bay, and Port Ludlow. Revenue Cutter Service sailors were familiar with the Trapdoor Springfield, U.S. Krag carbine, and the Model 1892 Colt revolver in .38 caliber, "Navy Type."

Meanwhile, on the other side of the world, in the Atlantic, Adolf's brothers were getting their sea legs on the old sailing barks. Harold was on the Norwegian 434 ton, 144' bark *Vidfarne* under Captain Jorgensen sailing out of Bristol, England. Gustaf was on the bark *Hugh Fordescus* under Captain H. Gelmordan. Several letters survive from the period of 1893-96, written in Norwegian. In them the boys describe some of their encounters. Harold writes his mother, "I am writing to tell you that we have arrive safely in America after 2 months at sea. We had good wind and nice weather for the most part." In another letter to mother dated July 15, 1893 he writes "I would now like to tell you that we were safe in Bristol. We took 22 days to cross the Atlantic and we had good wind every day. We came here 9 of June and we are now unloading our load and then we'll go empty and sail back to Shediak again." Later in the same letter Harold laments

"When we were sailing out from Shediak we sailed aground, so we were late by a couple of days. We were 33 men to get the boat off ground and they were all Norwegians." *Shediac* is in New Brunswick, Canada, just above Nova Scotia. Gustav writes his mother, dated May 30, 1894 "I have to write you again and tell you where I shall go. *Demerara* that I was on last year is a Bark from Arendal, it is a good ship I am on. The Captain had his wife and children on board and a maid and I like all of them so I think I will like it onboard." The letter is sent from South America. *Demerara* was engaged in the sugar trade from British Guiana in the warm Caribbean to the British Isles, *Arundel* being in the Orkney Islands north of Scotland.

In August of 1894 Harold writes to Adolf.

> We had a 31 day trip and thanks to the weather we ended up going too far north by New Foundland, where we encountered large icebergs and fog. So much ice none of us had seen before. I counted to 128 icebergs right away ahead of us. It wasn't good with the fog and we could only sail at 2-3 mile speed, but when the weather cleared we sailed full tilt to get away from the ice and it was a miracle we made it.

In 1895 Harold would return to Kristiana, as his mother Johanne was ill. She died that fall. Harold decided to attend a maritime school, which he did in 1896, and would one day become a captain. In a letter to Adolf dated April 24, 1896 Harold tells Adolf how things are going at home, and tells him that when he is done with school he's going to catch a ship to America because there is no chance of getting a job at home in Norway. In the same letter Harold states "I've heard that you've bought a real estate in Port Townsend. I've sailed with men who has worked there ashore, and they say it was the best place on earth for there it grows all sorts of plants they said."

There are no letters from this time on from Gustav. Gustav had been sailing on a ship down to South America. It is quite possible that he was killed in late 1895. In letters to Adolf during the holiday season of 1895, Harold laments to his brother "you are the only brother I have to write to." Also in 1895 it appears that Marie got married.

Back in the Pacific, Adolf was to see some action during the Spanish-American War of 1898. He served on the *Grant*, which had been taken over by the Navy for the Pacific Service. The war only lasted a few months. It was started over Cuba, when Cuba was in a war of independence with Spain. There was the famous naval battle in the then Spanish controlled Philippines at Manila Bay with Commodore Dewey, May 1, 1898. Then there was a naval blockade at Cuba, and one naval battle in July. The Americans were resoundingly victorious in both, and the war ended shortly thereafter. The *Grant* was released from the Navy August 15, 1898. She had been patrolling the seas from San Francisco to the Alaska gold fields with the Pacific Squadron, as there was concern for the safety of the gold laden ships. This was still in the height of the gold rush.

The United States gained control of the Philippines and Guam as a result of this war. Following the war was the Philippine Insurrection (1899-1902), in which revolutionary forces then rebelled against United States rule of their homeland. Following this was the Moro Rebellion. In some of the outlying battles U.S. soldiers fought with the passionate Moro tribesmen, their small caliber guns often not having good effect on the crazed warriors.

Adolf seems to have gone to the Philippine Insurrection for the rest of 1898 and 1899. Between this Pacific tour, and also a couple of later ones, he visited places like Japan,

Famous U.S. Revenue Cutter **Bear.**

Puget Sound Maritime Historical Society

China, Borneo, and the villages of Moro tribesmen in the Philippines.

About 1900, Adolf was assigned to the famous Revenue Cutter *Bear.* The *Bear* was a 198 foot, three-masted barkentine of about 1700 tons, with a steam auxiliary of 500 shaft horsepower. She was originally built in Scotland for service in northern ice laden waters; and her hull was six inches thick, with an iron prow.

The Revenue ships had first been sent to the Bering Sea to look after the fur seals due to an international controversy over the seal herd. Improper hunting methods were decimating the population. The ships of several countries were hunting the seals, besides the American ships. The seal skins were an economic asset, and this was the basis of the controversy. The conservationist aspect came to the fore at this time, however, as experts saw that the seals were being driven to extinction.

Even at this time the *Bear* was well known. In the 1880s and 90s, the Bear had grown famous under the command of her most famous master, Captain Michael Healy[1], "Hell Roaring Mike." The son of a successful Irish immigrant and a mulatto slave woman, Healy was the only member of his family that didn't enter the church. He kept his mother's heritage a secret his entire career. Healy was concerned for the welfare of the Alaskan natives, and acted out this concern on a regular basis. Though a heavy drinker himself, Healy vigorously enforced laws preventing the sale of liquor to the native peoples. Healy is known to history as a complex character, he could be both benevolent and vengeful, a deliberate man of internal conflict. The main mission of the *Bear* was

---

[1] One day the Coast Guard would name a polar icebreaker for Captain Healy.

Rugged Alaska.   Photo from the Benjamin Parker collection

Photo from Adolf Loken collection

economic in nature, protection of the fur seals, but the ships became known for their humanitarian deeds, deeds done of their own volition.

The Revenue Service cutters became regular transporters of scientists and naturalists to the polar regions, as one of their many and varied duties.

The *Bear* and her northern cruises had been the subject of a feature article in *National Geographic* magazine in January 1896. The *Bear* was immensely important to the state of Alaska, as she was almost the only law, or hospital, in the northern parts. Outside of the main cities, she was the principal government presence in coastal Alaska. Whaling was still legal at this time and *Bear* rescued stranded whalers every season.

The *Bear* and the *Grant* were stationed out of Port Townsend at the turn of the century, then later the *Bear* with the other Revenue Service ships were moved to West Seattle in 1913. The *Grant* was taken out of government service in 1906. The *Bear* was sailing every year through the warm months on the Bering Sea patrol, with a usual destination to Point Barrow, Alaska. Life on the *Bear* was a constant adventure, rescuing mariners and Eskimos alike in the icy northern territories of Alaska.

In November of 1900 the *Bear* was ordered to patrol Puget Sound and the general area around Port Townsend and Cape Flattery. The following spring, she made for the Bering Sea and a stop at Baroness, Karp Bay, Siberia. In 1901 she made the usual stops: Unalaska, Port Townsend, Seattle, Bremerton Naval Station, San Francisco, and San Diego.

An interesting event that first happened in 1892 and continued through the turn of the century, and was in the Port Townsend newspapers, was the introduction of reindeer to Alaska. The following was written by Adolf Nils Loken on one of his travels.

When Uncle Sam's sailors became Reindeer herders. By Adolf N. Loken U.S.C. & G.S.S.

Preface

Reindeers were first introduced into Alaska in 1892 by Dr. Sheldon Jackson at that time, head of the board of Education for the territory. The first herd of twenty deers were brought over from Siberia on the coast guard ship "Bear". For several years small herds were brought over. Three hundred reindeers were also bought and sent from north part of Norway. Laplanders were hired to care for them on their long travel to Alaska. From these herds there are in Alaska at present over four hundred thousand reindeers, and there is ample feeding ground to support more than six million.

Arriving at Unalaska, Behring Sea in the month of May 1, 1901 on the old coast guard cutter "Bear" from San Francisco, California we were surely surprised to receive orders to proceed for Siberia after a load of Reindeers. Our destination every year as usual has been Point Barrow, Alaska. After a few days stop at Unalaska we left for the Siberian coast where we arrived ten days later and anchored off the Russian town, Petropolasky. The governor of Siberia resided here, and we had to get his official permission first, before we were allowed to deal with the Reindeer owners. After receiving the governor's approval we left Petropolasky, for Baranoff bay, where we arrived three days later after a fine run up the coast, and came to an anchor off the small Indian village of same name. This place had been reported to us, as being the best place to get in touch with the reindeer herds; but we found the place all deserted of reindeers. When the natives told us, that the reindeers were thirty miles inland, we sent a couple indian runners away to tell the reindeer owners, that we were here to buy deers.

The Alaskan reindeer herd was the subject of a feature article in the April 1903 edition of *National Geographic* magazine. In it the *Bear* is mentioned several times, and is pictured. The reindeer were introduced to Alaska to feed the Eskimos, as at that time over-hunting and over-whaling were driving their usual food animals away.

National Geographic magazine was Adolf's favorite periodical. He used to tell his children that it was the only magazine worth reading. In those days especially, it was a publication for the gentleman of worldly and academic pursuits. People did not travel as much as they do today, and the world was a much larger and isolated place. This magazine brought the world closer and made it smaller. Adolf would have been very proud to have his ship's endeavors a subject of *National Geographic*.

CHAPTER III

A Belle from the Naze

Cornella Berntsen was from a town on the southern coast of Norway called Farsund. Farsund is a small town that occupies a little peninsula on the southern tip of Norway, about 150 miles from Oslo, then Kristiana. It is typical of the Norwegian coast and is surrounded by bays, lakes, islands, and other peninsulas. The area is not mountainous. The southern coast of Norway is not terribly different than the Pacific Northwest. It is similar to the Anacortes and San Juan Islands area in topography. A person from Poulsbo would feel at home here. Their family had lived in Farsund for centuries. Cornella was born Cornella Katherine Berntsen, June 10, 1878. Cornella's father's name was Bernt Berntsen Savik. The transmission of surnames in Scandinavia used to be different than what we know today, which explains the apparent discrepancy of Cornella to her father. The Oldest known of the Savik name was Lars Salvesen Savik born 1738 in Farsund. His son Bernt Larsen Savik, born 1768, had a son Bernt Tobias Berntsen Savik, born 1809, who had a son Bernt Berntsen Savik, born 1843, who was the father of Cornella. This Bernt married Karoline Larsen, Cornella's mother. Cornella had a sister named Minnie. At some point, Cornella had lived in Kristiana(Oslo).

Cornella seems to have been a dreamer, an adventurer, and an artist. She was a Victorian era European lady. She was fluent with music and culture, and very familiar with the music greats of her day like Edvard Grieg. Later in life, Cornella wrote a series of plays. In them, a girl named Sigrid wants to leave Norway and come to America to be a famous singer, or even an opera singer. The story starts in the 1890s. She consults a Gypsy fortuneteller, has a courtly romance with a lad from the village named Knute, makes it to New York and then to Chicago, from whence she ends up on a farm in Minnesota where she has more romance. It is not too difficult of a supposition to say that Cornella was musing about her own life in these plays. The following is the opening narrative from the heretofore unpublished work *The Search for the Rainbow's End* by Cornella Loken…

On the southern coast of Norway not far from the Naze, is a place called Solheld. Here we find Guri Ivorson living with her only daughter, Sigrid. The Ivorson farm was rather isolated, with the rolling of the waves, the sound of the foghorn on dark and stormy nights, and the weird cry of the sea birds. To most people it would seem a dreary place in which to live. To Sigrid all these things had a different meaning. Daily watching for passing ships, some coastwise, others headed for distant shores, her life was full of dreams. Every week a steamer for America passed by. Sigrid knew just when to look for it, and would stand and watch until only the masts were visible, disappearing like specks in the horizon. Mother Ivorson knew some of the secrets of the sea, because her father was a sea captain, and as a young girl she went on trips with

The house of Bernt Savik, Cornella's father, in Farsund, Norway. Photo c. 1900.

him, both to Archangel to load rye and to Spain and England with cargoes of fish. Guri's father died at sea when she was eighteen years of age. Young Ivor had been a mate with her dad. He loved Guri and asked her to marry him. She consented with the understanding that he give up deep-sea sailing.

Ivor Ivorson then became a coast pilot. But this also had its great dangers. A stormy night the foghorn kept blowing, there were signals of a ship in distress. Ivor must go to the rescue. He went but never returned. Both he and two other pilots lost their lives, that stormy night. Guri, now the widow Ivorson and Sigrid, their only child—then six years old, were now alone. Every night when a storm broke loose, and the foghorn sent out its monotonous warning, when the sea was beating high against the rocky coast, horrible memories of another stormy night came to her mind. To Sigrid the sound of the waves brought music to her ears. The sight of ships far out in the distance brought on dreams and filled her heart with longing. At such times Guri

would watch her daughter with troubled grievous looks. It was early fall, and the cows were still in the pasture. The Ivorson pasture led from the sea, up in the hill at the further end adjoining the farm of a neighbor, Eiliv Larson. Eiliv had a son named Knute, who had been Sigrid's childhood playmate. Their friendship continued up through the years, and hardly a day passed without Knute making some excuse for a visit over to Solheld.

Sigrid had passed her eighteenth birthday and Knut was a year older. It was milking time. Sigrid put on a pair of heavy shoes with woolen bottoms (worn a great deal in that part of the country) tied a kerchief over her head, picked up a milking pail, then bid her mother goodbye and started down the path leading to the pasture. The house and barn were standing on the hillside with full view of the ocean. Sigrid was want to do her milking on the lower hillside near the water, so she could watch any ships that night be passing by. Singing her favorite milking song, "Come Cow, Come Calf, Come Bossy," she stopped all of a sudden, shading her eyes with her hand against the glare of the setting sun, which then threw a glow on the calm water. Far out on the rim of the ocean a steamer could be seen. Sigrid was lost in thought. A rainbow appeared and with its beautiful colors reflecting in the water made the picture more enchanting. While Sigrid was admiring the scenery before her eyes, a familiar voice sounded coming from the woods over the hill, that of Knute. "You are looking in the wrong direction, the cows are up here." Sigrid turns around and calls, "Come Bossy, Come Bossy!" Knute had now come down the hillside and is sitting on a tree stump, he has his violin and as Sigrid calls again, "Come Bossy, Come Bossy" Moo, Moo, comes from his violin. Sigrid laughs, calls again, "Come Bossy!" then from the hillside, Bossy's well-known moo sounds and the cows, three in all, come trotting down the path.

The milking over, Sigrid and Knut start for the Ivorson home, talking about everyday affairs, laughing and joking as only youth can do.

Mother Ivorson was preparing the evening meal consisting of mush, milk and flatbread and butter and cheese. She was stirring the boiling mush with a wooden utensil, in Norwegian called a tvare. It was twilight and due time for Sigrid's return when merry voices were heard coming singing up the trail.

The winter was over, but patches of snow still lay here and there on the hillside. The early snowdrops were showing their drooping white blossoms from between their green leaves, whenever the sun had most power to bring them out. The first signs of spring were here. The cows and sheep were getting restless, after being in the barn all winter. They scented the spring air and wanted to be out in the pasture again. Mother Ivorson had put the last touches to the weaving of material for dresses for Sigrid and herself. This was woven from wool of their own sheep, which Sigrid during the winter months had carded and spun into yarn. The wool had been carefully washed and dyed a pretty blue, then dried which was a slow process this time of the year.

At last the goods was all ready to be cut down from the loom and Sigrid, watching her mother, gave a helping hand whenever it was needed. Mrs. Ivorson had after much pleading from Sigrid consented to her going to America. And this was to be her traveling dress. Knute came over later in the day to take the loom down because the planting time would soon be here, and after that the time for Sigrid's departure. There was other work ahead, the loom would not be needed and must be out of the way.

***

The following is adapted from Act I of *The Search for the Rainbow's End.*

It is at twilight in the early Fall. Mother Ivorsen is in her kitchen in a Norwegian country home in the early 1890s. Mother is sitting in front of the large fireplace, stirring a kettle.

Sigrid enters the kitchen with a milk bucket, and puts it down on the floor as she stops on the threshold, and turns halfway around in the doorway.

"Oh here you are Sigrid. Isn't Knute coming in?" Mother Ivorsen asks. Sigrid replies absentmindedly, while shading her eyes with her right hand "yes mother." "What is it Sigrid?" mother asks. Sigrid replies softly, as to herself, "I wonder what is beyond where sea and heaven meet—there is the American steamer, gliding towards the horizon…if I were only on it." Soft violin music is heard coming from the hillside. Sigrid continues, thoughtfully, "The strains from his violin, the tunes of my homeland resounding through our beloved woods and mountains makes me sick at heart, keeps me spellbound. But—the longing for the unknown is stronger. Ah…mother look—A rainbow in all its glorious colors. There it goes right down over the American steamer. Does that lead to the pot of gold the legend speaks of? Or is the future as uncertain for those on yonder ship as the end of the rainbow?"

"What would I find on the other side? A life of opportunities, or one of disappointments? Would the pot of gold…at the rainbow's end—be as far away then as it seems now? Even so, I will never be happy until I find out for myself. I am in a dreamland now full of vision and my thoughts are forcefully drawn away with the disappearing ship's masts beyond the horizon…" Etta, an old servant woman who was visiting, enters from the pantry and laughingly interjects "You will find a world quite different from your dreams."

Knute walks in. He picks up the milk bucket from the floor and places in on the long table, or Njokkenbank. "Good evening Mother Ivorsen." "God's peace Knute, won't you be seated?" she asks him politely. Knute places his violin on the bench, "many thanks mother Ivorsen." Knute remained standing. Sigrid gets a strainer and bowls(melke inger) out of the pantry, and is busy straining the milk. Knute turns toward Sigrid "I love the sea, Sigrid. But I could hate it when I see how completely it carries your heart away." Sigrid replies "it is not the sea, Knute, that I long for, I have it right here. But what is beyond, that I must find out." Knute adds "I pray to heaven, that your life will always be as free from worries as it is now. But should your longing be beyond control, God alone holds your destiny in his hand." "However, I shall follow you. If you need me, I want to be near to help." Sigrid, putting the milk away in the pantry, "Oh no, Knute. I want you and mother here. This is where my inspiration will always come from."

Mother Ivorsen, lifting a pot off the hanger and putting it down on the fireplace in front of the fire, stands up facing Sigrid "what has come over you lately, Sigrid? What great things do you suppose awaits you on the other side? Nothing but hardship—work in the kitchen or on some farm, from early morning until late at night. Stay home Sigrid. Here you have freedom, while there you will have to go by the clock, ordered around in a language you do not understand. A stranger in a foreign land." Sigrid replies "But mother, I will see and learn, and I promise to come back to you." Sigrid goes over to the window, looks out. "Someone is coming. It is Gypsy Martha. Now I shall have my fortune told."

A knock is heard at the door. Knute opens the door "good evening Martha." Gypsy Martha steps in, a sack on her back, a smaller one hanging at her side. A scarf is over her shoulder, a kerchief hid over her head, drawn back behind her ears showing large earrings. She has silver rings on her fingers.

Martha greets the house "good day, good people." Etta gets some coffee. Mother Ivorsen replies "good day Martha. Come in, take your sack off and rest a while." Martha loosens the straps fastening the sack. Mother Ivorsen inquires "It is a long time since I have seen you. Where have you been all this time?" Martha replies "long and weary is the road of the wanderer. Many parts of the country have I visited since I was here. Last summer I traveled around Satisdale." Sigrid interjects inquiringly "In Satisdale, did you tell fortunes to the young people there?" "Yah, that I did, many tokens did I receive from the pleased young maids, for my trouble. Brooches, belts and garters, see here!" Martha pulls out of her side pocket several trinkets. Sigrid exclaims "Oh, they are pretty! Would you tell my fortune if I make you some strong coffee?" "Yah! Bear me for some strong coffee and a sugar lump, and I will tell you anything you want to know."

Mother Ivorsen asks Knute "will you bring me some wood, then I will stir up the fire." "Yes mother Ivorsen, I will fix the fire for you also." Knute exits.

Sigrid turns to Martha "let me help you off with your sack Martha." Martha, with the help of Sigrid, takes the sack off and puts it in a corner. Mother Ivorsen smiles at Martha "come over here by the fire Martha, where it is warm." Martha moves over to the fire and stretches her hands out to warm them.

Knute comes back in with the wood, puts a few sticks on the fire. "Thank you, Knute" Sigrid says as she puts the coffee kettle over the fire. To which Knute replies "Oh, that is nothing worth mentioning."

Martha looks at Knute, "My! My! What a fine lad you have grown to be. When last I saw you, it was up in the mountains you were herding the sheep. A tourist came driving by, you ran to the Grind gate to open it for the stranger, and he tossed you two shining quarters." Knute replies wryly " and you asked me for one of them." Martha; "but you kept them both for yourself, and I predicted for you great sorrow." Sigrid joins the fray, "do tell me what sorrows are to befall Knute?" Martha answers "he is to loose what he most cares for in this world." Sigrid, taken aback, replies "I hope you will have something more pleasant to tell me." "Oh, yes. I always have good visions after a warm cup of coffee." Knute mutters "or bad ones when you don't get what you wish." Martha snaps back "often so, often so. Yah, yah."

Mother Ivorsen asks Martha "have you much wool in your sack today? I could use some." "Not this time. The farmers are all stingy with their wool nowadays." Knute looks at Martha "you sold two Kroners worth at Uncle Lars, yesterday." "Yes, yes, did sell some wool." While setting the table Sigrid winks at Martha "there Martha, Knute caught you at it." Martha laments, "oh, yes, let the lad have it out."

"Sit up here Martha; with your back to the fire that will warm you." "Thank you, mother Ivorsen." Martha takes her place at the table. Mother looks at Knute, "Knute, won't you join us in a cup of coffee? Maybe Martha will find some good news in your cup today." Sigrid seconds "yes Knute, do please." "Many thanks" Knute relents as he sits up to the table.

Mother Ivorsen turns to Sigrid "Sigrid, you may sit here next to Knute, and I will pour the coffee." She pours the coffee, then takes her place at the table. Martha looks at her cup, then glances around the table "my, my, but this warms the blood of an old woman." Mother tells her "drink out, and I will pour you another cupful." "Oh, many thanks, Mother Ivorsen." Sigrid points at a dish on the table "have some lefser, I made them yesterday." "Thank you, they do look inviting" Martha said. Knute passes the sugar "a sugar lump, Martha." "Thanks very kindly. It is not very often that poor old Martha is allowed to sit up at the table with good people like you."

Sigrid is looking in the coffee grounds at the bottom of her cup. "What do you see?" asks Martha. Sigrid hands her cup to Martha "it is not for me to know how to foresee my future." Martha reads the cup "great things are going to happen to you—but although this may be your greatest wish, it is not so to those who love you." Sigrid exclaims, "I am so thrilled! What do you see?" "I see a large ship, and I see you on it. You are looking over the railing waving your handkerchief. Now the ship is out of sight. But I see further you have turned away from the railing, you are crying. I see young folks dancing, a young man playing the harmonica, now another young man is trying to talk to you, but you are shaking your head. Here a kind

looking, well-dressed lady is walking on the deck on the arm of a gentleman—looks like a doctor. They are walking back and forth. Now the lady leaves the man and comes over to where you are standing. Here I see another land, the same ship is approaching. There is a mist—now it is clear. I see a gathering of people in a large room. All looking towards the side which has curtains drawn. The lights in the room go out. The curtains are opened showing a lighted space. And there in a glorious setting—I see you." Sigrid exclaims "oh, Martha, you are wonderful!!" Sigrid goes to the cupboard, then to Martha and presses something in her hand. Martha thanks her "many thanks, and God's blessing. I must go further now." Sigrid helps Martha with her sack "I will remember you as long as I live." Knute steps over "let me help you, Martha." "Thank you, my lad." Sigrid smiles at Knute "then I will help mother." Sigrid goes to the table and helps clear it.

Knute looks at Martha sadly "now I know where my sorrows will come from Martha, what you read in Sigrid's cup told me." "Yes, my poor lad." "Farewell, Martha" Mother Ivorsen says as Martha exits.

"Isn't Martha an interesting old gypsy" Sigrid reflects. Mother replies, "she seems to read your mind." "Her visions are greater than mine" Sigrid muses.

Knute starts to play his violin, and Sigrid hums to the tune of *The Last Rose of Summer,* and *Around the Gypsy Fire.* Knute looks at Sigrid " 'bet us forget 'bout the gypsies for the present. Sigrid, won't you sing *Aftmen er stille?"* Sigrid sings, Knute plays.

"Guess Martha will be late before she reaches Week, where she usually gets a night's lodging" Mother Ivorsen said. Sigrid replies "these wandering gypsies will go down in history, and the children of the next generations will read about them in fairy tales." Knute throws in "yes, the government is making them settle, so the children can have an education. They all have to get married now." "That will be a blessing" says Mother Ivorsen, while picking up her knitting "although some of them like Martha are harmless, there are many thieves and drunkards among them that often annoys peaceful folks around on the farms."

Knute puts his violin and bow away in their case, "it will be some time before Martha returns." Sigrid answers, "perhaps by that time I will know—how much truth there is in her prophesies."

Knute looks outside, "it is getting late, I must go." Sigrid goes to the door with him. "Good night Knute, come again soon" said Mother Ivorsen. "Thanks Mother Ivorsen, good night." Sigrid looks at Knute "good night Knute." "Good night Sigrid? I will see you soon." Knute exits as Sigrid stands in the doorway, watching him go. Mother calls "come in Sigrid, let us eat our mush and milk and go to bed." "Coming mother."

Six months later, mother Ivorsen is in her kitchen, sitting at her spinning wheel. Sigrid walks in with a bunch of Snowbells. "Look mother, aren't they pretty? The first sign of Spring. The snow is melting so fast now. And wherever there is a bare spot on the hillside I look for the little Snowbells." Mother Ivosen replies "they are beautiful Sigrid. Yes, the Spring will soon be here, but, I still have my weaving to finish. This wool here when carded and spun into yarn, will be enough to finish with." "By next week we can cut the material down. It is going to be very pretty. We will have to hurry; we better get Ingleborg over to help with the sewing of your dress. Mine can wait, I won't need it yet. I hate to think of it, but if you still want to go to America, we must hurry and get the work done."

Sigrid places the flowers in a glass, then picks up wool and starts carding, sits down on a stool "yes, I do want to go. And please do not worry so much, mother." "But you know Sigrid, all I have left is you. I have told you about how my mother died when I was a little girl, and father who was a sea captain took me with him on his ship."

"I did love to go with father. We went on trips to Spain and England with cargoes of fish. And every fall we made a trip to Archangel to load rye."

"Father died at sea, I was not with on that last trip, I was attending school. Your father was then a mate on Dad's ship. I was eighteen when he asked me to marry him. I did not want him

away to sea, so he quit deep sea sailing and became a coast pilot."

"We were very happy, especially after you came to brighten our life. Happy until that terrible night, when he went out for the last time to answer his call to duty, to help a ship's crew in distress."

"After that, I had only you. I dreaded the roaring of the sea. Hated the sound of the foghorn. The sight of ships brought back…sad memories. You see the way to your future in the direction those ships go. But they remind me of sorrow, and I hate to trust you to them."

Sigrid replies, "mother, won't you please look at the bright side of things for my sake. It isn't going to be easy to tear loose from all here that I love. But it won't be for long. I will be back, perhaps sooner than you realize. I will be back a wiser girl, and will then be able to understand things that now are a mystery. Oh, please mother, can't you see how it is and bear with me?" Mother Ivorsen laments, "let us not talk about it any more."

Sigrid changes the subject, "Knute told me yesterday that he would come over next week and take the loom down." "I am glad of that, I will have no more use of it this year and want it put away in the storeroom," said mother. Sigrid pauses for a while, then "I believe Bossy will have two calves this time." Mother says, "I must watch her closely now, but one calf is enough to feed." Sigrid adds "I was in the barn a while ago. Bossy was lying down." Mother replies "perhaps I had better take a look at her now." Mother Ivorsen steps out.

Sigrid takes the spinning wheel and spins while singing *The Fox Lay under the Birchroot*. After a while she says, "I wonder what is keeping mother." Sigrid thinks to herself "poor mother—it is going to be hard on her at first. But I will send letters every week and then she will feel better. If only Knute does not go away to sea, as he has threatened lately. Knute's uncle is a captain on the schooner *Rono*, and it is possible that he will take Knute with him. It may not be such a bad idea after all, for Knute's sake. But mother will be so lonely, at times like these I find myself weakening. But I mustn't, I don't want to grow old in this place without knowing what the rest of the world is like."

Mother Ivorsen steps in "Bossy has calved, but only one, thank goodness. I must mix her something warm, and then milk her." "Let me help you." "No Sigrid, it is better that you keep spinning. I must have all the wool spun by tomorrow." Mother Ivorsen takes a kettle of warm water off the fire, pours water in a bucket. She goes back outside. Sigrid calls after her "oh mother, you forgot the milking pail." Sigrid retrieves the milking pail, then goes to the door and gives it to her. Now standing in the doorway, mother says "thank you Sigrid. Now tomorrow I will make some nice cheese from the first milking" and shuts the door.

Sigrid resumes her spinning. She thinks to herself "I can't wait 'til I see the calf. What shall I call it? If it is a she I will call it Pearl, but if it is a bull calf, mother won't keep it long, so I will just call it calf." She hums while spinning for a bit, then thinks out loud "Well, I guess I will have to card some more wool." She starts carding, singing all the time. A little kitten playing around the floor gets a hold of a ball of yarn. "You naughty, naughty kitten." Sigrid picks up the ball of yarn, winds it up and puts it in the basket, which is standing on the floor. She then puts the basket up on the table. Sigrid picks up the kitten and plays with it. "Now will you be good?" Sigrid puts the kitten down again, goes back to her spinning.

Mother Ivorsen comes back in. Sigrid asks her "how is Bossy doing?" "Bossy is fine, and she has the loveliest she calf. Black and white with a spot above one eye, it is fat and so lively for a newborn calf." "Oh mother, I can't wait any longer, I must see it." "Alright Sigrid, but wait 'til I get some milk ready, then you give it the first feeding." "I would love to." Mother Ivorsen gives Sigrid a little pan full of milk, and Sigrid goes to the barn.

Mother Ivorsen sits down by the fireplace, muses to herself "what a joy and comfort God sent me when He gave me Sigrid. Her life radiates sunshine all around her. Now I must lose her. What have I done—since the one love left in my life is to be taken away? Perhaps I am being selfish...I must think of Sigrid's happiness. Encourage her! Let her try the wide world. If she meets with disappointment she still has her home to come back to. My love and prayers will follow her every step of her life."

She walks over to the spinning wheel and starts spinning.

"The weaving must be done, her dress must be made, before it is the time for planting. After that we will be too busy outdoors to even think about spinning or sowing. Sigrid will leave for America later in the Spring when the voyage will be more pleasant, and I will not persuade her against going."

Sigrid enters, "mother, I think Pearl is the most darling calf we ever had. Will you raise it, please mother?" "If that is your wish Sigrid, I will raise this calf." "Come here Sigrid" Mother Ivorsen says, as she stops spinning. "What is it now mother?" Sigrid puts the tin on the table, goes over to her mother. "I want you to go to America. I believe that I have been very selfish in trying to keep you from going. After this you shall do as your heart tells you, without any fear or interference from me. I have released you, may God keep you always." Sigrid embraces her mother "darling mother, thanks for all you have been to me ever."

***

The whistle had blown the third time, giving the last signal to delayed passengers. The landing was hoisted up, and all the lines fastening the ship to the dock were hauled on board. Then the engine started to give the noise that reminded the passengers of the voyage having begun. Mother Ivorson, Knute and a few neighbors and friends were at the dock talking to Sigrid until the boat shoved off.

This had been a busy day with Knute at hand, bright and early in the morning to drive them to Christiana where the American steamers landed. It was such a beautiful trip. The air filled with fragrance of the unfolding spring ground from the chirping birds and bubbling brooks, added music to the scenery along the road never to be forgotten. Now as Sigrid stood at the railing waving a last farewell, these impressions lingered in her mind. Looking through tears, those on the wharf grew dim, and soon the distance became too great. The steamer was going out between the numerous islands, that dot the Norwegian coast, and the passengers had their last glimpse of the mainland.

It was a very sorrowful girl we find at the railing looking back at the gray coastline. Back there was her home and her mother. All that was dear to here she had left behind, not knowing what would be in store for her in the future. A man tried to be friendly with her, but—he was not Knute—she shook her head. Life

seemed terrible empty right there. Her dreams were gone. The realities of life began to dawn to dawn upon her. How much different from her thoughts back there in the pasture on the hillside. There with her pets, and with Knute…his sweet music; with her loving mother, the sea and the rainbow.

"Will you pardon me sweet child?" a loving voice said. Sigrid looked up and smiled through tears. A lady with a face as beautiful as her voice stood there. Beside her a distinguished looking gentleman. "My name is Mrs. Brown and this is my husband, Dr. Brown. We have visited your beautiful country for several months, after the doctor ended his studies in other European countries. Your native land is a dreamland, you won't find another one as lovely." You are very kind, Mrs. Brown. It is so good to hear my land praised by a foreigner. My name is Sigrid Ivorson. I never realized how dear my homeland could be until now, when I have left it. But I wonder will the glamour of the new country, dim the love for my own? Mrs. Brown smiled, "My dear child, when you come to this new land, you will see life in true colors and not as in your visions. You will face facts and they will sometimes be shocking to your modest mind. But keep to your ideals, if you meet life with the highest that's in your mind you will solve your problems and claim your victor." " You are so kind Mrs. Brown, I only hope that where I go someone like you will

help me, when my problems seem just a little too much." "Perhaps we will be able to arrange that for you after we land. In the mean time be of good courage, and now, good-bye Sigrid, for the time being, we will see you soon."

It was evening. The fifteen days voyage was over, and the liner Thingvalla lay at anchor, outside Staten Island. The water was as calm and bright as a mirror. Boats large and small dotted the harbor of New York. The city itself an ocean of lights, showing the glamour, but concealing the horrors of a great metropolis. Again we find Sigrid standing at the railing. Amazed over the great sights. The Statue of Liberty, the Brooklyn Bridge, and the huge skyscrapers towering towards the skies like big black giants. These were not part of her vision but they were real here before her eyes. One building twenty-two stories high, a fellow passenger informed her. It is unbelievable, wonders after wonders surpassing all her dreams. There was a hustle and a bustle in the castlegarden over in Hoboken. Emigrants of many nationalities were waiting to pass the Immigration officers. Here was a Russian family huddled together, talking away all at one time. On the other side a Madonna-like Italian woman, with bare breast holding an infant in her arms, and several half-naked children around her. Then there were other people more like herself but talking in different languages. It was a perfect Babel.

Sigrid soon tired of watching and longed to get away. An officer called her by name. Over at the inspector's desk, her friends Dr. and Mrs. Brown were waiting. A sigh of relief passed from Sigrid's lips and tears of gratitude were in her eyes. It was easy with their kind help to pass the officials. The Browns also saw her safely to the train, and with their good wishes, their address in her purse, and invitation to visit them in Chicago in the near future. The journey by sail started Sigrid off for the little Minnesota town where her cousins lived.

The time moved slow at Solheld for mother Ivorson. Knute would venture in of an evening for a visit, but, he too was in low spirits. They would sit there and talk about the last letter from Sigrid, and secretly wipe away a tear. Knute had an uncle who was a sea captain. Ever since Sigrid left for America it had been Knute's wish to go with this uncle to sea. It was late in the summer when Knute received a letter from his uncle. He was with his ship at Liverpool loading, and Knute may if he wished join him there. The next visit to Solheld was a brief farewell. Knutes spirit was light, but it was with an aching heart that Mrs. Ivorson gave him her motherly blessings, as she lifted a corner of her apron to wipe away the tears.

"Rono" was a fourmaster schooner and a fine ship owned by a Norwegian firm. Knute had only been on board her a few days when they received orders to sail for South America. The time passed, Knute had been to many foreign ports. —Had seen the life and temptations of a seafaring man. The crew was made up mainly of hardened old-timers. Knute did not wish to become one of them. They were on their way to New York. Here Knute decided he would quit the ship. Captain Larson agreed to let him go. And with a years pay in his pocket, in cheerful mood Knute bid his uncle and the sea goodbye. Now knowing just what to do next, he wrote a letter to Sigrid and informed her of his arrival in New York. A few days later a letter came, which made him change his mind about going to where Sigrid was. Her letter was full of enthusiasm about her work at Browns and telling about her singing school and of the old professor who was taking a personal interest in her and wanting to study her privately. Knute realized that Sigrid was working her way towards the goal of her dreams. He could not do anything for her. By the help of a Lutheran minister he enrolled in a Norwegian Lutheran church school in the middle-west, with the object of studying English and the violin. The school helped Knute to secure a part time job. In this way he paid for

his expenses. During the summer months working on nearby farms, Knute managed to finish four years of college. After the graduating exercises with his diploma in his pocket and with his violin, Knute boarded a train for Chicago.

***

In Act II, scene I, Sigrid is in America, in a "large American city," (read Chicago) six years later, c 1900-1901. She is a maid in the house of a doctor. Sigrid is in a maid's union, to which she is very active. The union is going to have a social.

The father of a colleague of the doctor is a professor at a local university. This professor wants to promote Sigrid's musical talents.

Sigrid is befriended by the lady of the house, Mrs. Brown. Mrs. Brown muses about Sigrid, "Of all the maids I have had in my twenty years of married life, Sigrid has them all beat. But, oh dear! That housemaid's union certainly occupies her mind nowadays. Still, the world is progressing and it is also to a certain degree affecting those faithful souls in the kitchen. We must make allowances or we will find ourselves without help."

"Hmm—Dr. May who shares offices with Jack has taken a fancy to Sigrid. She has wonderful talents, he claims. After all, Dr. May should know because he is a singer himself of note, and organist in the largest church in the city."

"His father, Professor May, instructs in singing at the old university, and Sigrid has the opportunity of being in his class at the university settlement school.

It is a pity that so much talent is given to a poor immigrant girl who has little possibilities of ever having them developed to any great extent."

Sigrid confides to Mrs. Brown "yes Mrs. Brown, I do love to sing. I dream of becoming a great singer, of singing before a large audience. Back home my audience were our flocks of sheep. I used to sing to them, I fancied they understood, and I saw in them a real audience. Dreams sometimes come true—just now I am glad to be here with you and the doctor. You do understand me."

"Today I met professor May. He has given me special lessons for sometime, and he wants me to sing solo at our coming social. This will only be for a trial."

"Our choral club at the settlement school is giving a grand concert later in the season. I am to be one of the soloist and Prof. May will have some friends there connected with the grand opera. I may get a contract later on to sing in the opera. I will need to practice a lot for that great concert so it will take me away from work."

Mrs. Brown tells her "We will arrange all that. I am glad to hear that Prof. May has taken such an interest in you and we shall try to attend your concert. I knew when I first saw you on the steamer that you were different. You did not mix with the other young people, but kept to yourself. I said to the Doctor: That little girl is lonely and is therefore in danger. I am glad that you trusted me when I spoke to you."

Sigrid relates to her "Knute spoke about destiny. It was my good fortune to meet you and the doctor. I was lonely and so bewildered; almost sorry that I had left home. I had the address to some cousin in Minnesota. But the rainbow's end grew more distant all the time. I was beginning to feel that the pot of gold always would remain a fairy tale, and that I would have enjoyed it more by staying home. Then you spoke to me, and your kindness awoke new hopes within me."

Mrs. Brown; "yes, it was the good fortune of both of us—that the doctor and I decided to visit the land of the midnight sun, after the doctor had ended his studies in Vienna. And Providence brought us together with you on the same steamer bound for America."

"I wanted to ask you to come home with us right away, but after talking it over we decided perhaps it would be better for you to go to your relatives first."

"Yes, Mrs. Brown, but when I came to my cousin Lena, things went wrong. Lena and her husband were kind, but very hard working people. They had no use of dreamers, as they called me."

"Lena got me a job on the Schneider's farm, I thought of my mother's warning, but it was too late now. I did my best, those few months on the farm. Lars the hired man asked me to marry him. That would seem like giving up life. I wanted to get away so I asked Mr. Schneider for my money, said I was quitting."

"Lars drove me to the station. His pathetic look aroused sympathy. I told him about Knute and about mother, of my dreams for a real future; and when he said goodbye, there were tears in his honest blue eyes. I did not want to go back to my cousin, so I came here."

"And we were glad to have you come. We did not expect you to stay on the farm." "Now I must dress or we will be late for the party."

Later that evening, Sigrid is sweeping the floor in the kitchen and musing to herself "Of all things doing. For the president of my society to appoint me leader of our next social doing. The girls promised to be here this evening for practice, because the missus will be out and this is our chance."

"Alice our president promised to bring her boyfriend. Ole is a swell harmonica player, and we will have him play for the folk dances. The girls are such dears and this is a great opportunity for me to appear in public. In fact, this is my first chance."

"Professor May is making arrangements to have me sing several solos. This will really be a surprise for the girls. At the singing school the girls are more cultured, but I can't tear loose from those who have been my friends since I came to this city a stranger. Of the girls attending singing school I am the only one who does housework. The same is the case on my evening classes at the business school. The one thing I have against the maids' is: They are too anxious to copy their missus in dressing instead of spending their money for education so they can better themselves and get out of drudgery. But the members of our union must not know about what I think or they won't like me so well. Now I am supposed to coach the girls in singing the different nations' folk songs. Ole will play for the folk dances. We will practice the songs tonight and rehearse the dances at our next meeting at the union hall. Here we go!" Sigrid waves her broom as if directing while she hums a tune. She looks at the clock, and puts the broom away. As she takes off her apron she says out loud "it is pretty near time for the girls to be here."

A knock on the door, Sigrid opens it "oh hello Alice." "Good evening Sigrid. Are we the first ones?" "Yes Alice, you are the first. Hello Ole, I am so glad you came." Sigrid stretches her hand towards Ole. "Hello Sigrid, I would not miss this for anything, but I almost broke my neck getting here." Sigrid takes his hat "did you bring your harmonica?" "Yes I did. Here it is." Ole produces his harmonica. "Let me take your wrap." Sigrid takes the wrap to the closet. She comes back in "won't you be seated? The girls should be here soon." "Thank you" replies Alice as she sits down. Another knock is heard at the door. Ole says "there are the girls now." He opens the door. Jenny and Katherine come in. Sigrid greets them "oh, hello girls." Katherine addresses the room "good evening Sigrid, and hello Ole, how are you?" Ole cracks a smile "swell, how are you?" "Hello Sigrid" says Jenny. Sigrid replies "how are you? Let me take your things girls." Sigrid gets their wraps and takes them to the closet. Katherine asks "I haven't seen you for some time Alice, how have you been?" "Fine, I missed you at our meeting this afternoon." "Sorry, but I was late getting off."

"You have all Thursday off Jenny, I believe," states Alice. "Yes, all Thursday and evening too, but believe me I will have to make up for it tomorrow." Ole chimes in "well, you should worry about that." They all laugh.

A knock at the door again. Sigrid returns from the closet and opens the door "hello Marie." "Good evening everybody. Guess I am late." "No, not at all" Sigrid consoles her, as she takes Marie's coat and hat. "How are you Sigrid?" "Well, thank you. Be seated while I put your wrap away." Marie sits next to Alice. Another knock at the door, Ole opens it "well, that is something, look here Sigrid—the rest of the bunch." In come Sally Ann, Karen, Clara, Ester, and Lena. "We all happened to be on the same car," informs Sally Ann. "Oh, good evening girls. Take your things off and now that we are all here, we will get to practice right away." Alice gets up "let me help Sigrid."

After returning, Sigrid points at the chairs "be seated girls." They all find a seat. Ole asks "now where do we start?" Sigrid looks at Ole "can you play Yankee Doodle? Want to Town?" Ole starts playing. "Lena will you bring your Dutch boyfriend and dance for us?" "Yes, I will bring Hans and also my wooden

shoes." "Fine, and you will be first on the program. Ole will play 'Oh Where Oh Where Has My Little Dog Gone.'" Lena replies "I will look for the doggie and find Hans. Is that it?" Sigrid instructs "No, Hans will look for someone and meet you. Afterwards you will dance to that tune. Try it Ole." Ole plays the chorus and the girls sing to it. "That is good, now Katherine you will be next. You will sing some popular German folk tunes and the girls will all join in the dances."

Katherine sings *Ach du lieber Augustine*, and the girls join in. Sigrid directs "Jenny—you are a good singer. You will come in dressed as Joan of Arc and sing the first verse to that song, then all the girls will sing the chorus. The orchestra will play with us." Jenny walks center stage, poses as Joan of Arc, holds out her hand in salute and says: "Vive la France!" The girls applaud. Jenny says "I never knew that Joan of Arc could sing." Sigrid replies "well, she is going to sing this time anyway." Ole asks "who is going to sing the *Vulger Boatmen?*" Sigrid looks at Marie "oh yes, Marie you are going to be the Volga Boatman." Marie comes back "will the boatskie be there?" The girls laugh. Sigrid looks at Ole "can you make a skiff?" "I think so." "Bring it to the hall for our next meeting, Marie will need some rehearsing." Ester pipes up "oh, I was so seek when I came over on de sheep that I—." Karen interrupts "don't say it—Clara and I were on the same boat, we know." They all laugh. Clara adds "yes, it was a Danish liner."

Sigrid directs: "next, Mary, will be your turn." Mary turns her nose up snobbishly "I told me Missus, 'Here are all those foreigners going to put on a show in their old-fashioned dresses. I am going to wear me very best black frock, white cap and apron, and I will make a curtsy that would grace a queen.'" Sigrid says to her "and you will sing and dance to the tune of 'London Bridge is Falling Down.'" Sally Ann interjects "I hope it falls." The girls laugh.

"Next, Sally Ann will sing 'It is a Long Way to Tipperary.'" "Aye; and won't Pat be proud of the likes of me" said Sally Ann. "He should if you sing it well," said Sigrid. Ole plays the chorus, and the girls sing.

Sigrid perks her ear "I hear someone, it must be the missus." Alice rushes for the girls wrap.

"Don't rush, it is perfectly alright." Sigrid helps them with their wraps.

Later that evening Sigrid is relaxing. Mrs. Brown is in her drawing room with Professor May. She says "I will call Sigrid." She pokes her head out the door "Sigrid!" "Yes, Mrs. Brown." "Come here a minute." Sigrid come in. Professor May shakes Sigrid's hand "good evening Sigrid." "Good evening, Professor May." Mrs. Brown informs Sigrid "the doctor was called on a case, we had to leave the party early so Professor May walked home with us. He wants to go over some places with you, and give you some instructions." Sigrid informs her "the girls were here this evening, we practiced some songs for the social." "That was perfectly alright, Sigrid."

Professor May states "I am encouraging Sigrid in taking part in this program which her union is putting over. It will give her some experience in appearing before the public and she will get over her self-consciousness. You see, Mrs. Brown, Sigrid hasn't had the opportunities that most our young folks have, who receive the public school training in this country. They all have more or less chance to appear before an audience. Every genius knows his own worth, but it is the attitude of his surroundings that often brings him down."

"Sigrid's longing to come over here was based on her wonderful talent which craved expression. You, Mrs. Brown, are her lucky star, guiding her this far."

"You will have your reward in seeing her some day one of the foremost singers in the world."

Mrs. Brown replies "I have not done anything which calls for a reward. We liked Sigrid when we saw her, and had no further thought then to have her with us to do our work. She is trustworthy and good. But your discovering her talent makes some difference, still I want her here until she has established herself, and can make her living with her singing." Sigrid moves towards Mrs. Brown and looks at her lovingly "you make me very happy."

Professor May takes the paternal stance "yes, Mrs. Brown, that is something I wanted to talk to you about. It is absolutely necessary for Sigrid to have the shelter of a good home. And a place where she will be allowed to practice,

without that my work would be fruitless. It will be almost like making Sigrid a member of your family, instead of being your servant. I have talked to a ladies club, who will help with the financial part, and make arrangements for her appearing in concerts from time to time."

Mrs. Brown states "as far as Sigrid's status in this family is concerned…Sigrid has breeding enough to know her place at the right time, and I will see to it that she has time for practicing."

"And now I will say goodnight, Professor May. I know you wish to go over songs with Sigrid, and it is getting late, good night." "Good night, Mrs. Brown." They shake hands, Mrs. Brown leaves the room, and Professor May retires to the piano.

Professor May turns his attention to Sigrid "now we will go over some exercises, first let us have the breathing." Sigrid practices her exercises. "Now go over the songs you are to sing at this coming social, just hum." Sigrid practices the songs by humming them. "As you enter the stage, walk to center front, hold your hands clasped or in some other comfortable position; look over the audience, not at them. Wait thus a few seconds or until all attention is focused on you. The accompanist will then give you the cue to start. But you must not appear excited or in a hurry. Now go out the side door and enter as if entering the stage." Sigrid does as he instructs.

Sigrid stands as if before an imaginary audience "I see them all there, oh, I want to look at them—see if I recognized any of them—but I mustn't, I must act as if no one was there, as if I were alone—or else I will get perplexed." The professor confirms her "that is right, you do that and you won't be nervous." Sigrid asks "and after I have sung, what then?" "You will know your songs well. And they will be well received, those facts will make you forget your self-consciousness. Now practice entering the stage." Sigrid does as instructed.

The professor instructs Sigrid "now hum your song." Sigrid hums. The professor applauds, Sigrid bows smiling. "Hum the second number." Sigrid hums. The professor applauds, Sigrid bows, backing off the imaginary stage. Sigrid re-enters the room "now what shall I do?" "You must be prepared for an encore. You must always satisfy your audience. But we won't have time for that tonight. I will find some pieces suitable for an encore, and you can practice them at the settlement tomorrow night. Now, I must be leaving." The professor picks up his hat and cane, shakes hands with Sigrid "goodnight Sigrid." "Good night, Professor May." Sigrid goes to the door with him, then sits down on the piano stool, and brushes her hand across her forehead. She whispers softly "am I dreaming…or is all this really happening to me." With that, Sigrid slips out the door in a dream.

Several weeks later, it is the night of the maids' social at the union hall.

Knute has caught up with Sigrid, they have shared a reunion after several years' separation. Knute has volunteered to play violin in the orchestra for the night's production.

Alice, the president of the maid's union, is arranging flowers in a garden outside where a stage is set up.

"This has indeed been a busy week. The girls are so enthusiastic and have practiced so faithfully for tonight's program. I do hope it is a success. Professor May has got the United Women's Organization interested in Sigrid. The professor has great hopes for Sigrid and calls her his very talented pupil. It certainly has boosted the ticket sale, which will be of great help to our union. Strange things do happen in these modern times, but quoting Robert Burns: 'A man is a man for all that,' and someday the social barrier will be broken down and men will be what God meant them to be, equal." Alice moves some plants, looks around, and makes some finishing touches here and there. She goes inside.

Ole arrives playing his harmonica, crosses the stage with the girls in tow, each wearing their national costumes. They take their places.

Alice enters the stage. "Good evening friends, it is my privilege to introduce to you one of the leading ladies of this city who will be the Mistress of Ceremonies for the evening: The chairman of the United Women's Organization."

The Mistress of Ceremonies takes the stage "in behalf of the maid's union who is giving this program and the United Women's Organization, who are acting sponsors, I wish you all welcome. Professor May, our distinguished teacher of singing, has made some great discoveries in his work at the settlement school. One whom he is very proud of is, a member of the maid's union, and who has worked hard to help make this program a success. Through Professor May's influence, our organization has decided to make his star pupil our protégée and see to that her talent is developed to the fullest extent. And it is for her coming out we act as sponsors here tonight. I will now introduce to you Sigrid who will act as leader for the girls."

The M.C. exits the stage, and Sigrid enters. The orchestra starts a lively tune. Hans, the Dutch boy, looks around shading his eyes. "Lena promised to meet he here, she will bring her guitar and she will sing for me. (Longingly)Ah—well, I remember the time when we played by the old windmill. Lena tried to hide, I ran to catch her, and she lost her wooden shoe. Oh, here you are Lena, and where is your guitar?"

"Mamma would not let me bring it, so, just let us dance, like we used to do." The orchestra plays *Oh where, oh where is my Little Dog Gone?* They dance, the girls join in chorus. The orchestra plays a popular German tune. Katherine leads the girls in folk dances, then they form a semi-circle. The orchestra plays *Joan of Arc*, enter Jenny dressed as Joan of Arc, she sings, then the girls dance around her in a semi-circle. Ole plays the tune on his harmonica and leads them back to their seats.

Enter Marie as the Volga boatman, pulling a skiff, while the orchestra plays, she sings the boatman song, the girls join in the chorus accompanied by the orchestra.

Sigrid directs. The orchestra plays a Scandinavian tune, Clara, Ester and Kari form a tableau. The girls join around them and they all dance and sing Nordic folk tunes played on the harmonica by Ole.

Enter Mary, she walks to the middle of the stage, the orchestra plays *London Bridge is Falling Down*, the girls join hands and dance around her.

The orchestra plays *It is a long way to Tipperary*. All pepped up, Sally Ann steps center stage and sings, the girls join in chorus. The curtain falls for the intermission.

After the intermission, the Mistress of Ceremonies enters through the curtain. "I now take pleasure in introducing to you our protégée, your friend and ours, Miss Sigrid Ivorsen.

Sigrid sings…   Knute looks on…

***

This is the end of *The Search For The Rainbow's End.* Knute is left hanging.

Cornella Berntsen was living in Chicago c. 1901. Cornella's sister Minnie was living out on the west coast in the new state of Washington, in a booming little coastal town.

Cornella had an uncle, whose name is unknown to history, who had a sheep ranch near Crescent City, California. He had been shipwrecked there while on a Norwegian ship bound for Port Townsend, Washington. He liked the spot where he had been shipwrecked, and had decided to plant his roots there.

The intrepid Cornella, by some combination of train and ship, came out to visit her sister Minnie. During this time, their uncle in California had developed a cancer in his throat, and was dying. Cornella took a stagecoach down through the redwoods to see him. The stage passed through Wolf Creek, Oregon, near Grants Pass on its way down. He offered to give her the ranch if she would stay with him, but Cornella wanted to go back to her sister, and left, declining the ranch. It seems that she had had enough of farm life.

Cornella, on left, with best friend Amalia
at Chicago.

CHAPTER IV

A Victorian Romance in Bustling Port Townsend

Andrew Benson grew up in the southern Norwegian town of Farsund, his childhood sweetheart was a pretty girl named Minnie Berntsen. Andrew told Minnie that he was going to go to America and earn his fortune, and come back for her.

Andrew sailed from the Norwegian port of Kristiansand, not far from his native Farsund. It was March of 1888. He was sixteen years old. Andrew made his way half-way around the world to the booming seaports on Puget Sound. He got a job with the Puget Mill Company at Port Hadlock, Washington. Port Hadlock was at the south end of Port Townsend Bay. Andrew had never seen anything like this. Hadlock was a rowdy full-fledged Wild West town with saloons and hotels, drunken sailors, and very little law. Sailors from around the world called at busy little Hadlock to take on stores of fresh cut Northwest timber bound for worldwide ports. And the trees! Giants! They blocked out the sun!

There were mill hands who had come from wild and wooly Seabeck on Hood's Canal, who's mill had burned to the ground a couple of years before. Andrew was told tales of the local Indians; that it was once believed that in the center of the great and foreboding Olympic Mountains there was a central plain where a tribe of headhunters presided, that perhaps they held a cache of gold. The local Indians were reverent and fearful of the circular mountain range, and never ventured into the core. They thought it was the home of the Great Spirit. Only in the last few years had expeditions ventured into the outer ridges. Word was that there was interest at the local Fort Townsend to take an expedition through the center. The soldiers had started an expedition a couple years' previous, but had only made it in a few miles. There were early Indian troubles on the Sound in the 1850s, but they had been small scale and the atmosphere was peaceful now.

There was a legend; that years ago the local Chemakum Indians had been massacred at nearby Kala Point by raiding Indian tribes from Vancouver Island, and that one girl had escaped to a cave in a giant rock at the center of the Quimper peninsula. A British sailor who had jumped ship in the early 1850s married the girl and started a homestead in a beautiful inland valley. The same Vancouver Island tribes had gotten into a small battle with the U.S. government at the mill at Port Gamble near the mouth of Hood's Canal.

The local Klallam Indians had had an intertribal war at nearby Dungeness two decades before. At Port Townsend the Indians were known to be friendly and the great chief Chetzemoka, who had been a promoter of peace, died that year.

After only a few months, Andrew's heart grew lonely for his beloved Minnie. He remembered strolling through the flowered Norwegian countryside with Minnie on the way to Sunday school, the morning sunlight playing through the curls in her hair.

In 1893 Minnie immigrated to the United States, going to live with relatives in Chicago. The two were one step closer.

Andrew became a naturalized citizen of the United States March 17, 1896 at Seattle. He worked his way up the hawsepipe as a mariner, becoming a licensed officer and Master of Steam Vessels.

In 1896 Andrew became the master of a crab boat operating out of Port Townsend. He lived in a sailor's boarding house on the Commercial Wharf at the end of Polk Street. Around the corner and a block away was one of Port Townsend's notorious brothels.

In Port Townsend Andrew met who was to become a life-long friend, Adolf Loken, who was an oiler on the famous Revenue Cutter *Bear*. The two became fast friends and Andrew told Adolf of his beloved Minnie. Achieving a measure of success, Andrew was finally able to send for Minnie. Andrew and Minnie were at last married on April 3, 1900, by the Reverend Brooke Baker in Port Townsend.

Minnie convinced her sister Cornella to make the journey to Puget Sound as well. Cornella had been in Chicago and Minnesota with other relatives. Cornella made it out after the diversion to Crescent City, and took up work as a house servant.

In 1902 Adolf was promoted to Chief Oiler on the *Bear*, as a warrant officer.

Adolf became smitten with the young Cornella, a dignified lady from back home, charming, musical, literate, and cultured. He tried to shake the infatuation, but he couldn't. Cornella was a rare gem in this hive of corruption and lust that was Bloody Townsend. A ray of light from back home. Whenever the ship was in port, Adolf desired to spend time with Cornella. One imagines Adolf relaying romantic tales of world travel to the young Cornella. Of evenings spent listening to Cornella at the piano, playing the music of Edvard Greig, singing lovely songs next to the Christmas tree. In the Springtime, the two taking a ride in a buggy, the horse trotting gingerly down country roads, flowers in bloom all around, the birds chirping their songs in the air, the Olympic Mountains rising majestically in the distance. In such a divine setting romance flows quite naturally. Perhaps they rowed a small boat around the bay, or strolled through the green meadows, while reminiscing about life in the old country. A love letter from Adolf to Cornella survives.

U.S. Steamer "Bear"
San Fransisco
January 26th, 1903

Dear Cornella
    I got to San Fransisco yesterday. After we left Port Townsend, we went to Union B.C. and stopped there for 8 days. We had 8 days from Union to Frisco, and bad weather all the way down. I don't know what time we will leave for San Diego. I don't think it will be before middle of next

-2-

month. As I am writing to you, our mailman is calling for me, "Mail for A. Loken." You know, I only get mail once or twice a year, so it is such a surprising thing to me when I hear the mailman calling my name. When I saw the Port Townsend mark on it, I knew it was from Andy or you; and when I opened it and saw it was from you, than I knew, I had

-3-

one friend and a true and good one, that will stand by me through thick and thin, and one that will make our mailman sing out "Mail for A Loken!" Many times when I have been up north in Bearing Sea and we go into Dutch harbor for our mail, and sacks of mail will come onboard. Everybody will get letters or papers; but there never used to be any for me. It used to make me feel sad.

-4-

When you were home in Norway Cornella, Andy and (Minnie) his wife used to josh me about you; but I told them that girl was not borne yet, that I will fall in love with. I know lots of girls around the Sound, but none I care for. After I had seen you 3 or 4 times, I felt like a new man. I tried to shake that feeling off me; but I couldn't. I went around with the boys trowed the money all around me; got drunk; but I felt downhearted all the time. Only when I was together with you; than I felt happy.

-5-

Than first I knew, I was in love. My first thought than was to leave Port Townsend for good, as I thought you may have a fellower in Chicago or some other place. One that works ashore and will be home with you every night if married to you. I always thought it was not wright for a fellower, that makes his living at sea to get married, as he is away so much. But I have changed

-6-

my mind. We boys to sea struggle and work harder, face more danger and hardships than men ashore, and I think, that we are entitled to a little happiness in this world too. Well Cornella I am going to cut this letter short , before I get too sentimental. I thank you very much for your letter. I knew that you cared for me. I could see it on you. I will get a lisence out as an Engenier and I will make enough

-7-

to keep us comfortable. My time is not up before 1st of June 1904 but I think that I can get clear the 1st of May this year. We will forget the past and live for the future. I promise to be a good husband to you Cornella, if we are married. If you have some one in Chicago or old Country that you think more of than me; than I don't want to cut him out. I rather try to forget my love for you and be like a

-8-

brother to you than cut any other fellower out. I give my heart free and clear of any other one, and I want my girl to do the same thing. Tell Andy, that the "Golden Gate" is coming north but not before the new boat is ready. I stand a good show to get on her.----
Give Bendixsens and Olsens my best regards.
I think I finished 4 pages Cornella, I am going to close up now.
With my best wishes to my dear girl

> I remain yours
> Adolf Loken
> U.S.S. Bear
> Custom House
> San Fransisco
> Cal.

Give Andy and his wife my best wishes.

My first letter to a girl! What do think about it?

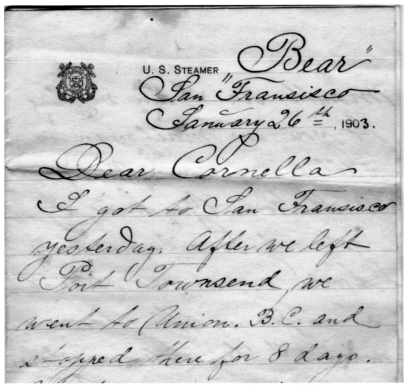

A portion of the first page of the letter from Adolf.

On November 19, 1903 Adolf and Cornella were married. They were married at Saint Paul's Episcopal Church in Port Townsend by Rev. Brook Baker. The Church still stands today, but in those days it was down by the water in the downtown area, and now it is moved up on the hill above the downtown. Their wedding announcement was on the back page of the November 26 edition of the Port Townsend *Morning Leader.*

On the front page of the *Leader* that day was the usual business about the town trying to coax the big railroad men to link up the Port Townsend Southern Railroad with the main line. Included with the usual advertisements was the typical ad for the Pacific Coast Steamship Company, the steamers *Umatilla, Queen,* and *City of Puebla* departing Union Wharf for San Francisco, and *City of Seattle* or *Cottage City* for Alaska. Also, the ad for the Puget Sound Navigation Company steamers bound for all points around the Sound; the steamers *Clallam, Alice Gertrude, Rosalie, Lydia Thompson,* and *Prosper.* In the shipping news section of the *Leader*, the dispositions of twelve ships in the harbor from all over the world are given, including two of the Pacific Coast ships, and the freighter *S.S. Lyra* of the Boston Steamship Company, which had embarked from Tacoma and Seattle with cargo bound for distant Asia. Of the twelve vessels, three were schooners, three were barks, three were "ships," and three were steamships. Four of the vessels were British, and one was Norwegian. Port Townsend still had a little steam in her boilers, but it was bleeding off fast. Ever since the Great Northern Railroad had went to Seattle, and then the Klondike gold rush of '97, everything had shifted to Seattle, and Port Townsend was almost a ghost town by comparison.

In the Spring of 1904, Cornella was with her sister taking care of her. She had had an operation of some sort, and she was expecting. Adolf was away at sea on the *Bear,* which was in San Francisco. The ship had been ordered back to Dutch Harbor, which

Adolf Loken. As a true gentleman of his day, Adolf always had a handkerchief in his uniform pocket in all the early photos.

Cornella Berntsen, taken in Chicago.

Andrew, taken in Port Townsend.

The church where they were married in Port Townsend today.

This is a period photo of Andrew and Minnie's house in Farsund, Norway. Note the painted decorations above the windows, the eves, and the roof.

Andrew and Minnie   *Thelma and Arnold in Farsund, Norway.*

meant that Adolf would be near home again and the newlyweds could be together again. But on the way the Ship was struck by another schooner and ended up back in Oakland, California, for repairs.

In the spring of 1904, Adolf and the *Bear* were in San Francisco Bay, over at Sausalito. From there they were ordered to the Bering Sea directly June 2 to enforce the protection of fur seals. June 4 they were 700 miles out of San Francisco when a schooner, the *Spokane*, rammed the *Bear* slashing a hole in her side and penetrating ten feet into the *Bear*. The point that the ship struck was at the warrant officers quarters on the *Bear* and they were all trapped. If the ship had sunk from the damage the warrant officers would have been drowned for sure. Fortunately, the seas were calm that day, and the two ships were separated without sinking them, and a piece of canvas was stretched over the gaping hole. So, they were spared from a worse fate and the *Bear* made it back to Sausalito. The ship put in for repairs at Hoabs Ship Yard, Oakland. This must have been very distressing for young Cornella, and as soon as she got Adolf's telegram, she joined him in San Francisco.

The ship did not go north in 1904. Instead of heading north as usual, the *Bear* made a trip to Honolulu, Hawaii that December.

In May of 1905 the *Bear* made its regular trip to the waters off Alaska, to Dutch harbor, Nome, St. Lawrence Island, and Siberia. That November she made it back to San Francisco.

Cornella returned to Port Townsend and they had their first child, Thelma Johanne, August 1905.

December 1, 1905 the *Bear* was taken out of commission with the Revenue Service, and eventually spent time in Mare Island Navy Yard receiving repairs. At this time Adolf was a Warrant Officer and Chief Oiler. When the *Bear* was taken out of commission, Adolf received the ship's flag as a souvenir, which is still in the possession of the family.

The *Bear* was again placed in commission in December 1907, and was in regular Revenue Service and Coast Guard service until 1926. She was very famous in the Northwest. She made regular cruises into the North Pacific often going as far as Point Barrow. After government service she was a museum in Oakland, California for a while, then she was purchased by an oceanographer. She made two Antarctic cruises before she sank off Nova Scotia in 1963.

Adolf must have been stationed at Oakland California for a while as he was there for the 1906 San Francisco earthquake and fire. He and his ship fought the great fire from the San Francisco Bay. The events of 1904-5 must have caused some tension in the new marriage. He must have been going through a difficult time about now as he resigned from the Revenue Service, which he had been in for sixteen years. Shortly after, he became ill with typhoid fever and was laid-up for four months. He officially left the service October 4, 1906. This was not a good year for him.

Adolf intended to work on boats on Puget Sound. They had their next child Byron Arnold in the summer of 1907.

Andrew and Minnie Benson went back to Farsund in 1909 to be with family. Andrew returned to Seattle and pursued his career as a master, leaving Minnie in Farsund for the time being. He lived at Seattle and New York City for the rest of his career. Andrew was not able to bring back Minnie for several years more than he anticipated, because of WWI. He finally brought her back to Seattle in 1921.

CHAPTER V

The Coast and Geodetic Survey Service

The Coast and Geodetic Survey Service was founded in 1807 to chart the coasts of America. It was a very respected and scientific service. Its job was charting the coasts, making soundings of the bottom of the bays and ocean floor near the coasts of the mainland, and islands belonging to the United States. They did highly scientific work like magnetic surveys of the affected parts of the globe. The Service was the subject of twenty-one *National Geographic* articles just in the period from 1888 to 1914 alone. The work of the service is carefully explained in these articles. In May 1906 there is an article on the San Francisco earthquake of the same year. The Service participated with other similar organizations in the world to determine the actual size and shape of the Earth. The Service ended up becoming the National Oceanic and Atmospheric Administration (NOAA) and still exists today.

Adolf worked on Puget Sound for about a year, through 1907, but he could not get used to shallow water sailing. It appears that maybe Cornella wished him to be nearer home. But, in any event, the call of the sea was greatest and Adolf joined the Coast and Geodetic Survey Service in April of 1908. He signed on to serve initially as 2nd Assistant engineer, then later 1st Assistant engineer on the *Explorer* in Alaskan waters.

The 135', 450 ton, wooden steamer *Explorer* was built in a Wilmington, Delaware yard expressly for the Coast Survey in 1904. She was a beautiful yacht-like craft ideally suited for meandering the Alaska coastline. She had a triple-expansion steam plant of 400 indicated horsepower, which could drive her at 10 knots. She was equipped with all the latest scientific observation equipment, including equipment for magnetic observations. Her compliment was 7 officers and 40 men. In 1908 her commander was W.C. Dibrell.

The usual season for Alaska surveying was March-April through September-October, typically 7-8 months per year, the actual survey work often not beginning until June. The crew would then lay off in the winter at Seattle, unless they had some warmer southern work.

Surveying the coast involved frequently putting ashore for triangulation and topographic measurements. Hydrography involved soundings and wire drags to gain the information used to make nautical charts.

In the summer and fall of 1908, the *Explorer* was surveying Shelikof Strait, Alaska, above Kodiak Island. She left at the end of the season October 15, and arrived in Seattle November 1, continuing on, she reached San Francisco November 9. *Explorer* made surveys in San Francisco bay and the lower portion of Suisun Bay through the winter.

Cornella decided to go back home to Farsund in Norway with Andrew and Minnie Benson and her two young children to be with family; she stayed there for four years. Meanwhile, Adolf would get established. Long separations were the way of the mariner.

USC & GSS Explorer *in Alaska. She had a graceful, yacht-like countenance.*   Photo from Adolf Loken collectic

Sailing north in the spring of 1909, *Explorer* reached Bristol Bay, above the Aleutians, May 26. She returned for the next two years. In command was W.C. Dibrell.

At the close of the 1910 season, *Explorer* with Adolf went to survey the Hawaiian island of Oahu. *Explorer* surveyed the sultry waters of Oahu through the winter to February 1911. *Explorer* was then sent to San Francisco for repairs, which took place from March of 1911 to July of 1912. H.W. Rhodes took command of *Explorer* briefly.

From 1912 to 1915, *Explorer* was commanded by Raymond S. Patton, who would go on to be an Admiral and Director of the Coast and Geodetic Survey. Adolf was 1st Assistant Engineer on the *Explorer,* but then he made Chief.

During the 1912 season *Explorer* did surveys in Kuskokwim Bay, north of Bristol Bay. That winter she had more repairs done at Bremerton Naval Shipyard and then had wireless radio equipment installed. In 1913 she returned to Kuskokwim Bay.

In 1914 it was the approach to Juneau: Icy Strait. In the middle of the season *Explorer* was diverted to work in Cook Inlet at the request of the Alaska Engineering Commission, in preparation for a railroad terminus. It was noted in official reports that *Explorer* was starting to show signs of weakness, as a result of being in rough open seas. It was recommended she be used in protected waters. In late 1914, *Explorer* was sent to parts inside Prince William Sound.

Adolf on the **Explorer.**

In March and April 1915, *Explorer* got work close to home and performed wire drag surveys of Rich Passage in Puget Sound. After that she was sent to Cook Inlet again. On her return in September, *Explorer* made stops at Seward, Haines, and Juneau. On arriving at Puget Sound in October, *Explorer* resurveyed Port Gamble off of Hood Canal.

In 1916 *Explorer* made her way to Dixon Entrance at the south end of southeast Alaska, and surveyed the coastal islands north of Cape Muzon. She had a new skipper, F.H. Hardy.

In the early spring of 1917, Explorer again made hydrographic surveys of Rich Passage. In May she sailed again to the coast north of Cape Muzon. Her skipper was T.J. Maher. The season was cut short, as the crew of the *Explorer* were deserting the ship for higher paying jobs when they reached Alaska. This had been occurring for some years now, but had reached a chronic level.

This was the year the United States entered WWI. Adolf resigned to enlist in the Navy on a wave of patriotism, as a Chief Machinists Mate. In the 1918 Annual report of the Coast Survey submitted to the Secretary of Commerce, it was noted "The work of the party was seriously handicapped by the desertion of a number of the crew and the resignation of the chief engineer." *Explorer* was laid up in Lake Union when she was taken over by the Navy May 16, 1918, for use as a patrol boat in Alaska. Some of the men took jobs on U.S. Shipping Board ships.

Adolf's Navy pay was very low and Cornella was not happy with that, and after a

DEPARTMENT OF COMMERCE AND LABOR

REPORT OF THE SUPERINTENDENT

OF THE

COAST AND GEODETIC SURVEY

SHOWING

THE PROGRESS OF THE WORK

FROM

JULY 1, 1908, TO JUNE 30, 1909

WASHINGTON
GOVERNMENT PRINTING OFFICE
1909

Flag of the USC & GS

Utilizing Triangulation, Topography, and Hydrography, the service did its work.

Maps are from the 1913 report of the progress of the Survey.

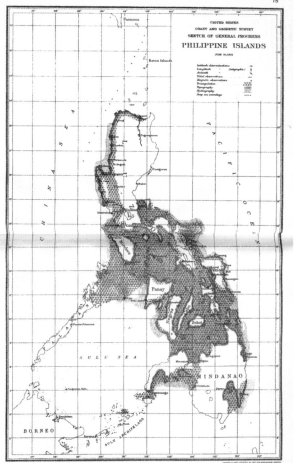

short while neither was he. A month after joining the Navy, Adolf was offered a Chief position on a new 8000 ton ship, but he couldn't take it as he had enlisted for four years. Well, through much wrangling on Adolf's part, he was commissioned as an Ensign, and was an engineer again.

Adolf saw service in World War I on a French liner as 2nd Assistant Engineer, and the *Mount Pelier* as 1st Assistant, probably. The *Mount Pelier* was a troop ship headed for France. The ship was apparently torpedoed or suffered damage from an explosion and this in turn caused a ruptured steam pipe or boiler. Adolf risked his life to handle the situation, receiving severe skin burns to his legs in the process; it had not even been his watch. In the process he saved several persons, but ironically, Adolf was the only one injured. For his actions in this incident Adolf received medals, and permission to be buried at Arlington cemetery.

The *Explorer* returned to the Navy Yard in the fall of 1918. Adolf returned to Seattle, but he was put on shore duty inspecting engines on the new government ships being churned out of the Seattle shipyards by the dozens. Firms like the new Skinner & Eddy shipyard were building modern 424', 8800 ton steel cargo ships for the new United States Shipping Board's Emergency Fleet Corporation as a result of the war, and the Puget Sound shipyards' output were recognized as amazing. Puget Sound yards were also producing copious quantities of wooden steamers as well, and that would be the source of controversy after the war, as they were surplused, and eventually scrapped.

Sometime in late 1918 to early 1919 Adolf shipped out on the new 8800 ton *West Congo*. This trip took him south where he caught up with his brother who he had not seen in twenty years. Captain Harold Loken had been for some time the Harbor Master of Colon, Panama. Adolf's ship put in at Balboa and was going to go through the canal the next morning. After telephoning and informing his brother Harold that he had found him, Adolf took a train over to see his long lost brother and his sister in law. This was to be the last time Adolf and his brother were to see each other.

Captain Harold Loken has an interesting and tragic story. After surviving a career at sea, and after he had retired from thirty years of being a Harbor Master in the Panama Canal Zone, Harold returned to Oslo. When Harold was seventy-three years old he made a trip to Los Angeles for a visit of some kind about November 1951—or at least he planed on going to Los Angeles. He was on the ship *Bataan*. He was in his bed in his stateroom when a fire broke out that eventually lasted for thirty hours. Harold, the *Bataan's* captain, and a woman were killed in the flames trapped in their staterooms.

After going through the Panama Canal, the *West Congo* headed for war ravaged Europe. The following letter is dated April 15, 1919.

Dear Wife and children.

As you see I am now in Trieste, Austria; but this city belongs to Italy now. There must be about 50,000 Italian soldiers in charge of the city. The whole Austrian Navy fleet was handed over to the Italians.

All work is at a stand still here and most of the population is starving.

We are taken all our flour ashore here. From here we go to a place called Spelaria, where we will take 100 american sailors back to New York. We may also get a cargo back to New York also.

Everything you want to buy here cost more than in the states. Most of the stores are closed. Half of the houses are empty or occupied by soldiers. All you see is soldiers everywhere.

I sent a letter to yours from Gibraltar.

I hope you are all well and that the allotment is arriving regularly.

I have been very busy since we arrived here as we are cleaning and overhauling all our boilers, and as [fau?] in charge of them, so it is up to me, grease and dirt from morning to night for the last 8 days. We have the best time when we are at sea, just standing our engine room watches. All the other officers went for 3 days trip to Venice Italy, I could have gone too if I wanted; but I could not afford it. I may make a trip out to the trenches and see them, when I get through work on the boilers.

There are 8 american destroyers here and 6 american submarine chasers.

I hope your garden will do swell this summer, and all your fancy rosebushes. Plant potatoes between the rosebushes, so that ground is rich. I tried to buy myself a [mershium?] pipe, but there is no [mershium?]pipes in the whole city, I still take a smoke on my corn cob.

Trieste is a very old city and there are fine buildings, churches, and monuments hundreds of years old. Lots of the buildings have been bombarded by Italian aroeplanes. And they killed a lot of the population. 1 little boy was on board to day(about 8 years old) He had a deep scar all along one side of his face from an aroeplane bomb. You can be thankful you are in Seattle and not over in these European countries. In all the places over here is misery and starvation.

Best wishes to you all from your Husband and father.

Tell Bernice to write a few words in the next letter

The *Explorer* was returned to the Coast Survey in 1919, but lay in Lake Union until February 1920. In 1920, Adolf was back in the Coast Survey Service as Chief Engineer on the now very familiar *Explorer*. Concern had been expressed over her seaworthiness in unprotected waters, and the graceful *Explorer* would spend the rest of her career in the protected waters of southeast Alaska on the beautiful Inside Passage, where she would become an icon in Alaska. During the survey season she was based out of the capital of Juneau.

In the 1920s, Adolf and Cornella were living in West Seattle, where they were to live most of the rest of their lives.

From 1920 to 1926 *Explorer* surveyed and performed wire drags of Lynn Canal and Chatham Strait, Icy Strait and Cross Sound, Gastineau Channel, Stephens Passage, Taku Harbor, Gambier Bay, Hobart Bay, and Frederick Sound. Some time was spent near Ketchikan as well. *Explorer* was commanded by N.H. Heck, J.H. Hawley, and F.B.T Siems during this period, but *Explorer* had only one Chief Engineer.

In the summer of 1921 the *Explorer* entertained the Governor of Alaska and even had a full band on board. Like the *Bear* had been, *Explorer* had become important to the state of Alaska, and she was very prominent at Juneau and the important locales on the Inside Passage. The Chief Engineers were a fraternal group, and Adolf Loken would become acquaintains with one of the top Chief Engineers at the most prominent steamship line to Alaska, the Alaska Steamship Company[1]. This engineer was Benjamin Parker, who sailed for Alaska Steam on the ships *Alaska*, *Victoria*, *Aleutian*, and *Alameda* in the '20s, and *Denali* and *Yukon* in the '30s. Both men called Seattle home, both were in the same local of the M.E.B.A., and both men were prominent in their profession, particularly in Alaska.

[1]The Alaska Steam story is given in Chapter VIII, pages 91, 93, and Chapter X.

Explorer *at Juneau entertaining dignitaries. In the harbor is the* **S.S. City of Seattle**. *A popular Alaska gold rush steamer, the Pacific Coast Steamship Co.'s* **City of Seattle** *had seen such prolific passengers as Wyatt Earp and "Soapy" Smith.*

Sitka, Alaska.   Photos from Adolf Loken collection

Eskimos in Alaska.

Photos from Adolf Loken collection

*This bear was after Adolf in Alaska. The companion in the picture killed it before it got
Adolf. They were on a trip looking for oil fields the story goes.*

Winter retreat Alaska style.   Photos from Adolf Loken collection

Next Adolf was to make a dramatic change of climate and participate in the survey of the Philippine Islands on the survey ship *Pathfinder,* embarking from Seattle in November 1926. He had surveyed Hawaii years earlier, but this was a warmer still climate, and humid. There was no air conditioning on ships in those days and the engine room would have been hot! Adolf recollects that he had to change his socks six times a day! What a change from Alaska. But this is the life of a sailor. For over two years Adolf served on *Pathfinder* while they surveyed the Philippines in 1926-29. The survey of these islands had been going on since 1901, and was starting to reach completion.

Upon joining the ship in December, a resurvey of Manila Bay was in progress, and was carried out the remainder of 1926. This was the civilized core of the Philippines, the rest of the expedition would be spent in the more primitive regions then being explored.

It is unfortunate that not too many of Adolf's own sea stories still exist in his own words. The South Sea Islands, numbering in the thousands, in those days were still very primitive. In the outlying Philippine Islands there were still headhunters and cannibals. In these areas the women still went about their days bare-breasted and wearing nothing but grass skirts, like in the old movies. The men wore almost nothing. They lived in huts made from poles and leaves. Later in life, Adolf recollects how he was fascinated by the nighttime dances around the campfire by the native cannibals. The survey ships would have meandered around the remote islands much more than the passenger steamers and merchantmen. The sailors would have better opportunity than most to observe the local cultures. We can see this world that Adolf witnessed first hand in the period articles from *National Geographic.* One letter does exist, however, and is quite interesting.

Aparri, Luzon island
July 1st, 1927.

Dear daughter.

I received your welcome letters, and that you liked your bracelet. I will be sending some more black coral bracelets, when I get back to the Sulu islands. We are still working around the northern islands. And will not be back in Manila till 1st of August. I shall send you postal card pictures of these people and places out here, and you ought to save them. I hear Arnold fixed up the front room, had it pepered and bought swell electric light fixtures. That was very nice. They make some swell looking reed furniture out here and if I can make a bargain, I may buy some and send to Seattle, for your swell sitting room. These people here on these islands, they live in grass huts, they have small farms and plenty of Cattle. We buy meat from them, and ave pay 10.00 dollars for a cow. In Manila we have to pay a high price for meat; because it is all imported from Australia.

Here is plenty of flying fish. The natives fish when it is dark and they carry a big burning torch in the bow of the canoe. The fish see this light, and fly for it, and fall into their canoes. The flying fish has wings like a bird. They use bow and arrows, when they go hunting.

Well, Dora, I suppose you are having a good time now during the vacation.

Are there plenty of roses. Our garden must look very nice in summertime, when everything is in bloom, don't you think the same.

Too bad we did not trade for that new big new house.

We don't sleep in our staterooms here; because it is too warm, so we sleep on deck in camp beds with big mosquito screens around every bed. I like to sleep in open air.

Best wishes to Dora and everybody.
God be with you.

From your
Daddy

American woman with Moro tribesmen on the Sulu Archipelago. The tribesmen are all carrying their Barong *and* Bolo *knives. The note on the back of the picture says "they are always on the warpath." Moro pirates had been plaguing the waters of the Sulu Sea for centuries, finally being subdued in the early twentieth century. Following the Insurrection was the Moro Rebellion. The Moro warriors were known to fight as fanatical berserkers.* Photos from the Adolf Loken collection

Top right: *Pith helmet worn by Adolf Loken.*
Far Right: *Moro bow from Ben Parker collection.*
Right: *Moro Barong short-sword.*

Above and below: *Borneo.*   *North Luzon, Negrito people.*

Photos from the
Adolf Loken
collection

For most of 1927 and 1928 *Pathfinder* surveyed the southern islands of the Philippines in the Sulu Archipelago, at the southern parts of the Sulu Sea, going as far south Borneo on the Equator. From January 1927 *Pathfinder* was engaged in the Sanboy Islands,

Fitted out for the hunt.

Photos from the Adolf Loken collection.

Above right:
*Negrito headhunters
of north Luzon Is.*

*By this time, the
Philippines were the
subject of dozens of
articles in* National
Geographic Magazine,
*particularly June
1898, March 1904,
April 1905, March
1911*, Sep. 1912*,
and Nov. 1913*.*

*The Survey of the
Philippines were in the
Dec. 1903 and Jan.
1911 issues.*

Photo from the Benjamin
Parker collection

halfway down the Sulu Archipelago. Working around the monsoon season, some time was spent in the Luzon Strait in 1927. *Pathfinder* resumed surveys in the Sulu Archipelago through 1928, then back again to the Luzon Strait. *Pathfinder* made her way to the Davao Gulf in September 1928 to March of 1929.

Upon returning from the South Seas, Adolf sailed back home on the American Mail

In the Tropics.

Photos from the Adolf Loken collection

Crew of the **Pathfinder.** National Geographic *featured articles on the Coast Survey of the Philippines and* **Pathfinder** *in the December 1903 issue and January 1911 issue.*

Period post card from China.

Mt Fuji. Period post card from Japan.   From Adolf Loken collection

Line liner *S.S. President Grant*[1]*,* a luxury cruise ship even by today's standards.   The American Mail Line brought travelers from around the world to the Far East and beyond.

In March of 1929, Adolf was assigned to the *Explorer* again, which would head to

---

[1] A period description of a voyage on *S.S. President Grant* is given in Chapter XI, pages 152-172.

southeast Alaskan waters once more, surveying Wrangell Narrows and Duncan Canal. The big news at the beginning of the season, in May, was the sinking of Alaska Steam's *Aleutian* up at Kodiak Island. The Coast Survey steamer *Surveyor* went to the rescue to pick up survivors, all survived but one. This was not the first time a survey boat rushed to aid a vessel in distress in the frigid Alaskan waters.

In 1930 *Explorer* carried Adolf to Behm Canal, not far from Ketchikan in the southernmost part of Alaska. Alaskan's were glad to have him back. The following article from the Ketchikan Sunday Chronicle dated August 17, 1930, tells a fitting story of Adolf's life at sea:

Chief engineer of Explorer Life's History Makes "Trader Horn" and London Fiction Pale Into Insignificance

"Trader horn" would look like a piker and the Fiction of Jack London would seem pale along-side of the life story and experiences of A.H. Loken, chief engineer of the United States coast and geodetic survey boat Explorer, now doing survey work in Behm canal close to Ketchikan.

This veteran in the service of Uncle Sam has sailed the seven seas. He drove the old cutter Grant around Cape Horn. He was in the Chinese, Philippine and Cuban service, and in the rumbling hold of transports, far below the waterline, he manned engines on transports through the submarine infested seas during the big scrap.

But it was in the Arctic among the sea-roving traders and matching against the ice, that was the richest part of his long and varied service. Born in Norway, battling against great odds is probably in the blood, for it is a generally known and accepted fact that the hardy Norsemen are the most numerous among the fishermen in the north seas where conditions are the most harsh.

Here in 1893

Chief Engineer Loken first came to Alaska in 1893, and has been making the trip, first in the old Grant and then in the Bear nearly every season since then, except during intervals when called to foreign service. He visited Point Barrow and Herschel island and was off the mouth of the Mackenzie river in the Arctic in early days, when sea traders and whalers braved the north waters in windjammers.

In those early days natives parted with valuable fox skins for $1.50 each and a string of beads or trifles they swapped furs which are now almost worth their weight in gold.

According to Loken's mates, when he can be prevailed upon to tell about some of his more exciting experiences, they are more interesting than any novel. He will pass lightly over the war, the Spanish American service, close shaves in China, and invariably swing back to the Arctic where his heart seems to be. He will even admit that he would like to be in the Arctic service today.

He was asked his views yesterday of Ketchikan and replied: "This climate makes it the natural home for Norsemen. One can see their handiwork on every hand. The fine boats which go from here to the halibut grounds tell their own story. Many of the residences and homes were built from the sea.

"I am not surprised to learn that the Alaskan fisherman have extended their fishing operations into the Bering sea. They will extend them into the Arctic, if they can find the fish there. That is their nature. The more risks and dangers which attach to fishing, the more the Scandinavians are at home."

USC & GSS DISCOVERER.   Photo from Adolf Loken collection

In 1931 Adolf was given the Chief's job on the *Discoverer*, a much newer and stouter ship. He was back in the open north Pacific again, surveying on the Kenai Peninsula to the north part of Kodiak Island, which carried on through the 1932 season.

Adolf lived in a time of rapid technological advancement, yet still, the modern world was very much in its infancy. It is interesting to note that these ships that Adolf was on were "Science Vessels," incorporating some of the latest technology (or should we say "gadgets") of the day. With that in mind we find the following letter particularly amusing.

Seward, Alaska.
July 5th, 1931

My dear daughter Florence.

Thank you very much for your letter that I received sometimes ago. The "Discoverer" arrived in Seward yesterday morning, so we celebrated the 4th of July in Seward. Looked at the baseball game between the ship's crew and the Seward team. Discoverer's team won.

Took in the movie in the evening. This is a bum town and plenty of snow here yet. We were in Seward a week ago also, brought in a badly hurt man from a salmon cannery. They sent a wireless message, broadcasted, from the cannery for medical help and our ship picked up the wireless message 100 miles away. And went full speed 15 miles pr. hour, to this cannery. We brought the man, badly hurt, to Seward hospital. 200 miles away. He was unconscious for 2 days, but he is now getting along fine. The wireless is a great invention.

I am feeling very good, better than last summer.

The **Discoverer** *plowing through the seas.*   NOAA

How are the roses and the flowers you planted?
How did you finish in the school?
Did you take in the 4th of July parade?
3 months more, I will be back in Seattle again.

Best wishes to you and everybody.   From your
                                                     <u>Daddy</u>

   Note the mention of the "wireless" set being a miracle of technology! This is a good example of the kind of side work the survey ships performed in the remote northern waters.

CHAPTER VI

The Roaring Twenties in West Seattle

Well, probably about 1912, Adolf bought a house in West Seattle, after his island expeditions, at 3242 35th Avenue South West. Cornella had not yet returned. The house had spacious grounds and was provided with many fruit trees and berry bushes all about.

The government ships were having their home port moved to West Seattle at that time. In those days, West Seattle was a resort area of Seattle proper. Many people in the city had summer houses across Elliot bay there, and there was a regular ferry that shuttled across. Also in West Seattle were Luna Park, a popular waterfront amusement park, and Alki Beach Park where people could take the ferry or streetcar over for a good time.

Cornella returned from Norway and set up housekeeping in her new house in West Seattle. In the fall of 1913 Adolf and Cornella had their second daughter Bernice Catherine, then in the fall of 1915 their third Florence Dora, and finally in the fall of 1917 their fourth Lilian Margaret.

In 1917 World War I was on. On a wave of patriotism Adolf joined the Navy as a Chief Machinists Mate. His pay was much lower than he and Cornella were accustomed to ($10 per month, and a small government allowance to Cornella) and Cornella was not at all happy. To make matters worse, Adolf was offered a position a month later on a new large ship, which paid $200/month, but he could not take it as he was in the Navy for four years. Cornella tried to get Adolf to do something about the situation, but his hands were tied, he was in the Navy. Cornella wrote to the Commandant of the Navy Yard to try to plead her husband's case. In letters to Cornella, Adolf complains that he is "losing money in this service."

Well, after Adolf had wrangled with his superiors for a couple of months, he was commissioned as an Ensign by May of 1917, and working as an Assistant Engineer with pay of about $150/month. Adolf travels all over Europe and the Mediterranean in his Navy service. He writes Cornella about how cheap fancy lace is in Spain and Italy and buys her some. He often asks how the berry bushes in the yard are doing.

When the *Explorer* returned to the Navy Yard in the fall of 1918, Adolf was in Seattle to take a position as her Chief with pay of $195/month, much to the relief of Cornella. This was after Adolf's incident on the *Mount Pelier*, where he was badly burned and then hospitalized at Newark. However, he was stuck on shore duty at this time in the shipyards inspecting the engines on the new government ships.

Shore duty was not to keep him forever though, and Adolf eventually found himself on a ship going through the Panama Canal where in nearby Colon he caught up with his long lost brother Harold, who was now addressed as Captain, and was the Harbor Master of Colon. This was the last time he would ever see his brother.

Young Thelma Loken.

Adolf was a good father, so much as a man at sea could be, and he kept an active interest in his children's education and development. In a letter dated September 4, 1920 from Juneau, Alaska Adolf addresses his teenage daughter Thelma.

> I received your letter a few days ago. I am glad to hear you had a good vacation on Bainbridge Island. You can have this trip every summer. Learn to be a good swimmer, that is a great sport. Well, I suppose your summer vacation is soon over now and that means schooling again. I want you also to take singing lessons at the Cornish school this winter. We have had lots of blueberries up here this summer. When a person goes blueberry picking in Alaska he has to carry a rifle with him as the woods are full of Bears. I have been shooting after 2 Bears this summer, they both got away. It is going to be a long season up here this year, least 2 months more.
> I had a letter from Arnold also and I see that he has been to the boy scout camp in Hood's Canal[Camp Parsons]. I suppose he is tooting the bugle for the scouts.

Note the reference to Arnold's going to the Boy Scout camp, Camp Parsons, on Hood's Canal. This was very near the first years of the camp's existence. The only way the boys got to the camp in those days was on a small steamer like the *Virginia V*. And also note the reference to Thelma's trip to Bainbridge Island as if it were a far off

wilderness!

In another letter to Thelma dated July 6th, 1921 from Juneau, Alaska, Adolf further shows his fatherly support.

> I received your welcome letter and I am glad to hear you are attending the Broadway shool.----
> I know that you were handicapped the first 2 years in shool because you did not know the English language very good, but I knew all the time that you had as good a head and a little more when it came to a show down. You do the best you can, I will always be with you.----
> I sent Arnold a letter to day with 1.00 dollar in it addressed to Orcas Island. I was at the dinner given by the Governor of Alaska 3 weeks ago and the Explorer is going out the 14th of this month and meet the new Governor of Alaska, coming up from Seattle.----
> We had a nice 4th of July here. Big parade led by Fort Seward band. We are going to have a band Onboard when we go out to meet the new Governor.----

Thelma was fifteen years old when she received this letter. Adolf always signed his letters to Thelma "from your Father." In later letters to Bernice he signs "from Daddy." His letters show formality, and at the same time tenderness. In his letters to Bernice he is often mentioning how he is sending her money for college and books and extras.

At the center of the Loken family were music and the arts, a common theme in this era, but especially well represented in this house. The piano was a dominant feature of the home, the strains of the violin ever present.

It was common among Scandinavians immigrating to not speak their native language to their children, and not teach the children their native language. They believed "we are Americans now," and they lived it. They did reminisce about the old country though, and formed organizations such as the Sons of Norway, and the Danish Brotherhood.

Adolf wished for all his children to be well educated. Arnold would graduate from the University of Washington with a degree in music, he was a musician at heart and played in bands. In 1923 Thelma was going to Pacific Lutheran "college" as it was known at that time, now of course Pacific Lutheran University.

For the most part, except for an incident we will treat shortly, the roaring twenties were good to the Lokens and they enjoyed over a decade of prosperity. Adolf was firmly entrenched in the Survey Service: He was a senior engineer, his job was secure, and, he made good money.

In July of 1927, Bernice went to a "church camp fourteen miles west of Bremerton." "It was the Congregational Young People's Conference. They have one every year. The place where we were is called Seabeck, although it is not the real town of Seabeck." She writes her father "I had a lovely time, swimming and rowing every day."

During the prosperous years of the Loken family, the period being mostly during the roaring twenties, Cornella used to take the family out on a big summer outing every year. Around 1928, Cornella made arrangements to take the family on their summer outing to the wilds of the Olympic Peninsula. At this time Thelma was suffering from her "condition." The Olympic and Soleduc Hot Springs were thought to have a medicinal effect on those that bathed in the steaming pools.

On the trip were Cornella, Thelma, Bernice, Florence, and Lilly. Little Lilly was just nine years old. From Seattle they embarked on a mosquito steamer bound for Port Angeles. Florence believed that they traveled on the *Virginia V,* but the memory was not exactly clear. From Port Angeles they took a bus to the store, now gone, that used to be on the highway right where it crosses the Elwha River. The store was right inside the bend in the road at that spot.

In those days there was not yet a road up to the Olympic Hot Springs, so, the women young and not so young had to hike up twelve miles to the resort. Florence recalls how they were afraid of bears along the way. Once they got up there they found the rustic resort area: there were little cabins that they lodged in, there were small bath houses that housed the mineral pools, and there was a swimming pool full of crystal clear river water. There was no lodge at that time according to Florence, but there was a store that they bought pancake flour, & etc. in. They cooked in the cabins.

While they were camped out up there, Arnold and a friend came up to meet the women and girls. Arnold had driven out to the store on the Elwha by car and had left his car at the store. They hiked back down the twelve miles and Arnold drove them all back to Seattle. It must have been a big car!

Florence would always remember this trip, it was quite an adventure for her. Except for Thelma's "condition," this was the good 'ole days. She would not return until the 1940's, however, with her husband Jim and another couple. Apparently at that time the resort was still there. The first time the author remembers going to the Olympic Hot Springs was with Florence. Chris was a young boy. This was in the 1970's and the resort was gone, but there was a park campground you could drive to. Now, once again, you have to hike up there. And, no resort, it is all natural setting today.

About 1929, the same year the Depression hit, Adolf and Cornella bought the house next door which was much bigger and nicer, but did not have the yard with all its fruit like the other. The address was 3248 45th Ave. S.W. They rented out their former house. Here they lived until 1938.

Sheet music cover.

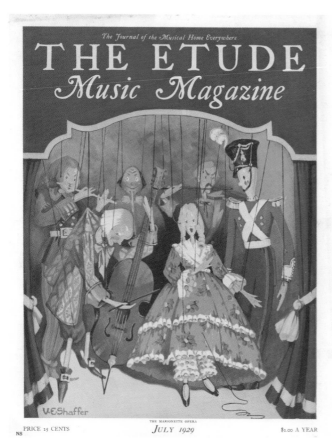

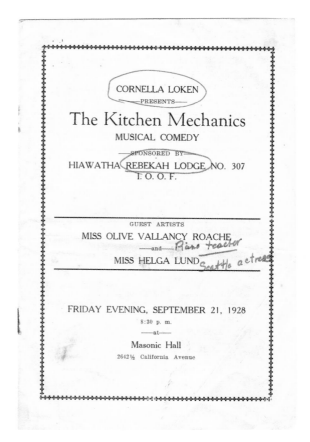

Cornella Loken, 1930s.

In this play Arnold provides the musicians, *"His Peppy Band."* The cast has fifteen characters, Bernice is one of them.

The Loken residence from 1929-1938 in West Seattle. 3248 45th Ave. S.W. The Lokens lived in this house during the height of their prosperity. After the death of Adolf in 1933, the Depression made life difficult.

This bronze lighthouse is from the Loken residence of the twenties and early thirties. It lights up, and the glow alternately gets brighter and dimmer, simulating a real lighthouse. The loken women used to keep this lighthouse plugged in, and on, the entire time Adolf was out to sea. When he would return home safe, it was unplugged until the next time. The doily it is sitting on was also a favorite of the Loken residence. **Right:** *Model ship* **S.S. Pacific** *built by Adolf and crew while on* **Bear**.

Thelma Loken.

Arnold Loken.

Bernice Loken.

Bernice on right and Lily? on left.

Florence. When young she went by Dora.

The Alki Beach, Municipal Bath House, SEATTLE U.S.A.

Photo by Webster & Stevens.

Post Card c 1910. For more on the history of West Seattle, see Seattle's Luna Park *by Aaron J. Naff.*

Adolf's retirement plans were prosperous as well. He writes to Florence in 1929.

U.S.S. "Explorer"
Wrangell, Alaska.
July 7, 1929.

My dear daughter,

Well I received your welcome letter. I had been looking for a letter from you for sometime. Well I sure would liked to have been at the school, when graduation was going on. Well Florence I shall buy you a new dress, when you start in the High School. We had our 4th of July in Wrangell with a very quite day.

The old Explorer is working in the finest part of Alaska, Wrangell Narrows. Deer and black bears are walking around everywhere. No one is allowed to shoot them.

Well, Florence how do you like the new house. I am sure it is better than the old one. I am going to buy one more house 20 miles from Los Angeles, California. This house will have from 1 to 3 acres of land to it. So I can have plenty of fruit trees, roses, chickens, and pidgeons. Thelma shall take care of the chickens and pidgeon. We shall live in Seattle summertime and California wintertime. I want you to take up drawing, scetching as one subject at the highschool, as you are a very good artist in drawing. Draw me the dutch kids and I will send you 1 dollar for the picture. Sign your name to the picture. Mamma gets her check from Washington every month.

Best wishes to you and everybody.

From your
Father

Later that same summer Adolf writes Florence again. Florence is fourteen at this time.

Wrangell, Alaska.
August 4th, 1929

My Dear daughter Florence.

    I received your picture "The Dutch Kids" and also your letter. The Picture is very good, everybody think it is fine. Artistie. I am going to frame it and hang it up in my room. When I get back to Seattle, I am going to buy you <u>water colors, pencilbrushes,</u> and <u>scetching table</u>. You sure know how to draw. At the High School you will take up drawing and commercial course as main courses.
    We have had rain here all the time, so we expect a little sunshine in August. The woods are full of blueberries, so we have blueberry pie all the time. I am sending you 2 dollars, I think the picture is worth it.
    Best wishes to you and all

From your
<u>Father</u>

    As we have seen, the Loken household was a proper, formal one. Adolf had endeavored to become an officer in the military as a young man, and then actually did become a marine officer. In those days a son of such a man would be raised to become a success. The daughters of such a man would be raised to become ladies: so that they could marry a successful man. Such girls would be schooled in the arts, music, and the social graces; so as to be as charming as possible. Boys were raised to be men, and girls to be women, feminine. It was a proper world of ladies and gentlemen. Of upper classes and lower classes. Of evenings spent by the piano listening to dear daughter play. The 1800's had seen a tremendous emphasis on the arts, and this had spilled over into the first half of the twentieth century. In those days, even the arts were proper for the most part, though things were already starting to change.
    In the first years of the Depression, Cornella found herself in a position to be benevolent and would feed any out-of-work man that came to the door. She would serve them on the back porch; a hot plate of food and some hot coffee.
    The following year Florence received her usual letter.

Ketchican, Alaska
August 2nd, 1930

My dear daughter Florence.

    I received letters from my 3 girls this time and I am sitting down to write letters to all of you included "Thelma." Arnold I shall send a doz. handkierchiefs to a week from now. I am also sending you a picture of the ship's goose. This goose was picked up in the woods, when it was very small. Could hardly walk, and it has grown very big since. It is very tame, eats from our hand and follow us around ashore like a dog. It is a wild goose, but is tame now. I may get it, and let it walk around the yard. We also have an Alaska Eagle. The weather has not been very good this summer, rain and plenty of wind.

There has been a lot of tourist coming up here this summer; and times up here is very good. Plenty of fish, salmon, and all canneries are working night and day. Blueberries are plentyfull.

It cost 75 cents to go and see movies up here. I want to hear grand opera for that much money. I hope you are having a good time this summer.

Best wishes to you all.

From your
<u>Daddy</u>.

The first years of the Depression did not affect the Lokens much, but then tragedy struck. In 1933 Adolf was going to be assigned to the *Surveyor*, pride of the fleet. It was March, and Adolf was getting ready for the season. He collapsed walking downtown Seattle on his way to work, and later died in the hospital. Adolf Nils Loken had served in the government service for forty-two years.

Thelma was a beautiful young girl who, as we saw earlier, grew up in her youngest years in the old country of Norway. She spoke Norwegian and probably had a thick accent when she was very young. She was musical and had a beautiful singing voice. She attended the Cornish School of the Arts in Seattle. Thelma even performed on the Seattle radio as a singer.

The Loken family had a dark secret that even the younger children Florence and Lily did not know about: and would not know about most, or all, of their lives. Florence remembers her childhood days being dampened by a dark cloud that she knew as Thelma's "condition." As Florence grew up she noticed that not many people came to visit at the family home because of this "condition." As a young girl Florence remembers that her family did not talk about things of a personal nature. They for sure did not talk about sex and things of that nature. They were very Victorian and old world European. Their household was a warm but formal place. Florence remembered that after the children would go to bed Adolf and Cornella would converse in Norwegian. They liked their privacy. Not even Cornella, Florence's own mother, would ever let the secret out. Florence would not know the cause of Thelma's "condition" until a couple of years before her older sister Bernice's death in the 1980s. Lily would never know. Bernice *did* know however, and this might have colored her entire life. Arnold no doubt did know, but it did not seem to affect him so badly as it apparently affected Bernice. And it appears that Arnold never spoke of it either.

The secret was—Thelma had been tragically raped by a gang of boys in Seattle when she was eighteen, in 1924. The incident greatly affected her for the worse and she never got over it. She was a diagnosed schizophrenic from the time of the incident on, and she was on medications for it. At least in the later years of her condition, Thelma was not in touch with reality and was described as not talking and catatonic, not aware of her surroundings. It appears that Adolf did not approve of anyone in the family talking about the incident. A matter of pride apparently, a fear of scandal, and perhaps a desire to shelter the others. In any event, it was a BIG *dark* thing that no one was supposed to speak of. Thelma was taken care of by her mother until she died. Thelma died just three years after her father died. Her father's death might have been the last straw for her. Adolf was the pillar that the family depended on. Arnold drove Thelma and family to see a psychiatrist or specialist of some kind in Chicago in an attempt to save her, but it was to no avail. They apparently tried one in Minnesota as well. Cornella tried everything she could, except talking about the cause of the trouble openly.

When Thelma died she was extremely thin and bedridden. The house was cold as it was winter and they had no money for heat. Cornella had been offered a load of firewood by the local American Legion post, but had turned it down out of pride against taking charity. Even the lights had been turned out by the power company. These were dark depression days in the Loken household. Just before Thelma died however, her mind cleared up and she remembered the names of her family members. Her heart gave out at thirty years of age in the winter of 1936.

Florence got a job at Sears in May of 1936 playing the piano in one of the departments, and things were okay for a while. However, Cornella could not afford to keep the family house without Adolf's income, and those were depression days, which had hit everyone hard. Arnold got jobs here and there, and that helped, but not enough to keep their former lifestyle going. Bernice was the smart one and was going to college in the mid thirties, and so was not much help with money.

About 1937, Cornella and her younger daughters went over to Brownsville to spend a weekend at a place owned by her life insurance agent, who was a friend. Cornella was impressed with the spot and was able to buy a lot there very cheaply. It is about a quarter mile north of the present day marina, which was not there then. At that time there was only a mosquito fleet era car-ferry dock. The ferry came across from Fletcher Bay on Bainbridge Island. The Brownsville store was there then, however.

In 1938 Cornella had to give up their house to its builder, Mr. Nelson. Apparently, by this time she had already sold the rental house. Mr. Nelson wanted to do something for Cornella for giving up the house. Cornella told him he could build a shack on her lot in Brownsville. Instead of a shack, Mr. Nelson built a fine little summer cottage for Cornella. He said to her, "I don't build shacks." Cornella owned her summer cottage in Brownsville all her life, and she and Lily visited there often on weekends and summers. The address was 2605 Fernglen Street, which is off of Ogle road, which at that time was the Keyport Highway. Even though it did not have water or plumbing, i.e. outhouse, Cornella loved the place and would enjoy going over and taking care of it, raking the leaves, etc. Florence would later live in the cottage at Brownsville one winter in 1943-44 when her future husband, James Carter, was in the war, and she was working at Keyport Torpedo Base as a typist. Florence had her baby boy Gary there and Cornella was there to care for him. The cottage has since been removed and a larger residence put in its place. Of course in those days there was only a handful of houses in that area, but now it is quite a neighborhood.

Cornella and Lily lived in West Seattle on 35th Ave in some project apartments for the rest of their lives. As a young girl Lily is thought by Florence to have been the prettiest of the girls. Lily acquired diabetes and always lived with her mother. She became quite heavy. She is said to have been a nice girl and a pleasant woman however. Cornella did her best to care for Lily, but without her husband Adolf, they never had much again. Lily never married and she also died a little before her time at about fifty years old.

Cornella was a writer and wrote articles for a couple of political magazines such as *The Northwest Technocrat*. She tended to be a liberal and socialist, and a big union supporter. She wrote two plays which survive: *The Search for the Rainbow's End* and

Sunrise Again. She tried to make them a success through a New York agent, but was unsuccessful.

The specter of living with Thelma's "condition" was to have a lasting effect on this family. The inability of one man to cope with his daughter's tragedy would have long reaching implications. Only two of the Loken children would themselves have children, Bernice and Florence. These days of the twenties and thirties would stay with them forever. Bernice was on the "inside" of the family politics, party to keeping things under wraps. Florence was younger and more sheltered, on the outside of this issue. Bernice, the brainy one, finished college but would have her husband, William McKinley, leave her after a few years, and she would die despised by her children. Kind and elegant Florence, artistic and musical, would also be left by her husband later in her life, but was loved by her children. Perhaps the life of Cornella, the young girl in Norway who had her fortune told by the gypsy woman—proved tragic?

Arnold would always be a source of great help. Cornella remained active in veterans organizations due to her husband's war service in the Spanish American war and the Great War(World War I). Cornella received a widow's pension from Adolf's Spanish American war service until she died. Cornella died aged eighty-nine years in Seattle in 1967, beloved by her family.

Arnold Loken was always warmly remembered by his sister Florence. He was a tall man of six foot three, which was especially large in those days. Yes, he was a big Norwegian but a gentle man as well. He was a talented and well-known musician in 1930's Seattle. He played in popular music bands in downtown clubs. He worked as a musician on cruise ships also. Later he would play first violin with the Seattle Symphony.

Along came World War II and Arnold became a Boeing machinist, probably about 1940. In 1942, working alongside Rosie the riveter after the war started for the United States. Those were the days when Boeing built the famous B-17 and B-29. Arnold represented the Scandinavian lads of Seattle who built Boeing from the little company of the 1930's, to the world's premier aerospace giant of today. He worked at Boeing for over twenty years, through the era of the B-47, B-52, and the groundbreaking 707 jet airliner. Arnold was a steady and sober Norwegian man, he went to work and he came home. He always looked after his mother. His diversion was playing in the Seattle Symphony. He eventually retired from Boeing in the mid 1960s.

Arnold Loken married Geneva Courtney, whom he later divorced. They had no children. He had a second wife, Bernice, but they had no children either and so this branch of the Loken name in America became extinct. Harold Loken, the Harbor Master of Colon, Adolf's brother, had no male children either, so this branch became extinct also.

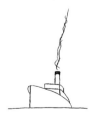

CHAPTER VII

Out of New England

Benjamin Poole Parker was descended from a prosperous New England family. His puritan ancestor, Thomas Parker of Derbyshire* in old England, sailed to America in the year of our Lord 1635. With a group of fellow puritans, Thomas had settled the town of Reading, Massachusetts, which is just outside of Boston. The Reading Parkers boasted members who fought, and died, in the French and Indian War, the Revolutionary War, and the War of 1812. Captain John Parker of the Lexington Militia, April 19, 1775, who received the message from Paul Revere that the British army was marching their way, and acted upon it, was a third cousin. Similarly, the Reading Parkers were related to the Rev. Theodore Parker, famous early nineteenth century Boston theologian and outspoken abolitionist. The usual family business was carpentry, furniture, and lumber.

For six generations this Parker family dwelt in Reading. Then, one Lt. Loae Parker of the Reading Militia, who fought in the War of 1812, and his wife both died before their time, in 1814. The couple had four children. The four children were dispersed among family. Ben's grandfather was sent to live in New Orleans. When Ben's father, who was a doctor, died at age thirty in 1879, Ben was just three months old. A couple of letters written by Ben's grandmother on his mother's side bespeaks of his southern ancestry. They were written when Ben was in college, dated 1897.

*According to tradition, this branch of the Parker family of Derbyshire, England, was founded by a thirteenth century crusader, Reginald le Parker, who attended Edward I, the "Longshanks" on the Eighth Crusade, and so was given a grant of land.

Your dear [mother's] grandfather Duke (my husband) was what [some] most erroneously called a Rebel. He was engaged in the navel engagement on the Mississippi River. He was second officer on the Gun Boat Gov. Moore, in which engagement he was quite seriously wounded. After this he was captured & was a prisoner under Farragut for five months, paroled by his friend Genl. W.T. Sherman, who had known him from his boyhood. So if you ever read Genl. Shermans book on the war, you will see where he speaks of the brave rebel Capt. No name I believe is given, but those who knew your grandfather Duke know full well of the efforts [ ] [ ] [S?]. [A?] there are but few left now of a once large & happy family. Your grandfather Poole was 90 years of age when he left us. He was for many years stationed at Ft. Moultry S.C. as also at Charlston S.C. resigned, went to New Orleans & there practiced law. He was a ready writer & gave many articles of great merit to many papers not [any?] at home but in California where his Articles on the Chinese question merited much comment.

Benjamin Poole Parker at ten years of age, in 1889.

Continued...

I hope dear boy that you will devote much of your [study time] to reading-- as nothing so develops the mental powers as the close study of great minds, read carefully it will greatly assist you in spelling correctly[.] O do be careful about writing[,] you can alone learn to use your pen handsomely [by?] practice only, it does not require a master -- Tom Acee although a poor scholar[,] writes a fine hand[.] A student only gave him a little training in the muscular movement[.]

I trust dear child that you may have a lovely time at Xmas. I hope to go to Church, this will constitute my Xmas feast. I will honor Xmas in my heart. I will live in the cherished past. "The stars that shone in Bethlehem shine still and shall not cease; And we listen still for the tidings of Glory and of Peace.["]

Harrison Parker.

Ben's mother died when he was just fourteen. The boy was no doubt devastated, and he ran away to sea for a while. But, he came back. It was in this way that Ben was reconnected with his New England roots.

Through some family connection, Ben came into the generous care of one of his uncles, Harrison Parker of Boston. Harrison Parker was also descended from Lt. Loae Parker of the Reading Militia, who had fought in the War of 1812. Harrison Parker, with his wife Fanny Fletcher Parker, cared for Ben his last few teenage years. A couple of letters survive that are correspondence from Ben to his "aunt Fannie." These letters were written when Ben was at sea, apparently on his school ship, and nearby Boston. In them Ben describes his time on the ship and the ports they pull into. His letters exhibit a close

Part of an advertisement for the Palmer & Parker Company.

and personal nature, as if written to his mother. In one of the letters Ben asks "and will you ask uncle Harry to take some money out of the Bank and send it to me right away. I had to get some fire room shoes and underware for the fire room." This shows the close custodial connection of Ben to his relatives Harrison and Fannie. When Ben later had a son, he named him *Charles*, no doubt after his father, and *Harrison*, probably after Harrison Parker who was the only father he ever knew.

Harrison was one of the Parkers in the wood veneers business. He was from the same branch of the old and well established Parker family of New England.

Harrison was a partner in the Palmer and Parker lumber and veneer company of Boston, Massachusetts. They imported and manufactured hardwoods and veneers. Harrison was the kind of man who could rub shoulders with the likes of Senators and such. His family was indicative of the success of the Parker name in New England.

Harrison was born in New York City. His parents were unable to care for him so he went to live in the family of his uncle, Harrison Parker of Winchester,

Massachusetts. The uncle Harrison was in the business of manufacturing mahogany veneers, as well as veneers of other fine woods. The younger Harrison then got his start in the veneer business under the tutelage of his uncle.

At nineteen years of age Harrison enlisted in the United States Army to fight in the Civil War. He saw action in North Carolina and was wounded there. After his military service, Harrison returned to Winchester to again work for his uncle in the veneer business.

Harrison married Fanny Fletcher June 12, 1875 at Winchester. They had had two children when they moved into the south end of the house of the senior Harrison Parker, about 1879. The house had twenty-two rooms and was known affectionately as "Red Roof." Harrison and Fanny were to have five more children. In the 1890s, with his family expanding, Harrison Parker II purchased the estate from his uncle and occupied the entire house.

With Fanny Fletcher directing the activities, the house known as "Red Roof" was to be well known in the community as a center of social culture and church activity. She was known as a Christian of deep spirituality. Local groups such as Art Club, Shakespeare Club, the Browning Club, and the Mothers association met at the house regularly. Fanny was known as a woman of artistic and literary tastes of the finest kind, and entertained many friends with the same interests from all over the world. The gardens were known as the spot for lawn parties and picnics of the School Teachers, the Church Cradle Roll and other groups.

When the senior Harrison Parker died, Harrison the nephew took over the business, and with his brother-in-law, Irving S. Palmer, started a new company, the Palmer and Parker Company. Harrison was a very successful businessman and was still the president of the company at his death.

Like his wife, he also was a man of taste and a lover of beautiful things. Harrison was known as a humble man as well as a man of generosity. He was a pillar of the local first Congregational

Church of Winchester and was a member for over fifty years. He was a Deacon for twenty-one years. Friends would say of him, "He was my ideal of a Christian gentleman." Harrison's son, Asa Merrick Parker, would become Reverend Asa Merrick Parker, Congregational minister. Harrison's daughter, Esther Parker, would marry the Rev. Dr. Sidney Lovett, who became Chaplain of Yale University. Harrison and Fanny's other son, Gordon Parker, spent a number of years with the Palmer and Parker Company himself. During the First World War Gordon served as a Navy Lieutenant. Later he would become President of the Parkwood Corporation, another veneer manufacturing company. In addition, Gordon was a member of the First Congregational Church of Winchester, which he served as treasurer and committee chairman. Eugenia Parker, one of Harrison and Fanny's daughters, built and ran Camp Blazing Trail for girls in Maine for twenty five years, and was herself a president of a Congregational Church and Sunday School teacher.

So, it is obvious that many good things sprang from the household of Harrison and Fanny Parker, and it is fortunate that Ben had the opportunity of being in their household and experiencing the benefits of such a home.

Ben graduated from the Massachusetts State Nautical School in 1898.

Ben would start his career with the Boston Steamship Company of Boston, Massachusetts circa 1900. He started his marine career here as an oiler for forty dollars per month.

Fanny Parker late in her life at **"Red Roof."**

It is clear that Ben was actively seeking to make his sea going career prosperous, as he changed jobs often his first years at sea, usually for the better. In 1901 Ben went to work for the Metropolitan Dredging Company, of New York, again as an oiler,

Young Ben in uniform, 1899.

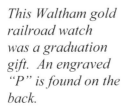

This Waltham gold railroad watch was a graduation gift. An engraved "P" is found on the back.

but eventually for more money.

In 1902 Ben went back to the Boston Steamship Co., again as an oiler, but soon he made Third Assistant Engineer, the position which his schooling had trained him for. As an oiler Ben had belonged to the International Association of Machinists (I.A.M.) union, but on his being promoted to Third Assistant Engineer, he then joined the Marine Engineers Beneficial Association (M.E.B.A.)

In 1903, Ben was working for both the Boston Steamship Co. and the Metropolitan Dredge Co. as a Third Assistant Engineer, making a salary of seventy dollars per month.

In 1904 Ben was working for Metropolitan Dredge the first part of the year, but sometime that year Ben signed on with the Great Northern Steamship Company of Seattle, Washington as a Third Assistant Engineer and that is where the Parker Washington history begins.

This was a dynamic time to be getting into marine engineering. There was a great movement of technological progress in the last decade of the nineteenth century and the first decade of the twentieth. The immigrant trade from Europe fueled a demand for larger and larger, and faster and faster steamers to streak across the Atlantic[1]. Some of the ships were more than 600' in length and could gallop across the sea at greater than twenty knots, thus earning the distinction of being a "greyhound" of the Atlantic.

---

[1]There are numerous excellent books covering the great North Atlantic era of steam such as: *Steamboat Conquest of the World* by Frederick A. Talbot, 1912, *Ocean Liners of the 20th Century* by Gordon Newell, 1963, *The Only Way To Cross* by John Maxtone-Graham, 1972, *Sail, Steam, and Splendor* by Byron S. Miller, 1977, *Great Ocean Liners* by Ian Dear, 1991, *Passenger Liners from Germany* by Clas Broder Hansen, 1991, and a whole library of others.

CHAPTER VIII

Great Northern, Klondike, and Seattle

When the first railroad surveys were undertaken out west, it was noted than the northern route had one desirable quality—it was cold—and therefore conducive to hauling perishable cargoes. Silk was the major export of Asia at this time, and needed temperature controlled transport. Also, the east coast of the United States desired a link with the markets of Asia—China and Japan, and the northern ports were hundreds of miles closer by sea than San Francisco.

Portland and Astoria, where Lewis and Clark emerged on their famous trek, was an early favorite for a northern port, but it had one drawback—the mighty Columbia itself; the notorious bar at its mouth, making it a difficult and dangerous port to enter. Plus, Puget Sound was even closer to Asia than Portland.

The saga of the railroads coming to Puget Sound is one full of drama. Where would the railroad terminus be? What city would benefit from this boon? There were several early contenders on the Sound: Olympia, Port Townsend, Tacoma, Seattle, and Bellingham. Port Townsend, the "Key City," had been the prominent seaport from the early days, and had the best harbor, but it was far more isolated by land. Easier to sail a ship a few more miles by sea than build a hundred miles of railroad track. After much wrangling and cajoling by railroad tycoons, and the various cities doing their level best to attract the railroad terminus, the favorite seemed to be Tacoma, the "City of Destiny," with the arrival of the Northern Pacific Railroad in 1873, a year that also saw the advent of a depression.

Seattle, the "Queen City," did not take these events lightly, and started to build its own railroad, which was taken up by the large railroad concern, and was connected to the transcontinental road.

The Great Northern Railroad of James J. Hill, which had made its way from Minnesota and across the west, in 1893 clambered over Stevens Pass and meandered to the shores of Everett, then down to Seattle. Unfortunately, 1893 also saw economic depression, and growth was stymied for a few years.

Port Townsend had thought itself a major contender, but the depression of 1893 spelled its doom. The town held out for a railroad until the advent of the twentieth century, but to no avail. From 1893 on, the population began to decline. On the east side of the Sound, just the opposite was occurring, as the city of Seattle was growing by leaps and bounds. Seattle was forging industries, and was a center of shipyards and shipping.

The Great Northern Railroad made Seattle an economic force to be reckoned with. The Klondike Gold Rush of 1897 did the rest, as Seattle became the outfitter town of choice for miners heading north. Overnight, there were not enough ships in the northwest. The principle method of travel in the Northwest was by water, as the land was totally covered by enormous trees. This fostered the growth of many large and small shipping companies. The road to

Alaska was only by water, and would remain that way for many years. This prompted regular ocean-going passenger service from Port Townsend and Puget Sound cities to Alaska.

In the days of sail, Port Townsend ruled the game, but as the market shifted to steamers, Seattle began to hold sway. By the turn of the century, Seattle and Tacoma had overtaken Port Townsend as the most important seaport cities in Washington and service ran from Seattle-Tacoma to the ports in Alaska.

In addition, the U.S. Government had an increasingly abounding presence on Northwest waters, and in the Pacific Ocean at large. The Revenue Service, later the Coast Guard by act of Congress in 1915, had been operating out of Port Townsend for many years at this time, and the Coast and Geodetic Survey Service was busy charting the U.S. possessions in the Pacific Ocean and the Bering Sea. The U.S. Customs House moved from Port Townsend to Seattle in 1913, and the Revenue Service had moved most of its operations to the booming city of Seattle. This marked the effective end of Port Townsend as a viable seaport and industrial city.

In the international maritime trade, the Europeans dominated the game. The American Civil War had had a ruinous effect on the United States Merchant Marine. Blockades, commerce raiding and many sinkings had decimated the American fleet. Before the Civil War the United States had had a strong trading presence on the Atlantic, but post war in the late nineteenth century, foreign shipping companies like England's Cunard line and Germany's North German Lloyd dominated the international trade across the Atlantic. The immigrant trade was in full bloom, and provided the impetus for an ever increasing quantity of larger and faster steamships. Another prime incentive were government mail contracts; "mail boats" were always the fastest in the fleet, by government requirement.

In the days of sail, travel by sea had been brutal. But in the age of the steamships, getting there had become a pleasure for many. Steady speed to get you there soon, warm cabins, good food, music, dancing, and many other relaxations had become the norm of sea travel, at least for the well heeled.

England's sprawled worldwide empire was based on shipping and they were not about to let it decay. The Americans had a stronger presence in the Pacific, but in that ocean there were competitors as well, such as the Japanese. Trade with Asia was an emerging market.

The Europeans had carried on a trade with the markets of Asia for centuries, but their route was a long and arduous one around Africa. The Suez Canal opening in 1869 shortened the route considerably, but some espoused the route across the Pacific, connecting by train across North America, and on to the markets of the American east coast and Europe.

Some American industrialists were clamoring for a viable international-oriented U.S. Merchant Marine. Railroad baron James J. Hill was one of those. Lumber baron turned steamboat operator Robert Dollar was another. A bourgeoning U.S. Merchant Marine was in the works.

By the turn of the century Jim Hill had control of both the Great Northern and the Northern Pacific Railroads. He was the man of the times.

One of the things that Hill wanted for his great railroad was a steamship line to connect with Asia. In 1900 he formed the Great Northern Steamship Company and had two ships ordered in a back-east shipyard, the Eastern Shipbuilding Company of New London, Connecticut. These ships, the *S.S. Minnesota* and *S.S. Dakota,* would be the largest ships ever built in America at the time of their launch at 630' in length and 28,000 tons, and boasted refrigerated cargo holds and first class passenger accommodations. *Minnesota* and *Dakota* were twin-screw, but they were not fast, and a voyage on them to the Far East would literally be "a ride on a slow boat to China."

TWO SEA MONSTERS

And Their Relation to the Commerce of the East

By J. Ellis Higbee

The late evolutions, revolutions and developments in the far East have attracted to that prolific section the attention of the world, and especially that of commercial America.

In taking advantage of this new trade which is sure to form a large part of the business of this country, the Great Northern Railway has had built two enormous steel ships, to ply between Seattle and the Orient, which will go into service during the coming Summer.

These vessels are the largest that have ever been constructed, their capacity be-

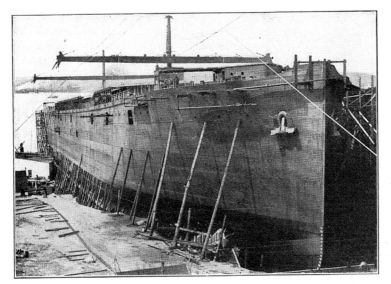

Bow View of Steamship " Minnesota " in the Ways, Just Before the Launching

ing 28,000 tons of freight, which is 9,600 tons more than the deadweight cargo capacity even of the "Cedric." They will have a capacity for nine hundred thousand bushels of wheat, or the equivalent of an ordinary railroad train seven miles long; or a mixed cargo that would require two thousand five hundred cars to transport. There will be accommodations for nine hundred and twenty passengers.

Each vessel is six hundred and thirty feet long, seventy-three and one-half feet extreme beam, fifty-five feet six inches deep.

One of the unique features of these vessels is a cellular or double bottom, the two shells being six feet apart, and extending the whole length of the vessel. The space between the inner and outer bottoms is divided into small cells five feet by twenty-seven to thirty inches. The space is also divided into large water-tight compartments, called tanks, so that in case of the outer skin or shell being punctured the

water could only fill one or two of these tanks, and there would be no danger whatever of the vessel sinking. This also prevents the possible damage to the cargo from water, as so often happens in the ordinary vessel. These tanks are also arranged so that they can carry fresh water with which to supply the engines, or sea water can be admitted, when desired, for ballast.

The vessels are provided with a double keel running the entire length of the bottom, about eighteen inches off the center on either side, and are the only ships built with more than a single keel. A set of bilge fins are so arranged as to prevent the rolling of the ship in the trough of the sea, thus materially lessening the discomforts of seasickness.

The vessels will be provided with the finest electrical system with which a vessel has ever been equipped, and will be the only vessels in existence that will handle their cargoes by electric power. In fact, with the exception of the propelling power, all of the machinery of the vessels will be operated by electricity.

The cold storage rooms for the accommodation of the ships' provisions have a capacity requisite to feed fifteen hundred people for four weeks, and the coal bunkers will carry five thousand tons of coal.

Each vessel will be equipped with two propelling twin screw engines of about ten thousand horse-power and capable of a speed of fourteen knots per hour.

There are five decks. The cargo will be carried below the main deck, upon which are accommodations for the second and third-class passengers, steerage passengers, live stock and some cargo. Above the main deck, there are three mid-ship decks for first-class passengers, making eight decks in all, including the bridge deck.

The cooling as well as the heating of these vessels has been given the most careful attention, so as to make them comfortable in any climate, and no luxury that can possibly add to the comfort, convenience and pleasure of the passengers has been omitted.

All of the usual features of first-class passenger steamers are included among the accommodations of these boats, but it is the purpose here to merely mention the novel features and facilities which give these vessels a unique place among the craft of the world.

The "Minnesota" was launched at New London, Connecticut, April 16th; the "Dakota," her twin sister, will probably produce. This means that they are able to keep busy something like three freight trains daily in and out of Puget Sound harbors.

In order to develop this amount of business, the commerce of the United States with the Orient will be pushed with great aggressiveness.

Japan to-day has a commerce of something like two hundred and fifty million

The Steamship "Minnesota," the New Queen of the Pacific

be launched in June. They will run from Puget Sound to Asiatic ports, over the northerly route via Bering Sea.

With a speed of fourteen knots, they will make the 5,800 miles from Seattle to Hong Kong in about two and one-half weeks and, allowing ten days at each end for receiving and dispatching cargo, will make the round trip within something like sixty days. This implies that in every sixty day period, if these vessels succeed in getting full cargoes, they together will take two hundred trainloads of freight from Puget Sound and return 200 trainloads of Oriental

dollars a year, of which we get less than twenty per cent. China has a foreign trade of only one dollar per capita, as compared with Japan's seven dollars per capita. Should the commerce of China be developed to equal the per capita commerce of Japan it would, with China's 400,000,000 population, produce a foreign trade equal to that of the greatest civilized nation.

These giant ocean carriers have had blocked out for them that important international mission, and they appear to be of the proportions and capacity for just such a tremendous undertaking.

1903 article from the New York magazine, the "Four Track News." Even in this era, the business of transporting freight was in the realm of mathematics and statistics. The ton-mile of freight, or cost to move a ton of freight a mile was the measurement employed.

The *Minnesota* arrived at Seattle in 1904 and the *Dakota* in 1905. At this time the railroad tunnel under Seattle was bored, and in 1906 a glorious new terminal building was completed at the waterfront. Seattle smiled.

Hill had intended to build three more ships of the same size, but instead he made an arrangement with the Boston Steamship Co. to run its two largest ships, the *Shawmut* and *Tremont*, with his *Minnesota* and *Dakota*. In addition, three more Boston Steam ships and three from a New York line were running in Great Northern service. These, the largest ships in the Pacific, were running a trans Pacific connecting service linking up with the Great Northern Railroad.

The *Minnesota* and *Dakota* made the Asian run with the contracted *Shawmut* and *Tremont*. The *Shawmut* and *Tremont* were fast twin-screw 535' liners.

Funnel colors and flag.

In the Victorian era, most steamships that operated in the northern latitudes wore black hulls with white superstructures. Some lines that operated in the tropics wore white hulls.

A steamship line's livery consisted of the colors on the smokestack, known as the funnel, and the line's flag.

Any steamship line of note had a host of things with the line's logo on them, such as china, silverware, glasses, towels, matchbooks, ashtrays, and playing cards.

Playing card for whiling away the hours at sea.

The Great Northern Steamship Co.

Runs the largest ocean liners used on the Pacific Ocean, over the shortest route from the United States to Japan, China and the Philippines. These mammoth twin-screw steamships

DAKOTA AND MINNESOTA
28,000 TONS

are palatial in their appointments, and arranged so that every cabin is an outside room—something found on no other ocean liners.

¶ The Minnesota and Dakota follow the mild Japan current from Seattle to Yokohama, and connect with the two great transcontinental lines, the Great Northern and the Northern Pacific Railways.

For berth reservations and full particulars address
Any agent of the Great Northern or Northern Pacific Railways

W. W. KING, G. P. A.   G. G. BURNHAM, G. A.
Great Northern Steamship Co., Seattle   *209 Adams Street, Chicago*

GREAT NORTHERN STEAMSHIP AGENTS

413 Broadway, New York   220 South Clark Street, Chicago
319 Broadway, New York   208 South Clark Street, Chicago
201 Washington Street, Boston   303 Carlton Building, St. Louis
207 Old South Building, Boston   210 Commercial Building, St. Louis

S. S. Minnesota Sails from Seattle, February 1st
S. S. Dakota Sails from Seattle, March 12th

The Great Northern Steamship Line represented the bulk of the early U.S. foray into the Pacific foreign trade. Without an immigrant trade such as was had in the Atlantic, in the Pacific the sea going commodity was freight. Passengers were taken more to offset the operational costs—to make freight hauling rates more competitive.

Japan—China

Rich in tradition—with every nook and corner permeated with the mysticism of their centuries old civilization, with their odd customs, famous gardens, and unique shrines and temples, Japan and China offer an unusual number of different and curious attractions. The best time to see Japan is in April during the

Cherry Blossom Season

The cherry blossom is held in high honor in Japan and the cherry blossom festival is an annual national event. The tree is cultivated for the blossom only and produces in the greatest profusion a flower of unusual size and beauty. You will arrive in Japan in time to see the buds burst into bloom if you go on the

Steamship Minnesota

Sailing from Seattle March 2, 1908. Largest, most comfortable ship in Trans-Pacific service First cabin accommodations are all outside rooms. Suites de luxe consisting of bedroom with commodious brass bed, sitting room and private bath are designed to meet the requirements of the most fastidious traveler. All staterooms are electrically lighted and heated and provided with private telephone.

For literature and further information address any representative of the Great Northern Railway, Northern Pacific Railway, or

Great Northern Steamship Company

A. L. CRAIG, General Passenger Agent, St. Paul, Minn.
W. C. THORN, Traveling Passenger Agent, 209 Adams St., Chicago, Ill.
W. A. Ross, Ass't. Gen'l. Pass'r. Agt., Seattle, Wash.
New York Offices, 319 and 379 Broadway.

Towards the end of the 19th century, the travel agent began to come of importance to satisfy the vacation needs of the middle and upper classes. With the power of steam on land and water, travel for pleasure and education became more and more prominent, as well as a hallmark of the affluent. The travel agent could arrange between train and steamer connections, hotels, tours, and etc.

The exotic Far East provided much allure for the traveler of means.

One day one of the world's great airlines, Northwest Orient, which was also based in Minneapolis, would serve the same routes as the combined Great Northern Railway and Steamship lines.

1907 magazine ad.

Funnel and flag of the Pacific Coast Steamship Company. The Pacific Coast Steamship Co. was the reigning line in the West Coast "coastwise" trade.

S.S. Pacific

Other major steamship lines on the Seattle waterfront were the Pacific Coast Steamship Company and upstart Alaska Steamship Company, both coastal operations, and both heavily invested in trade to Alaska. The Pacific Coast Steamship Company was originally a San Francisco based operation, which grew out of an 1860's partnership. In 1875 the steamship line gained the dubious distinction of having the worst maritime disaster of the west coast. The rotten wooden steamer *S.S. Pacific* rammed a sailing bark off Cape Flattery in foul weather. The rotten *Pacific* broke in three pieces shortly after and all but two on board perished—hundreds. The sailing bark suffered light damage in the collision, but ended up on the beach.

In 1877 the company was formed as the Pacific Coast Steamship Company, and served west coast ports from Mexico to Alaska.

Alaska was the newest frontier, being acquired from Russia in 1867. Gradually, shipping filled the need for

the fisheries, and even some tourism. The dramatic scenery of Alaska, the fjords, mountains, and glaciers, soon found fame. After the Klondike Gold Rush, the traffic from Seattle to Alaska was so heavy the company made Seattle its main hub. Pacific Coast Steamship Company maintained extensive pier and office facilities in Seattle.

In 1905-06 the Pacific Coast Steamship Co had twenty-one steamers serving the coast. The passenger steamers serving southeast Alaska were the *Al-Ki, City of Seattle, City of Topeka,* and *Cottage City.* Set apart for excursion service was the steamer *Spokane.* Traveling to the far north at Nome and St. Michael were the *Senator* and *Valencia.*

Running south to San Francisco from Puget Sound, Victoria, and Port Townsend were the passenger steamers *Umatilla, City of Puebla,* and *Queen. Umatilla* was the largest in the fleet at 3069 tons. *Umatilla* was noted for having been the onetime command of famous Pacific master "Dynamite" Johnny O'Brien.

Later on the run were the larger and new *President* and *Governor*.

The Alaska Steamship Company was formed in December 1894 at Port Townsend. The company purchased its first ship in 1895, the small wooden steamer *Willapa*. The Alaska Steamship Company entered the Alaska market as a bitter rival to established Pacific Coast Steamship Company. The Alaska Steam ships operated out of Seattle. The *Willapa* fiercely battled the Pacific Coast ships for business in 1895-96, but then rumors of gold started to lure prospectors north. The Klondike gold rush of 1897 meant there were now not enough ships to service Alaska, and Alaska Steam was here to stay.

After 1904, Alaska Steam had four small steamers, the largest of which was the new 207 foot, 1600 ton *S.S. Jefferson*.

Steamship lines sailing to Alaska made extensive use of the Native American theme.

*Alaska was billed as a scenic vacation wonderland. The **Spokane** was set aside for the summer excursion season, May through September.*

Passengers were allowed 150 pounds of baggage. All meals were included in the ticket. San Francisco to Puget Sound steamers would "connect" with Puget Sound to Alaska steamers at the "hub" of Port Townsend. Most steamship runs had at least two steamers serving them, so one would be running northbound while the other southbound.

If you can find a reprint, or original, a good description of this period and service is found in All About Alaska *by Alfred P. Swineford and the Pacific Coast Steamship Company.*

*Built in 1906, **S.S. President** was flagship of the fleet and one of the ships on the run from Puget Sound to California. Later she would be the **Dorothy Alexander** of the Pacific Steamship Company and **Columbia** of the Alaska Line.*

4193

STEAMSHIP "SPOKANE" ON LYNN CANAL, ALASKA-PACIFIC COAST STEAMSHIP COMPANY.   "TOTEM POLE ROUTE"

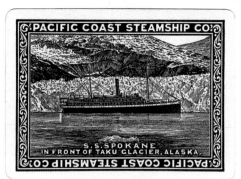

PACIFIC COAST STEAMSHIP CO.

S.S. SPOKANE
IN FRONT OF TAKU GLACIER, ALASKA.

PACIFIC COAST STEAMSHIP CO.

The ship's purser had various items for sale such as playing cards.

S.S. PRESIDENT. PACIFIC COAST STEAMSHIP CO.

S.S. Jefferson *of upstart Alaska Steamship Company, c. 1907. In 1908 Alaska Steam was taken over by the Kennicott Copper Corporation of New York that operated a copper mine in Alaska. From that point on the fleet greatly expanded with larger ships and Alaska Steam would be home ported at Pier 2 on the Seattle waterfront.*

CHAPTER IX

On a Steamer Bound for Puget Sound

Ben came out west to Puget Sound full of promise for the future. He had graduated from one of the nation's leading maritime academies, he was an engineer on one of the largest steamers in the world, and his career had just begun.

In those first years of the twentieth century, and making regular trans Pacific voyages to the Far East, life was full of adventure and excitement in the fullest sense of the sailor's tradition. Ben fell into his own and learned his trade well. His home port of Seattle was growing at an explosive rate and prospering in every way, and his employer, the Great Northern Railroad, was at the heart of it. Life was good.

It was during this early time in Seattle that Ben met his future wife Geneva, as she was known in her younger years. Genevieve E. Clark, of Cairo, Ill., raised in Wichita, Kansas, was working in the Great Northern Railroad office on pier 91 in Seattle in 1906, and that is where she and Ben met. Geneva must have been bold and adventuresome, to be employed so far from home.

Minnesota *checking through customs at Port Townsend.*

The "black gang" as the engine room crew was known.

And the men who led them, the Engineer's Assistants. Ben is second from left with his arm in the overhead. Photos from Benjamin Parker collection

Above: *The Engineer's Assistants. Ben is in front, second from left.*

Above right: *This picture is taken in front of a small observation bridge on the forecastle of* **Minnesota**. *Ben has his hand on his chief water-tender, his "right hand chinaman."*

In this Christmas card, the flag opposite the Stars and Stripes is that of the Great Northern Steamship Company.

Ben Parker collection

The **Minnesota's** engines were 4800 shaft horsepower each. The giant triple expansion reciprocating engines were several stories high, the engine room like a factory filled with machinery (see illustration page 4). Keeping the engines fed with 230 psi steam working pressure consumed enormous amounts of coal.

On the back of this picture Ben wrote "Coaling ship at Nagasaki. Man and woman pass the coal up in small baskets."

Ben Parker collection

(3) COALING THE "MINNESOTA" AT NAGASAKI. 景の込積炭石タソネミ船汽國米るけ於に港崎長

There was an affluent couple from Chicago, Fred and Mary, traveling to Japan in April of 1907. There is no connection to Ben Parker, but the description of their travel is interesting. We open with Fred, writing to family back home.

Pardon if I cover, in part, much of the same trail as Mary, for I see she has written many pages, and necessarily our material is largely the same.

The Minnesota is all we had dreamed and more, so also our special cabin. $30 is ridiculously cheap for the extra accommodations of bath, toilet, bed, and a sizable room.

Mary writes.

For one week and two days we have been going westward over the ocean waves. Farther and farther from the dear home we love.

As I might have expected—the first days were anything by pleasant. We left at noon and were in sight of land until after breakfast the next morning. It was then that the swells were large on the ocean and it was then that I rolled into bed and gave thanks most ardently, that Moma and Alice had decided to stay at home. It was some time during this day or the next that I told Fred I would never—no never—come to Japan with him again. He read to me a good deal of the time. We finished Gipsy Smiths' life. Well, finally I was up again and only once since have I missed a meal.

Day before yesterday there was a strong wind blowing—80 miles an hour—which is a hurricane. The sea was in a turmoil—and the wind would take the crest of the waves and make it look like a flurry of snow. I sat in a sheltered nook on the deck—and watched it there for hours. Part of the time the sum was shinning brightly and then we would pass through a snow storm and the sea would seem more terrible than ever. Our ship took the storm splendidly. However I went to bed rather than to dinner that evening.

Fred continues.

It has been fine for Mary to have no berth over her head when feeling a little "seedy." She has been awfully brave and if trying would present mal demer, she would have been well every minute.

It is not without its compensation, however, for when it is smooth, she seems to feel almost ecstatic.

The latter feeling has largely predominated, so you will know we have not had a rough voyage, considering our track, and the time of year. We were within a few miles of the Aleutian Is. But it was not quite clear enough to discern land.

Our course is the shortest between U.S. and Japan—4260 miles. The flatness of the Earth nearer the poles is indisputably proven by our track which goes N.W. from Seattle to get on a smaller circle, which we follow for several days, then turning S.W. So the shortest distance between two points (on the Earths surface) may be a circle.

At best, however, the Southern trip is much pleasanter in the matter of weather. It has been possible to be on deck, but always necessary to be well wrapped, and really comfortable only when exercising. Steamer chairs have been used very little.

It has been rainy, blowy, sunny, snowy, sometimes all in a single day, but uniformly cool. Now that we are only 24hrs. from Japan some moderation is noticeable. With these conditions obtaining naturally we have spent much time in our cabin, and more yet in the spacious foyer, music room, and library, all of which are luxuriously comfortable. As usual, we have accomplished less than we had resolved to do, but withal have read Gipsey Smith's autobiography & parts of two other books and some of the Bible every day, which appeals to us more and more as being indeed the book of books. We have done something to our scrap books—I have completed one up to date on tea.

The couple meets many fine and well to do people on board, and enjoys their social time immensely, they meet missionaries and other members of the clergy, and a wealthy couple from Milwaukee. Mary notes "There are some people on ship board who have worked hard and made their pile, and are now going to see the world." Fred conducts business.

Fred Oglevee and I have worked from 10 to 12 most every morning on tea business and have matters in hand ready for the buying season better than any previous year.

As usual, too, we have an excuse for not doing more. It is the same one as at home—too many chances for a good time.

A more congenial or jolly crowd seldom gets together. Deck sports, proposal parties, concerts, and various other forms of amusements have been on from morning until night. The most profitable has been two sermons from Dr. Whitman ex. Priest of Colby & Columbia (D.C.) Univ. & a lecture from Gen. Booth. Dr. Whitman's sermon this morning was such as you hear only once or twice in a lifetime.

Gen. Booth captured the sympathies of the most prejudiced, being given a birthday token of $150 by the passengers. He is certainly one of God's noblest. He is expecting to be accorded an audience with the Mikado.

Dr. Dobbins, another Baptist from Philadelphia will preach to-night. He is well acquainted with my uncle Will, a Bap. Preacher at Carbondale, Penn. He speaks very highly of Uncle Will, who it seems has made a specialty of harmonizing and building up weak and quarrelsome churches.

But the weaker and lower side of ship life has also been felt. For two days the pools on the ship's run were the absorbing topics. The pot was about $5 each day, first prize drawing half, & the two consolation prizes each [ ] 25%. Some who won a consolation prize were losers then, having bought so many tickets. Several times women bid frantically, giving one a little hint of what Monte Carlo must be. We didn't take much part in the sports, but Fred Olgevee won about $12 and a box of cigars.

Mary continues.

Yesterday was General Booth's birthday. He was 78 yrs old. Two of the children on board had a birthday then too. So we had a special dinner last evening, and some fine birthday cakes, candles and favors. The General told quite a little about his life and the work of the Salvation Army. He interested everyone and after his speech was over we all went up and shook hands with him. Then he retired, and we took up a subscription of $108 and sent it up to him as a birthday contribution to his work.

There is a Mr. Samson from England on board who has been around the world 20 times. We had thought just a little bit about coming home by way of Siberia and Russia.

As the voyage draws to a close, Mary recounts.

There is a fog over the ocean today and the deep fog horn is heard every few minutes. The Captain is most sincerely hoping that the fog will lift by night for we are too near land to be very safe in such a fog. The people on board are

arraying there plans for travel in Japan, and many are going about with guide books under their arms, and many questions & ask of the people who have been in Japan before. Fred has been doling out information for several days, and is a very popular man still. The food on this ship is not as good as on the other two ships.

Arriving in Japan, Mary recounts "We came into the harbor just at dusk on Monday evening, April 15th, just three weeks from the time I left home. We had dinner on ship board, and then got into the steam launch which brought us from the quarantine station (where the Minnesota had to stop) to the pier." "Yesterday we went to Tokyo to see the cherry blossoms. They were just a little passed their prime but still very beautiful, and we had a fine chance to see Japan in its most beautiful array." Fred muses "Somehow, it seems great to be here once more. The people, the blossoms, the sunshine, and life generally have a fascination for me which I fear I shall miss when I come no more."

When the *Minnesota* was still one day out of Japan, Fred included in his letter.

We are hoping to see something of the Dakota as we go in. Our Capt. & crew seem to feel there was no excuse for such an accident, as she ran on to a rock that was plainly charted & in the daytime at that. Rumor has it that both of these ships have been losing money; that the Dakota will not be replaced and this ship will be sold to the Japanese line N.Y.K.

The year 1907 saw the loss of the *Dakota*, and it was also the year a depression struck. The *Dakota* struck Shira Hami Reef, about forty miles from Yokohama, March 3, 1907 and ended a total loss. Jim Hill declared that the *Dakota* would not be replaced, as he concluded that a ship could not be run at a profit easily under the U.S. flag. Indeed the two ships had been something of an experiment on his part.

During this time the labor movement was rising across the country, with the attendant strikes, politics, and complications. Hill complained that the government did not make it easy for him.

The Seamen's Act of 1915, sponsored by progressive politicians, and backed strongly by the union lobby, had the stated purpose of

The Great Northern Railroad office on Seattle's Pier 91, c. 1906. This is where Ben and Genevieve met. Genevieve is on the right.   Photo from Benjamin Parker collection

helping out the American sailor, but unfortunately it had the opposite effect—and killed many of their jobs. For Hill it was the last straw, and he gave up. The big ships never made any money, and indeed lost a fortune, millions. The *Minnesota* was sold that year to haul men and material for World War I.

The Act had a similar effect on the Pacific Mail Steamship Company of San Francisco, the oldest trans-Pacific line. A 1915 *New York Times* article read "New Seamen's Law Leaves Few Vessels of Importance to Fly American Flag." With the collapse of the Great Northern line, a void was left in the trans-Pacific service on behalf of the U.S.

Many historians like to simply dismiss this with "Hill didn't understand the steamship shipping business," but, he was a captain in the railroad business, and therefore a transportation industry insider, so it would appear not so easy to dismiss the failure this way.

Meanwhile, the Japanese steamship lines were alive and well, running large steel steamships, with good service, and only too ready to pick up the slack. Hill left it to them.

The earliest postcard from Ben to Genevieve was dated November 1, 1906, and it was addressed to "Miss Gen. Clark, 3806 Evanston Ave, Fremont Station, Seattle, Wash, U.S.A." They were married June 8, 1907 in Seattle, Washington.

Genevieve Evelyn Clark was born September 3, 1884, to Jefferson Morgan Clark and Mildred Eliza Atkins Clark in Cairo, Illinois. She was to grow up in Wichita, Kansas, however, and she went to high school there, and would one day return for her fiftieth high school anniversary. She was a mid western girl. She was a young lady with a graceful countenance, befitting the Victorian period. Geneva went to Wichita Commercial College after high school, and graduated February 20, 1902 with a degree in business.

Ben continued to work for the Great Northern Steamship Co. on the *Minnesota* out of Seattle, by this time being promoted to Senior Second Assistant Engineer, at ninety dollars per month.

After Ben and Genevieve were married in early 1907, Ben sought a shore job, no doubt to spend time with his new wife. This changed his career outlook for a time, and he quit the Great Northern Steamship Co. From late 1907 through 1908, Ben worked as a machinist in Seattle for fifty cents per hour. Ben and Genevieve's first child was born January 11, 1908, their daughter Esther. Ben loved his wife dearly, but the sea was in his blood and a shore job could not keep him for long.

Ben and Geneva bought a house at 5211 1st Ave Northwest, Seattle. They would own the house all the days of their lives, and live there for most of them. Ben also purchased a ranch in the then rural part of south Seattle. At that time there was nothing but trees and a few farms down that way. This is where Ben and Geneva's children would be raised. Their next child, Mildred, was born October 31, 1909. It would be ten more years before Charles would be born.

Ben would write to Geneva often while he was at sea, but she was to live the lonely life of a sea going man's wife. She was, however, to accompany her husband on several voyages around the Pacific. She went to Alaska, China, Japan, various Pacific islands, India, and Australia. Even Ben and Geneva's children

would accompany them on the long voyages.

Life at home was still full for the rest of the family however. The majority of the time was spent on the "Ranch." This is where the children identified with home. The Parker Ranch[2] was a working farm and there was much activity.

The Ranch was familiar territory to friends and relatives of the Parker family as well. Genevieve's brother, Hugh E. Clark, lived in Seattle with his family as well and visited often. Hugh was an electrician and was in the electricians union, the IBEW. He was also a reserve Seattle Police Officer.

In 1909 Ben signed on with Uncle Sam and took a job on a government transport as a Third Assistant Engineer, at seventy a month.

Ben was soon sailing out of Seattle again and in January of 1910 was working for the Pacific Coast Steamship Company of Seattle, as Second Assistant Engineer. Ben was quite possibly on the Pacific Coast Steam's flagship, the passenger steamer *President,* on the California run.

This was to be a short stay also, on November 22, 1910 Ben signed on with the government again, this time the Bureau of Navigation, Manila, Philippine Islands, as Chief Engineer at more than double his previous pay.

His Pacific service saw Ben on the U.S. ships

---

[2] The Ranch was located in what is now the city of Burien about a mile or so from what is now Sea-Tac airport. Today there are apartments and such encrusting the land where the Ranch once stood. There is a road today that passes through the property, S 177th Place off of Ambaum Boulevard South.

Ben on the left, Esther, Genevieve, and Mildred.

Early days at the ranch, Genevieve on the right.

Young Ben and Geneva with Esther.

Esther June Parker, aged 12 years.

Ben with brother-in-law Hugh Clark, Ben on left.

Esther and Mildred at the Ranch.

A hay wagon day at the Ranch.

Ranger and *Corregidor*. Interestingly enough, a future relative, Adolf Nils Loken, a Norwegian, would also see service in the Pacific with the Coast and Geodetic Survey Service. Ben and Adolf were supposed to have known each other, but whether they met in the Pacific or in the Northwest is not clear.

Ben ended his U.S. service March of 1913 and went to work for the Pacific Cold Storage Company of Tacoma, Wa., as a First Assistant Engineer at ninety a month; he had been making one fifty in the P.I. He probably sailed on the *Elihu Thompson* from Seattle to Hawaii. But in 1914 he again entered government service as a Chief Engineer, at one fifty a month, working in the Panama Canal Zone. 1914 was of course the year the First World War began in Europe. Ben sailed for the government only part of 1914.

Later in 1914, Ben went to work for the Port Angeles Transportation Company and shipped out for them until 1915 as a First Assistant Engineer. For this company he sailed on the *S.S.*

City of Angeles between Port Angeles and Seattle, probably so he could stay close to home.

The *City of Angeles* was typical of the Puget Sound Mosquito Fleet steamers and ran a daily service between Pier 1 at the foot of Yesler Way in Seattle, to Union Wharf at Port Townsend, Port Williams and Dungeness at Sequim, and Port Angeles. Fare from Seattle to Port Townsend was $1.

The Mosquito Fleet was so named for the number and diminutive size of its vessels. It was the way people got around in the early days, and the mosquito fleet had thrived on Puget Sound for decades. It had a long and storied past of steamboat races, rivalries, local shipwrecks, and many of the boats were likened unto local celebrities. However, the fleet was in fact near the beginning of its end, as the automobile had spelled the fleet's doom.

The farmers at Dungeness on the Olympic Peninsula had endeavored to bring their produce to market on Puget Sound. They lived at the

Ben with crew in Philippines. Ben is on the far right in the foreground. Photos from Benjamin Parker collection

Ever since the U.S. had acquired control of the Philippines 12 years previous, it had been trying to maintain order and establish infrastructure. There were still Morro troubles. The Bureau of Navigation was officially an overseer of the merchant marine, but provided an all around government presence. For Ben it was a way to make some money, get sea time as Chief Engineer, and have an adventure.

U.S.S. Corregidor, *one of Ben's early ships in the Philippine service.*   Photos from Ben Parker collection

The **S.S. City of Angeles** *was typical of the Mosquito Fleet vessels plying Puget Sound.*

mouth of the shallow Dungeness river delta. To bridge over the shallows, the town built a three-quarters-of-a-mile long pier into the Strait of Juan de Fuca at the end of their main street[3].

The Port Angeles Transportation Company suffered from ill management, and was embroiled in litigation in 1915. So, in 1915 Ben again signed on with the Pacific Coast Steamship Co. and shipped out for them until some time in 1916. Ben would work at Todd Shipyards between voyages at least though 1918. During this time he would belong to the I.A.M. union again, in addition to the M.E.B.A.

Pacific Coast had been having troubles and the company changed hands in 1917, becoming the property of H.F. Alexander of Tacoma, who already operated a line of steamers known as the

---

[3] Not much of the old pier or town remains today, save for the *Three Crabs* restaurant which stands next to the threshold of the old pier, inside the great arc of Dungeness Spit.

*The **Niels Nielsen** in the ice at Vladivostok.*

"Admiral Line." The combined company became the Pacific Steamship Company and would be operated out of Seattle under the brand "The Admiral Line." Now there were two large coastwise steamship lines based in Seattle, the Admiral Line and the Alaska Line.

The Great War was raging away "over there" in Europe, and many believed that it was only a matter of time before the U.S. was involved. Some in congress had wanted to get the U.S. government into the shipping business, to bolster the industry up and bring it back to glory. Also, if the U.S. entered the war, they would need a lot of ships… They formed the War Shipping Board and, after official entry into the war, the Emergency Fleet Corporation.

In late 1916 Ben shipped out on the *S.S. Niels Nielsen*. The steel freighter *Niels Nielsen* was built by the Todd Dry Dock and Construction Corporation for the Norwegian firm of B. Stolt-Nielson, but the ship was constructed in the yard of the newly formed Skinner & Eddy Corporation in Seattle. The *Niels Nielsen* was the first ship constructed in the Skinner & Eddy yard and was the largest ship built in the Northwest up to that time. The company was formed January 1916, and the *Niels Nielsen's* keel was laid May 2. The Skinner & Eddy Corporation would go on to build the two sisters of the *Niels Nielsen*, twenty-five more of the type, and other state of the art steel freighters for the War Shipping Board and the government

owned Emergency Fleet Corporation by the close of the war[4].

The *Niels Nielsen* was a type 1013 design, or "Robert Dollar" type, and was 424 feet in length, with a 54 foot beam and 8800 deadweight tons. She was steam turbine powered. The steam turbine was a revolutionary design that was made famous a decade earlier with the advent of the renowned trans-Atlantic Cunard liner *Mauretania*. The geared steam turbine power-plant was further developed into the far more flexible turbo-electric power-plant that would be in wide use throughout the middle of the twentieth century. The steam turbine is particularly significant as the precursor to the gas turbine, or "jet" engine.

The steam turbines operated through a reduction gear, as they turned at higher RPM than the reciprocating engines. The turbine only operated in one direction, so a separate, smaller engine was required for reversing. The General Electric propulsion plant in the *Niels Nielsen* had a five-stage turbine for normal operation, and a two-stage turbine for reversing. She had three Scotch marine boilers delivering 210 PSI working pressure, which could burn oil or coal. 2500 shaft horsepower was delivered to a single

---

[4] After the war, when all this shipbuilding industry quickly subsided, there were plenty of surplus engineering resources and skilled labor available for a small seaplane company on Lake Union—owned by William Boeing—to take advantage of.

four-blade propeller 16' 5" in diameter to drive the ship at 11.5 knots.

Just launched in September, she sailed under charter to the Mitsui & Co., bound for Vladivostok in November. During WWI the *Niels Nielsen* had been taken over by the War Shipping Board. The Russian port of Vladivostok was a busy one before the communist takeover. During WWI American ships made a fortune hauling supplies to Siberia.

It was not German submarines that would haunt the *Niels Nielsen*, but bad fortune and cold weather. The *Niels Nielsen* was on her way to Russia with a full load of valuable war supplies, when she encountered a heavy gale off Cape Flattery. 220 miles from the cape the ships propeller fell apart, possibly due to an incident when the ship was launched[5], and the *Niels Nielsen* began drifting towards the shore of Vancouver Island. She sent out a distress call on her wireless set which was soon answered with the tug *Goliath* coming to the rescue, November 27. By the afternoon of the 29th the *Niels Nielsen* was finally sighted. By this time she was drifting dangerously close to shore in the area of Cape Cook, which is at the north end of Vancouver Island. The *Niels Nielsen* was given a tow-line and the ship was saved, none too soon. The ship had been drifting twenty-five miles per day since she lost her propeller. In tow by the *Goliath*, she was taken to Victoria, from where she was again towed to Seattle and fitted with a new propeller the first part of December. Her rescue was considered quite a fortunate success, and made all the local papers. Late in December *Niels Nielsen* was again on her way to Vladivostok with Ben probably her First Assistant or Chief. Ben wrote home about the trip.

Sea of Japan January 3, 1917

Sweetheart Gen & dear Babys.

Will commence writing my letter today as the ship will be at Vladivostok tomorrow if

nothing happens, and I will take a chance of a letter getting home before I do. There isent much use of my discribing the trip as far as the weather is concerned as you have been across at this time of the year and know what it is. But we did run into a couple of pretty bad gales. One of them smashed up things around decks a little and we had to heave to for several hours, but she is a fine sea boat at that. I had to stop the turbine the second day out to do a little work on the air pump and it hasent given any trouble since.

I have quite a log to keep and I take the Pressures and temperatures at noon and midnight so that I saw the old year out and the new in. The Capt. had a little extra spread for Xmas and New Years and it came in kind of handy as these people are nothing extra in the food line. I will have some work to do in Port so it will make the time pass more quickly. My won't I be glad to get headed home again and I hope we don't have to burn coal as it will be kind of hard steaming.

Later in the same letter Ben states:

2pm Vladivostok Jan 5th 1917.

Dearest. Well we got the Niels Nielsen here, now all we want is to get her back again. Talk about cold Gen well this is the limit and blowing a gale. The harbor is all full of ice and it has Alaska beat a mile. Yesterday afternoon the Telemotor for the steering engine froze up and it shut in thick so we had to anchor for the night. I worked on the telemotor until eleven o'clock last night and it was sure some cold up on the bridge.

Elsewhere in the letter Ben shows that he is not very happy and longs for home. He indicates that he will be taking a shore job in the shipyard when he comes back from sea.

Ben received the Merchant Marine Combat Ribbon for being on a merchant ship in a combat zone in World War I.

By this point in Ben's life, he had traveled all over the Pacific Ocean, from Alaska to India, and everything in between. He had seen native islanders in their relatively untouched state of existence, in those days still very much in their old cultures, with their traditional dress, and even some of them still headhunters and cannibals. He had been all over the Orient,

[5] When the *Niels Nielsen* was launched down the ways, her propeller started turning when it hit the water, at the same time the propeller fell next to one of the tugboats attending the launching, and the turning propeller chopped off the tug's stern.

ridden in a rickshaw, and even dressed himself up in a Kimono for a picture. He had seen true adventure and lived the life of a sea-faring man. But he was also a tender man, and ever since he had been married, he seems to have had an extra longing for a home life, especially since his life with Genevieve was so comforting to him.

Family matters seemed to have weighed the heaviest on Ben at this time in his life, and the death of Ben and Genevieve's daughter, Mildred, in 1919 must have been an extremely difficult time for Ben and especially Genevieve. No doubt Ben had to stay home and comfort his grieving wife. He worked for a couple of Seattle firms, one of which of course was Todd Shipyards, until their son Charles Harrison Parker was born, May 28, 1920, which in some part made up for the loss of their daughter.

Dry land, however, could not keep Ben forever and August 3, 1920, Ben again signed on with the Pacific Steamship Co. as First Assistant Engineer. He sailed for Pacific Steam until March of 1921.

Whenever he could, however, Ben would get home to spend a few days or weeks at the Ranch with Geneva, Esther, and Charles.

Charles Harrison Parker

Charles grew up in a prosperous environment. He had his own gun and his own horse, and later his own car, and all the space a young man needed to enjoy them. He had a pleasant older sister to care for him. He was a spoiled child no doubt. He did have a great respect and love for his father and mother, but it is said that Geneva had a difficult time keeping track of him. It would appear that the family lived in town at Fremont in the winters and during school, and at the ranch during the summers. Charles was known as a carefree and reckless young boy. He was a handful for his mother, and his father was away at sea most of the time.

He did have a proper respect for his parents, however. From a young age Charles wrote his father often when his father was at sea. He informs his father about the state of the ranch, how the animals are doing, how the fruit trees are doing, etc. He often lets his father know that

he is being a good boy in his father's absence, and adds statements to his letters such as "P.S. I am piling some wood."

Esther June Parker

Esther June Parker was a very sweet, pleasant child, and her parents adored her. She was naturally talented as a musician. She played the piano and organ. She was an organist at St. Paul's Episcopal Church at 15 Roy Street in Seattle. She took good care of her younger brother Charles, and Charles was to always have a warm place in his heart for his memory of Esther.

Esther was known as a very brilliant young lady, and she was also a very romantic girl. Esther graduated from Ballard High School in June of 1925. She was the senior class Salutatorian.

In 1925 Esther was to go to Massachusetts and visit with relatives there. Esther's travel by train was arranged by Eugenia Parker with Temple Tours located in Boston, Mass. Temple Tours was owned by Eugenia's sister and her husband; Reeve and Constance Chipman. Esther rode the Northern Pacific Empire Builder to Chicago, and from there to Boston. Winchester and Boston were the home of Ben's relatives, Harrison and Fanny. By this date, however, Harrison had passed on. Esther got to know the family of Harrison and Fanny: Rev Asa Merrick Parker and wife Adelaide, Constance and husband Reeve Chipman, Esther and husband Rev Sidney Lovett, Gordon Parker and wife Mary, and Eugenia Parker.

Esther left a diary of her 1925 summer trip to visit the New England relatives, her going to Red Roof, Gordon Parker's farm at Laughing Brook, going to camp, and the many other things she encountered in and around Boston and Winchester. Going through her diary of this summer we get a very good look at a very charming young girl, and we learn a lot about the back east Parkers of the day. She begins her saga as the train heads for the mountains.

> Here I am gazing at the surrounding country from a Pullman car window. Everything is fine for the beginning but you can't tell what

Genevieve with Charles.

Sister Esther with Charles at the Ranch.

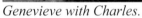

Genevieve on a summer day.

Ben with his son Charles.

Young Charles.

Genevieve always doted on her son.

A care free youth at play in the wilds of the then untamed parts south of Seattle, at the "Ranch."

Charles taking care of chores at the Ranch.

will be the end. The only thing I wish is that I had the two seats to myself. There is a gentleman opposite me going to North Dakota. He deplores the fact that he is going to such a hot and dry country, but it is only for two weeks. The country so far is just woods and hills. I don't know where the dining car is but I don't care as I have plenty of candy to last me a month. I have dirt of my face already.

The wooded hills give way to dry hills and the heat grows fairly intolerable. People are fanning themselves, walking up and down, sleeping, discarding their clothing, and drinking ice water. Absolutely futile attempts at cooling off.

Esther goes on to give the blow by blow of her journey. She makes it through the first day of train travel. The next day she has conversations with several of the train's occupants. There are two ministers traveling with her and she spends the day chatting and eating with them; "I just found out that one of the two people opposite me is a Catholic Priest and the other a Presbyterian Minister. The minister and I were talking about [study?] and

Seattle. He praises Seattle in the most flowery and exaggerated language." Esther meets an aviator going to Minnesota and a young man whose father owns eighteen factories. The next day she is found talking with the minister once again "The weather is lovely and cool and I am enjoying a conversation with the minister concerning evolution, logic, philosophy, religion, etc. It was very very interesting and he is very sensible and cultured. I never did meet anyone whom I liked better. He is extremely jolly and very humorous."

She spends four days on the train. The young girl is already homesick at this point; she writes the day before arriving at Boston "It was raining this morning and everything is gloomy. My heart is sore."

Arriving at Boston late Sunday, she is picked up by Eugenia Parker and taken to Red Roof at Winchester. There Esther refreshes herself with a bath, some supper, and a good night's rest. The next day Esther was taken to see an old couple by the name of Mr. & Mrs. Stevens who had known Ben Parker as a young boy and were disappointed that he was not with Esther. They told Esther what a good boy he had been and Esther told them "papa was the best man in the world and oh, there really never will be any better."

Esther is both impressed and bewildered by her new surroundings, "Everything is so old fashioned and quaint, the old brick roads and old fashioned buildings. I feel like I am in a foreign country." Esther thought New England an extravagant place; "We stopped to have dinner(lunch) at 'Ye Old Kentucky Inn' and paid $5.00 for just three meals. I think that atrocious." Esther is amazed by the busy city "Traffic here in Boston is simply awful. Seattle knows nothing of traffic congestion; great hordes of people trying to cross, street cars and cars coming from a thousand directions." (Oh—if she could only see Seattle now!)

Esther and Eugenia were to be fairly inseparable for the summer Esther visited, and Esther spent the majority of her days with her. They go to Boston to shop, dine, and visit places like the Boston library, which impressed Esther very much; "It was a most wonderful place, the marvelous paintings and beautiful marble staircase and statues." Esther even saw the President and heard him speak.

Not content with Winchester and Boston alone, Eugenia takes Esther around to see the local Massachusetts sights, such as Lexington, Concord, etc. They traveled all over "We had our lunch and then went to Salem and visited the House of Seven Gables and went up the secret staircase. It was quite creepy, the house is terribly old and oh so interesting."

Esther eats very well while at Red Roof, and makes a point of telling us what she has for

Esther Parker.

breakfast, lunch, and dinner every day "For supper Eugenia & I had waffles and ice cream with syrup poured over. It was excellent eating." Later she worries "I am afraid I am eating too much. I might suffer from it."

Every time Esther sees a dog she likes, it makes her think of her brother Charles and how she would like him to have the dog. She misses her family very much and even has nightmares that bad things happen to them. She dreams that her father's ship sinks, and that her brother Charles is dying and she can't save him, and her mother goes to sleep without blankets and freezes to death, Oh My. She laments "A train makes me homesick and one is just leaving town. Oh take me with you."

Esther had many opportunities to go to church and prayer meetings while in Winchester, and on July 5 she goes for the first time to the Reverend Sidney Lovett's church. She apparently developed a fondness for Sidney, and mentions him pleasantly elsewhere.

Esther also spent quite a bit of time in the company of her Aunt Fanny, who of course remembered Ben so well, even well enough to remind Esther of her father's birthday. Esther was to become quite fond of Aunt Fanny.

July 10 Esther and the whole household packed up and went to Gordon's farm in central Massachusetts. She loved the trip out there and was allowed to drive the car part of the way. She comments on the drive "The country was perfectly lovely, the beautiful rolling Berkshire Hills of New England, speckled with little villages." At the farm she met Mary, Gordon's wife. Mary ran the farm as Gordon worked in

Esther with her brother Charles.

Boston most of the time. Esther was to help Mary out quite a bit and spend a lot of time with her while at the farm. Almost as soon as they arrived at Laughing Brook, they changed clothes and went to work; "We went out in the field and turned all the wet hay over to dry and it was hot work." She thought the farm a very lovely place "Laughing Brook runs through the place, over rocks and pebbles and it reminds me of the ranch." Esther further comments, "The brook was lovely and the green fields bordering it were covered with yellow black eyed susans."

Esther spent a little time with Gordon as well "Gordon took us in his big Packard for a ride up further on the Mohawk Trail. We saw the loveliest scenery imaginable." Most of her time was spent with Eugenia and Mary though, doing work on the farm, building picket fences, raking up hay in the fields; "They were just taking in a huge load of hay and so we all piled on & had a ride to the barn." The visit was not all work though, and taking walks, swims, and other amusements filled the days; "In the evening we

all got ready and went to a sugar eat at Ashfield. It was held in the town hall and lots of people assembled. They gave us a great big dish of snow and a pitcher of maple syrup. When it hits the snow it hardens and gets nice and chewy. They give you all you can eat and a dish of pickles offset the sweet syrup."

July 17 little Esther and company packed up to go to her Aunt Esther and Sidney Lovett's place. The trip was 185 miles and Esther drove for 96 of them, which being a young girl she was quite thrilled to do. When they got there Esther was very impressed "The house is large and lovely." and "The view of the Mts from here is magnificent, with two lakes visible down below them." There were plenty of people there to keep them company "They have Freda the cook, the chauffeur's daughter, Bob the boy who works for them, Mary, Eugenia, Aunt Fanny, Sidney, Esther, the children & myself, here." Here Esther worked out in the fields as well, and traveled around the area. Esther sure liked to ride in their big cars "I went home in Gordon's car. It rides like the wind and as smooth as satin."

Esther liked to be in the company of Sidney Lovett "Sidney arrived at 11: P.M. from Boston as had the pleasure of his company all day." She goes on "Had a cherry eating contest at night & Sidney & I called it a tie for we both ate 70 & it would be foolish to open another can."

July 23 they went back to Red Roof and Winchester. Esther and Eugenia and Aunt Fanny spent the days doing their usual touring around, shopping, etc. Every other day one of the relatives would stop by to visit or have dinner. The Winchester Parkers were truly a jolly and close knit family.

August 1 Esther was taken to Maine to go to Merrick and Adeliade Parker's summer home "started off in their big Studebaker for Maine. Had a fine drive up along the coast even tho it was a bit misty and cloudy. We passed about every thing on the road and seemed to be flying part of the time." When they got there Esther was equally impressed "Their summer home is right on the sea shore and the view of the Atlantic is grand and such a wonderful smell. The house is fairly large and built for the summer and out of doors." The usual gaggle of friends and relatives are there. Esther takes advantage of the summer weather "Before supper all hands had a swim, the water was cold like ours." The local town is called "Old Orchard" and there is plenty of amusements there we are told.

Esther says that Merrick reminds her of her uncle Harry in Seattle. They spend an afternoon touring Portland, Maine.

It is a fine city and reminds me more of Seattle than any Eastern city so far. While Adelaide and Priscilla shopped, Merrick took me for a drive around the city and it was beautiful. We saw Longfellow's home, the one where he was born and the one where he spent his boyhood days, the latter right in the heart of the business district. Then we met the shoppers and went to a pipe organ concert, one of the largest pipe organs in the world. I certainly enjoyed the music and so did everybody else. After that Merrick took us into the best ice cream place and we had what they call a jap; any kind of ice cream with a syrup marshmallow whip cream and nuts in it.

August 8 Esther takes a train back to Red Roof again, Winchester is beginning to feel like home to her "Was glad to see Aunt Fanny and it was good to get back." They spend their days doing their usual domestic routines. Esther goes to the Palmers place. These are the Palmers of the Palmer & Parker Company. Esther remarks of the place "The house is beautiful and seems to shine." Esther played their piano for them while visiting.

August 15 Esther is hauled off to summer camp. Eugenia is there serving as a counselor and so keeps her company, and they have a good time.

August 29 Esther goes back to Red Roof and remarks "Glad to see Aunt Fanny and Winchester." Again all the relatives come over and there is visiting, touring, dining, having fun, etc. Esther seems impressed by the Palmers and remarks "Clara & Will Palmer came for me at 10:00 A.M. in the big car and chauffeur and took me on a drive to Swampscott, Salem, Revere Beach, Lynn Glauster, Magnolia, Everett, etc."

Over the summer of 1925 Esther had taken in just about everything New England had to offer, and had gotten to know the eastern branch of the family intimately. By the time she was to leave for Seattle, Esther had thought Red Roof almost home.

September 7 Esther's summer adventure is almost at an end, and she is taken to the train station amid a lot of farewell wishes and gifts, and heads across Canada for home in Seattle.

Esther studied music at the University of Washington in the late twenties. While at the U of W she attended and participated in many recitals, and is featured in many programs. Esther was a gifted student, and a very intelligent girl as the following political paper would suggest.

More power to you-- Pitkin-

W. Wilson, W. Harding and H. Hoover all failed lamentably as national leaders simply because each in his own peculiar way was unable to maintain dominance in important crises. F. Roosevelt succeeds primarily as a result of his easy dominance over people and affairs. Just what does this mean? Wilson could not assert himself in open conference; so he withdrew and thought alone, reaching decisions which failed to reckon cunningly with trends and wishes. Harding was easy-going, soft, and a moral moron; so his clever, strong, corrupt friends got the jump on him simply by telling him what to do in a compelling voice. Hoover was somewhat like Wilson in that he could not turn on his energies effectively in the presence of strong men who differed with him. But where Wilson was unable to do this mainly because he was a semi-invalid with a diseased ego, Hoover failed chiefly because he was too easily vexed and even enraged by opposition, sometimes to the point of speechlessness. Furthermore, Hoover must have been dimly aware of his own limitations as a leader; for he was always inclined to turn over every decision to a committee or to a national conference-and straightway to drop the matter. This form of "passing the buck" is manifestly one odd sort of self-subordination, not a matter of sugar-coated with the sweet name of "socialized group-action".

Franklin Roosevelt always acts dominantly. He gathers advice and information from all quarters. While doing this, he is open-minded in the finest manner. But as soon as he reaches a conclusion, he takes the reins firmly, issues orders, and brooks no opposition. The time for the opponent has passed. The hour of action has arrived. Action is a discharge of energy. Masterful action drives straight and true. Even when it leads to mistakes, men respect it because they understand that it is much better to put all one's energies behind a wrong decision than to wobble feebly all around a right one.

THE THREE DETERMINERS.

Your energy flow varies with changes in three major forces; the quality of the stimulus, your own energy habits, and the momentary tensions demanding prompt relief. The weaker any one of these, the stronger are the other two, relatively. The weaker the stimulus, the stronger relatively are habit and momentary desire. If, for example, I am asked to do at noon a task that doesn't interest me anyhow, I resist undertaking it; for at noon I am hungry and usually eat lunch. The hunger tensions are far more insistent on prompt relief than the mild tensions aroused by feeble intellectual interest. My noon lunch habit, too, is stronger. Hence, if I do the work, I do it with weak interest and attention.

If you use your energies in a hit-or-miss fashion and have few well-organized habits, you will be dominated more by the stimulus of momentary desire than by your habits. Children and adults of inferior mentality attend to very simple stimuli, and shift their attention from object to object without any strong inner direction of their energies and interests. They lean on an outer directing force. And "they want they want when they want it."

Finally, the weaker your momentary desire, the stronger are stimulus and habit. You have few impulses to relieve strong momentary tensions. If you are neither hungry, nor thirsty, nor otherwise moved by some craving, you are easily dominated by stimulating objects and situations, and by habit, whether good or bad. People who have they want either pursue each palling novelty or else stick in their comfortable rut.

The problem of attention is chiefly one of energies so well-organized relative to the task at hand that we use no more energy than absolutely necessary to achieve good results. To establish effective attention habits, then, we must eliminate as far as possible everything that interferes with the straight-line transmission of energy. nnn

Esther graduated from the U of W with a degree in music on the 17th of June, 1929.

Esther returned again, after college, to New England, and was involved in many activities there. She must have really loved Boston and the area. She had no trouble in finding a proper escort to show her about town. In the letter below she explains to her mother, "One of the conservatory boys has been taking me quite a few places lately and he is excellent company; recital, theatre, & I know the proper way to eat Spaghetti." Esther writes the following letter.

March 22nd.

Dearest Mama:-
    What a beautiful Sunday this is---warm and just like summer, and one that would take us to the ranch.
    Friday three of us rushed Symphony & waited in line two hours & it was cold I can tell you. But that is the only way to get in unless

one has a season ticket & we wanted to hear the famous pianist Vladimir Herowitz play the Tschaikovsky Concerto; such technique. But one number they played was terrible to listen to---very modern & unmelodic. You would have been horrified.

That same night we all went over to Jordan Hall to hear the Conservatory Orchestra, so the day was full of orchestra and Symphony.

One of the conservatory boys has been taking me quite a few places lately and he is excellent company; recital, theatre, & I know the proper way to eat Spaghetti.

Last night the boy I have been going with from Tech.(M.I.T.), took me to an entertainment put on by the students and in it the boys took the parts of girls. It was extremely clever & funny. It so happened that Walter's father is up here for the weekend so they invited me to come along; he is a very fine looking man & I know you would approve of both father & son.

My piano teacher wants me to memorize a piece & play it in a recital, so I am going to try & do that before I come home. As yet I haven't told him my plans.

Guess I will call cousin Clara & let her know that I am needed at the church.

All love to you,

Esther

She does well in her music at Boston, and she wins a scholarship to the New England Conservatory of Music. In a letter to her mother she pleads with mama to let her stay and finish a course of musical study.

Dearest Mama:-

Another letter, but different; Mr. Flanders has offered me a scholarship in organ which means that my organ lessons will be paid for. Oh mama it is going to mean a great deal to stay on and work hard and I can make enough to cover my incidental expenses such as carfare etc. They give scholarships to just a few people , and I am very fortunate, since a great many of the girls around here would give anything to have one; in fact Helen Wilson won't come back unless she can make one in voice. Well this $75 you sent me will cover my pullman(train fare) home and part of my next semester expenses. I have figured in piano lessons at 2 1/2 and organ

practice 3 times a week and you won't have to give me a bit more than $300 for everything. In order to be able to stay this next semester and get as much out of it as I can I would even borrow the $300 from you and pay it back when I get home. Couldn't I do that? I still would rather be home, but I feel like it is a case of duty to stay and take advantage of Mr. Flanders offer. Will you let me?

We are in the midst of a big snow storm and it is beautiful-- about 8 inches so far. Last night I was one of the 5 fortunates to recieve a box seat ticket to the opera " Die Valkurie." Our box was close to the stage where we could see everything and everyone could see us-- we were all dressed formally and you can tell the neighbors that it is a great thrill to sit in the Boston Opera House just opposite the Governor of Mass. This opera lasted from 8:15 until 11:45 and it was magnificent; my piano solo "Magie Fire" comes from it. So far I have seen $24 worth of Grand Opera for nothing. My piano teacher says that anytime I want an extra lesson or help of any kind I can have as much as I like. Of course the better I do, the more credit he gets so it works both ways.

Tes and I still have that $25 coming at the end so really $275 would be all that you would have to send for the whole time; my clothes are plentiful, and as I said before what little things I get I am going to pay for myself & that will be fun-- an incentive.

When June comes I will be ready to come home-- you know I would rather he home more than any place in the world & am much happier there, but this is education. I feel that I must stay the semester & work hard; don't you and papa think it best. Answer as soon as possible.

All love

from Esther

As an organist of St. Paul's Episcopal Church, and a member of the Western Washington Chapter of the American Guild of Organists, Esther played and attended recitals at many Northwest churches and music halls. She played at places such as the University Temple at 15 Ave N.E. and East 43rd Street, and St. Mark's Cathedral at Tenth Avenue North and East Galer.

CHAPTER X

Coastwise Lines

The traffic of the United States Merchant Marine was divided into two categories, coastwise voyages and foreign voyages. Every mariner documented every voyage he partook in as a coastwise trip or foreign trip in his discharge book (official government career log). These days we would compare this to domestic or international airline travel. There were fifteen coastwise steamship lines serving Seattle in 1919, not counting the twenty-two operators of the local Mosquito Fleet. The two principal coastwise lines operating out of Seattle were the Admiral Line of the Pacific Steamship Company and the Alaska Line of the Alaska Steamship Company.

Pacific Steam was a descendant of the old Pacific Coast Steamship Company of San Francisco. The Pacific Steamship Company was part of the Pacific Coast Company, rail and steamboat conglomerates. Their docks were south a few piers to Alaska Steam's, some would say "in more ways than one." Pacific Steam also ran its "Admiral Oriental Line," their international trans-Pacific line, which developed a reputation for first-rate service. Ben worked for the Pacific Steamship Company from August 3, 1920, until March of 1921. He was First Assistant Engineer.

S.S. H.F. Alexander *of the Pacific Steamship Co. in front of the Alaska Steam pier.*

Pacific Steamship Co.

Sailing Schedules
[Subject to Change Without Notice]

between

SEATTLE / PORTLAND / VICTORIA and SAN FRANCISCO / LOS ANGELES / SAN DIEGO

THE ADMIRAL LINE P.S.S.CO.

Effective July 1st, 1928

Read Down — SOUTHBOUND — Read Down

CITIES		H. F. Alexander	Ruth Alexander or Emma Alexander	Admiral Benson or Admiral Peoples	Admiral Dewey or Admiral Schley	Admiral Farragut
SEATTLE	Leave	Tue. 5:00 PM	Sat. Midnite			
VICTORIA	Arrive		Sun. 7:00 AM			
	Leave		Sun. 9:00 AM			
PORTLAND①	Leave			Tue. 5:00 PM	Sat. 5:00 PM	Wed. 5:00 PM
SAN FRANCISCO	Arrive	Thu. 7:30 AM	Tue.② 2:00 PM	Fri. 7:00 AM	Sat. 7:00 AM	Sat. 7:00 AM
	Leave	Thu. 5:00 PM	Wed. 3:00 PM	Sat. 3:00 PM	Tue. 10:00 PM	
LOS ANGELES	Arrive	Fri. 10:30 AM	Thu. 5:00 PM	Sun. 11:00 PM	Thu. 6:00 AM	
	Leave		Fri. 8:00 PM	Mon. 1:00 PM	Thu. 8:00 PM	
SAN DIEGO	Arrive		Sat. 6:00 AM	Mon. 9:00 PM	Fri. 6:00 AM	

Read Down — NORTHBOUND — Read Down

CITIES		H. F. Alexander	Ruth Alexander or Emma Alexander	Admiral Benson or Admiral Peoples	Admiral Dewey or Admiral Schley	Admiral Farragut
SAN DIEGO	Leave		Sat. 10:00 PM	Mon. Midnite	Fri. 10:00 PM	
LOS ANGELES	Arrive		Sun. 7:00 AM	Tue. 8:00 AM	Sat. 7:00 AM	
	Leave	Fri. 5:00 PM	Sun. 11:00 AM	Tue. 2:00 PM	Sat. 2:00 PM	
SAN FRANCISCO	Arrive	Sat. 10:30 AM	Mon. 1:00 PM	Wed. 9:00 PM	Sun. 9:00 PM	
	Leave	Sat. 5:00 PM	Tue. 5:00 PM	Thu. 5:00 PM	Tue. 5:00 PM	Sat. 10:00 PM
PORTLAND①	Arrive			Sun. 7:00 AM	Fri. 7:00 AM	Tue. 2:00 PM
VICTORIA	Arrive		Thu. 10:00 PM			
SEATTLE	Arrive	Mon. 9:00 AM	Fri. 7:00 AM			

① All PORTLAND vessels call at ASTORIA both north and south bound (except ADMIRAL FARRAGUT, which calls northbound only). Southbound arrival hour at ASTORIA is approximately 6 hours after sailing from PORTLAND.
② Northbound arrival hour at ASTORIA is approximately 8 hours before arrival at PORTLAND.
③ SS. EMMA ALEXANDER arrives San Francisco at 11:00 a. m.

A-314-1 JULY 1928 PRINTED IN USA 25M AP11647

1919

The Admiral Line operated principally down the coast from Seattle and Victoria, B.C. all the way down to San Diego. The line also had excursion steamers to Alaska, but by this time Alaska Steam dominated that route.

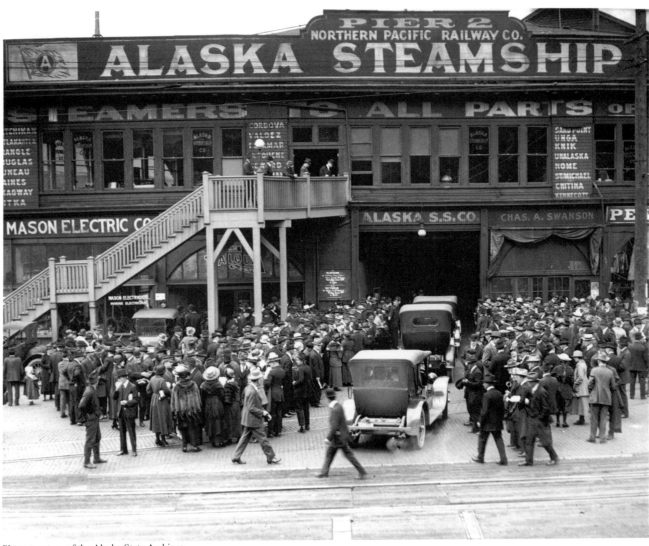

Photo courtesy of the Alaska State Archives

The Alaska Line

The Alaska Steamship Company was formed in 1895 to take advantage of the budding territory of Alaska, serving fishing ports hauling passengers and freight. Just a couple of years later in 1897 the Klondike Gold Rush really put Alaska, and the port of Seattle in Washington which served it, on the map. From this point on, regular steamer service to Alaska was nearly overwhelmed.

The original Alaska Steam was formed in Port Townsend with one small ship, the *Willapa*. By 1907 the line had four little ships. The company was bought by the Kennicott Copper Corporation in

1908, which also acquired the Northwestern Steamship Company and merged the two lines, together with still more ships, to form a new Alaska Steamship Company. The Alaska Steam ships were able to haul the parent company's copper on the southward bound voyages, giving the line a distinct advantage over the competition, such as the rival Admiral Line.

In 1920 the Merchant Marine Act, or the Jones Act as it was known, shut out foreign competition, and gave Alaska Steam a near monopoly in the Alaska trade.

By August of 1921, Ben had landed his best job yet; he signed on with the Alaska Steamship Company, a career that was to last

S.S. Northwestern *at Haines, Alaska situated on Lynn Canal between Juneau and Skagway. Typical of the scenes that inspired an Alaska tourist trade, c. 1920s.*

twenty years. One year as a First Assistant, and nineteen as Chief Engineer. A Western Union Cable survives to this day, sent by a D.L. Gray: "COME AS SOON AS POSSIBLE HAVE POSITION OPEN AS OPERATING ENGINEER. ASSISTANT TO MR MORROW SALARY FOUR SIXTY PER MONTH. WIRE ANSWER AND GIVE DATE OF ARRIVAL HERE". The address the cable was sent too was 5211 1 Ave Northwest Seattle, the address Ben and Genevieve were to maintain for many long years. The sending address is San Pedro California.

The Alaska Steamship Company was home ported at pier 2, later renamed pier 51, in Seattle, one dock south of the Colman Dock.

The line provided transportation for passengers and freight up and down the west coast. Alaska Steam also had a fleet of freighters. In addition, the line ran a fleet of cruise ships to ply the Inside Passage of southern Alaska, providing a first rate tourist experience and visiting all the important ports, as well as the breathtaking wonders of Alaska such as the glaciers. The early twenties were boom years for Alaska Steam, and wages were among the highest they would be for twenty years. Ben would one day be Alaska Steam's top Chief Engineer. Life was not to be without its difficulties from now on for Ben however, as he was to see several challenges with Alaska Steamship.

The **S.S. Alaska.**

Photo from Benjamin Parker collection

The ship that Ben was to first sail on at the Alaska Steamship Co. was the company's namesake, the S.S. *Alaska*. She ran out of Seattle until she was chartered by the San Francisco-Portland Steamship Co. in November, 1920. On August 6, 1921 she was making her way down the coast of California off cape Mendocino at night and in heavy fog. At 9:00pm that night the *Alaska* struck some rocks at Blunts Reef, tearing her hull open. She immediately started to list to starboard and sank beneath the California waters within fifteen minutes of striking the reef. The captain was directing the abandon ship efforts on the bridge when the ship's funnel crashed down into the bridge and killed him. The first boat lowered into the water was crushed against the ship's hull and everyone in the boat perished. Another boat was lowered into the foggy seas, this time making it safely away the ship. Then another boat made it away. The fourth boat lowered did not fair so well, as it capsized after being lowered and most of its occupants drowned. Ben Parker and the other engineers jumped into the sea just before *Alaska* made her final plunge; after a failed attempt of the officers to launch a boat. By this time the ship had too much of a list to launch more boats. Before *Alaska* sank, she got a wireless distress call out and the *Anyox*, just fifteen miles away, came to her rescue. The crew of the *Anyox* saved all the people in *Alaska's* boats and thirty people floating in the water who managed to cling to wreckage. Ben Parker was in the water, clinging to a part of the ship's deckhouse, until 6:00pm the next day and was finally picked up by a Coast Guard boat. In Seattle the front page headlines read "SCORES BELIEVED DROWNED WHEN STEAMSHIP ALASKA GOES DOWN." The wreck of the *Alaska* made headlines up and down the coast. The following is taken from the San Francisco newspaper reporting on the hearing following the *Alaska* wreck.

The morning session was opened with the testimony of the officers of the engine room. Chief engineer John M. Callfas, who has held his license for more than twenty years, testified he went to the engine room as soon as he heard the crash, ordered the engine crew to start the pumps working, at the telegraph signal he received from Captain Hobey, and worked with the crew to insert broom handles in the rivet holes, through which the water was pouring. Finding this of no use he plugged the openings with oakum, but the water forced the oakum back. Realizing the most important duty was to keep the dynamo going, Callfas stated he stood by with the engine crew to insure its working; had the crew put out every fire under the boilers, and was himself the last man to crawl up on deck.

Callfas stated the Alaska was making full speed, 14 1/2 knots per hour, at the time she struck Blunt's reef, and at no time did he hear the Blunt reef signal. He further testified frequent and efficient boat drills were held and that each boat was properly equipped.

TESTIMONY CORROBORATED

Callfas' testimony as to his conduct in the engine room was corroborated by the first, second and third assistant engineers, who also testified, and gave their names and addresses, respectively, as,:

Benjamin P. Parker, 5211 First avenue N.W., Seattle; Douglas Mertin of Portland, Or., and S.A. Carlson, 3853 Wrenton avenue, Seattle.

First Assistant Engineer Parker testified he received the order to start the pumps in the forward hold directly from Captain Hobey over the telephone, transmitted it to Chief Engineer Callfas and that it was immediately executed. Parker also declared he had charge of hiring the engine crew, and that he knew from experience they were efficient.

SCORES BELIEVED DROWNED WHEN STEAMSHIP ALASKA GOES DOWN

STEAMSHIP ALASKA STRIKES ROCK

THE steamship Alaska as she appeared in Seattle Harbor prior to being chartered to the San Francisco-Portland Steamship Company last November. She is now believed to be a total wreck on Blunts Reef, off Cape Mendocino, Calif.

The Maltese cross indicates the point where the steamship Alaska went on the rocks last night. It is thirty miles from Eureka, Calif., and 450 miles from Portland.

Portion of newspaper headline from a Seattle paper. Headlines were equally large in the San Francisco papers.

Ben Parker collection

And so ended the *Alaska*. When all was said and done, seventy crew and ninety-six passengers were saved, but over forty persons lost their lives in the tragic sinking.

The *Alaska* would be replaced by a new turbine powered twin-screw ship of the same namesake. The new *Alaska* was built in Seattle by Todd Drydock & Construction Company at the Skinner & Eddy yard. The *Alaska* was one of two new ships ever ordered by Alaska Steam.

S.S. Victoria *in front of the old Coleman dock in Seattle.*   Puget Sound Maritime Historical Society

One of the more well known ships that Ben was to sail on was the Alaska Steamship *Victoria,* known as "Old Vic" to many in the Northwest in Ben's day. *Victoria,* an iron hull ship of 3,914 tons, was originally built in 1870, at Dumbarton, Scotland, and was a Cunard liner under the flag of Great Britain. *Victoria* had already had a long career when she came to the Northwest in 1887 in the service of the Canadian Pacific Railway Company. Next she was purchased by the Northern Pacific Steamship Company. After the Klondike Gold Rush came another rush at Nome in 1899. *Victoria* became famous hauling prospectors too, and gold from, Nome, Alaska beginning 1900, leading the way through the ice after the Spring thaw. In the old days gamblers frequented her voyages, relieving prospectors of their money.

Next the *Victoria* was taken over by the Northwestern Steamship Company in 1904, and continued on the Nome run.

Victoria joined the Alaska Steamship fleet in 1908 when the Kennicott Copper Corporation merged the Alaska Steamship

Company and the Northwestern Steamship Company, the new combined concern being called the Alaska Steamship Company.

Old Vic was Alaska Steam's premier sea boat, and was put on the Bering Sea cruise to the far north of Alaska. She was always the first ship to Nome, as she was stout enough to break some ice.

From 1909 to 1919 the *Victoria* was commanded by the famous Pacific mariner "Dynamite" Johnny O'Brien, whose life and exploits can be read in *Tales of the Seven Seas* by Dennis Powers.

In 1924 the *Victoria* was completely overhauled and made into essentially a new ship. Ben was serving as Chief engineer on *Victoria* in 1925. That means he was put in charge of a new ship, and the most well known of Alaska Steam's ships. Ben had obviously come a long way in his career. How long he served on her is not precisely known, sometime in the late twenties. Ben served her well, and at least this one ship would be without incident for Ben.

Victoria lasted in Alaska Steam service until 1954. She was to have

Victoria *on an early brochure, 1915.*

*The **Victoria** at dock in Seattle after her 1924 overhaul, when Ben became her Chief.*   *Ben Parker collection*

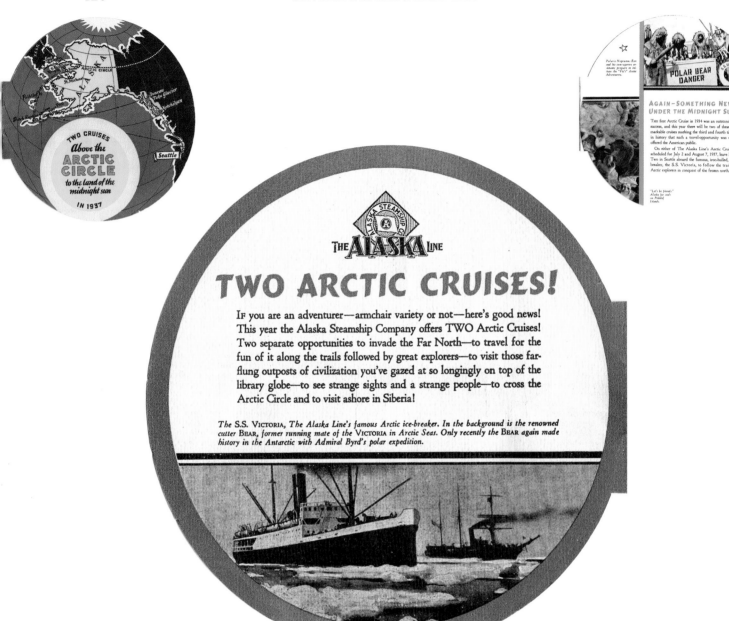

the longest steamship career on the Pacific west coast, and when she was retired after eighty-four years at sea, she was recognized as the oldest ship in the United States Merchant Marine.

The next Alaska Steamship Co. vessel that Ben was to sail on was the *Aleutian,* which joined the fleet in 1927. *Aleutian* was one of Alaska Steam's premier cruise liners touring the Inside Passage of southeastern Alaska, and as far north as Prince William Sound. This was a leisurely change from the open Bering Sea and icy Nome. The twin-screw *Aleutian* was built in Philadelphia in 1898 and was a vessel of 5,664 tons, 360 feet long with engines of 5,000 horsepower.

The Inside Passage may have been pleasant and scenic cruising, but it was fraught with dangers. Lacking radar, depth-sounders, and good charts, many ships ripped out their bottoms on rocks and shoals.

Aleutian struck a rock and sank in Uruk Bay, Kodiak Island on May 26, 1929. She sank in ten minuets. All passengers and crew except one escaped in the boats and were picked up by a U.S. Coast & Geodetic Survey vessel, the *Surveyor.* Adolf Loken was the Chief Engineer

S.S. Aleutian, *1927.*

on the *Surveyor* when he fell ill in 1933, but at this time he was Chief Engineer on the old *Explorer*, heading to southeast Alaska. *Explorer* likely heard the distress call, or heard the news being relayed from the *Surveyor*, however. It was a good thing to have the survey boats working here and there all over, as they were pressed into rescue duty more than once.

The Chief Engineers were a fraternal group, and they all belonged to the M.E.B.A. Both Adolf and Ben had worked on some of the most famous northwest ships.

The crew of the *Aleutian* were noted for their cool heads and professionalism during the evacuation of the ship.

The *Aleutian* would be replaced by a larger ship of the

ALASKA STEAMSHIP COMPANY
Copper River & Northwestern R·R·

THE ALASKA LINE

same namesake.

In 1929 Ben was Chief on the *Alameda*, operating out of Ketchikan, Alaska. The *Alameda* was a popular old boat, but, unfortunately, in 1931 the *Alameda* burned at the pier in Seattle.

Ben also served aboard the Alaska steamer *Denali*. The *Denali*, like so many of the ships of the Alaska Steamship Company that Ben Parker sailed on, ended up a wreck at Zayas Island, off northern British Columbia 3:00am, May 19, 1935. All aboard made it to safety. They were picked up by the Coast Guard cutter *Cayne* after receiving *Denali's* SOS.

Ben would spend the rest of his career with Alaska Steam on the Inside Passage runs where the sailing was smooth, but the dangers ever present.

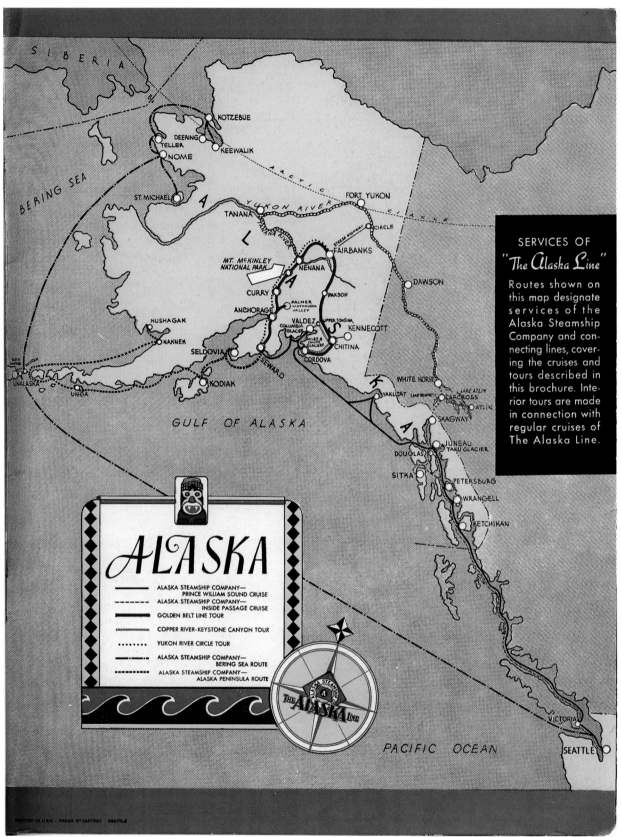

The routes of the Alaska Line from a 1936 advertisement magazine.

Alaska Steam funnel insignia.

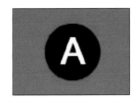

Flags

Luggage label.

Playing card.

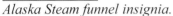

First — An Explanation

In this cruise-log we had intended to tell of *every* outstanding bit of beauty to be seen along the routes of THE ALASKA LINE. Before you've been in Alaska very long you'll understand why we have failed to entirely complete our purpose— so we've left some pages blank for you to try your hand at describing indescribable Alaska. We sincerely hope you'll find the following pages handy as a guide in entering your own memoirs.

★ The geographic names of any region may be likened to the coins circulating in a great sea-port. As these coins are stamped by various nations, so geographic names are stamped by a conquering, colonizing or exploring people. Alaska's history dates from its discovery by Vitus Bering of the Imperial Russian Navy, in 1741. Names along the coast of Alaska and British Columbia are derived almost exclusively from the following six sources, comprising the na-

tions whose explorations and settlements charted the course of Alaska's history until its purchase by the United States from Russia in 1867: Natives; Russians—1741 to 1867; Spaniards—1774 to 1800; English—1778 to —; French—1786; Americans— 1848 to —. ★ No attempt has been made to outline the various "Surprise Ports" into which your steamer sails while en route between the major ports described. These "Surprise Ports," located in picturesque sheltered coves, are unique as a feature of your Alaska Steamship cruise. It is recommended that while the steamer is loading or discharging cargo, full advantage be taken of the opportunities thus presented to explore and photograph the surrounding country. The half-hour whistle (two blasts) gives ample warning of departure, and these extra stops make it possible to add additional experiences to this trip through "America's Fjords."

3

Round-shaped tour book.

Trying to bolster the tourist business, during the Depression Alaska Steam embarked on an ambitious advertising campaign.

1936.

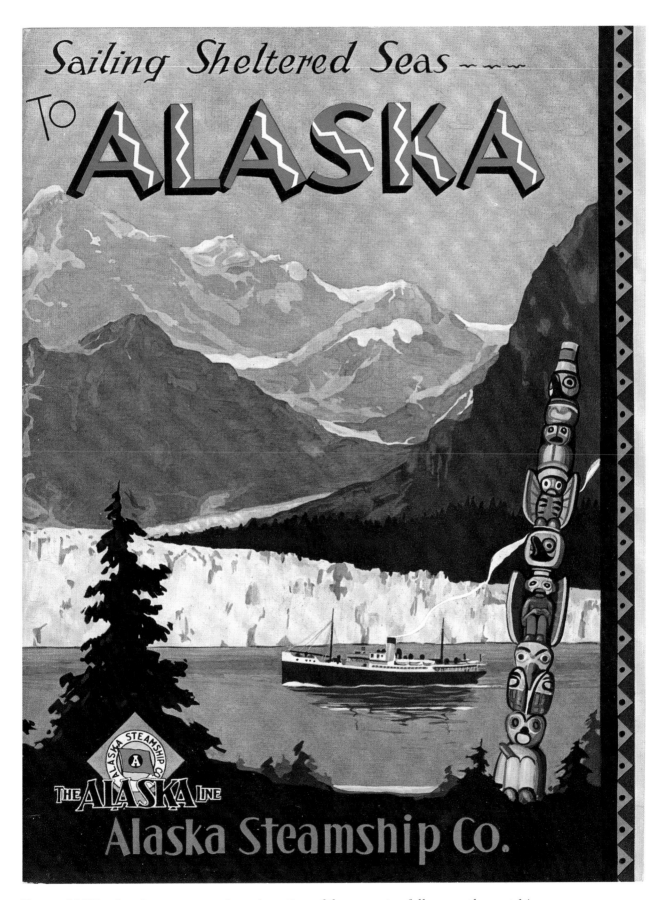

Cover of 1931 advertisement magazine. A portion of the magazine follows on the next 14 pages.

THE ALASKA LINE

SAILING SHELTERED SEAS

THE ALASKA LINE
ALASKA STEAMSHIP CO.

ALASKA STEAMSHIP COMPANY

PIER 2 ·:· SEATTLE

Sailing Sheltered Seas to ~
Mystic, Romantic Alaska

Newest of all the corners of this great continent . . . last of the borders to be made accessible . . . the scene of tomorrow's action and industry—Alaska!

Here are busy towns, strategically located for commercial gain . . . immense fish canneries whose products are shipped over the entire world . . . mines that yield the earth's rich minerals in abundance . . . fertile soil to produce luxurious foliage and food . . . a network of railway lines and air lanes . . . up-to-date methods and the most modern equipment for the pursuit of industry . . . a hospitable people, alert, energetic, ever proud to receive travelers and visitors.

Yet this marvelous territory retains its quaint, ancient charm—the charm of an old-world civilization that was transplanted on its shores a century and a half ago when Baranof was "the little Czar of the Pacific" . . . when the foundries of Sitka cast the bells for the old California missions . . . when Russian feet danced to Russian music in the castle on the hill.

A writer once said that here was God's workshop . . . an artist found all the colors of the rainbow here assembled. Yet no pen or brush can aptly tell the story that Nature here discloses.

As you sail sheltered seas you dream of the past . . . live in the present . . . conjure up the future. That is part of Alaska's mysticism.

The S. S. Northwestern in Southeastern Alaska   © WESTERN CANADA AIRWAYS, LTD.

[2

S. S. Yukon at Columbia Glacier, in Southwestern Alaska

THE Alaska Steamship Company offers a choice of several different voyages to this land of wonder; voyages that combine scenic grandeur and restful, carefree travel so enjoyably that in all the world their equal cannot be found.

Part of the pleasure of any one of these voyages lies in the boat trip itself, for Alaska Steamship Company liners are famous among travelers. Exceptionally comfortable accommodations, superior cuisine, efficient service and a constant effort to cater in every way to the passenger's enjoyment are factors that contribute to the fine reputation of this service.

These are the leading trips:

Cruise "A"—Nine-day "Inside Passage" Cruise.

Cruise "B"—Eleven-day "Inside Passage" Cruise.

Cruise "C"—Twelve-day Prince William Sound Cruise.

Tour "D"—Twelve-day Copper River-Keystone Canyon Tour.

Tour "E"—Nineteen-day Golden Belt Line Tour.

Tour "F"—Thirty-five day Yukon River Circle Tour.

Tour "G"—Twenty-three day Yukon River Circle Tour.

These and a few other interesting cruises and tours are described in our Cruise Folder, which carries complete information.

3]

SAILING SHELTERED SEAS

Ketchikan, a short two days from Seattle by steamer

S. S. Alameda in Wrangell Narrows

The trip from Wrangell to Petersburg, a lively fishing town, is replete with thrills as the liner glides through winding, twisting passages so narrow that passengers might carry on a conversation with persons on either shore.

KETCHIKAN, first port of call in Alaska, has many attractions. Its business district and shops are highly intriguing. Large salmon canneries, virtually in the city, never fail to interest travelers. At the nearby falls, in spawning season, salmon are seen jumping and working their way upstream.

[4

WITH "THE ALASKA LINE"

WRANGELL, second port of call, is one of the oldest towns in Alaska, having been established in 1867 when the United States negotiated the purchase of this territory. It was maintained for twenty years as a military post, and later became the outfitting center when the first gold strike was made in the Cassiar country, British Columbia. In Wrangell are found some of the oldest and most interesting Alaska Indian totems.

Brailing a salmon trap

Alaska is the world's greatest producer of salmon, with an annual pack of approximately 240,000,000 cans. In addition, millions of pounds of fresh salmon and fresh halibut are shipped annually throughout the United States.

5]

SAILING SHELTERED SEAS

SS. "Aleutian." Length, 416 feet; displacement, 9200 tons.

THE Alaska Steamship Company is the pioneer transportation company connecting Alaska with "the States." Its liners serve Alaska from Ketchikan, the first city, to Kotzebue Sound, in Bering Sea. The ships pictured on these two pages comprise part of the fleet that offers this service.

The service, accommodations and cuisine on each ship leave nothing to be desired. Every stateroom has hot and cold fresh running water. De luxe staterooms with adjoining bath are available. There is a barber shop and smoking room on every ship.

Music is provided during luncheon and dinner and for dancing in the evening. Deck games, shuffle board, quoits, deck tennis, deck golf and many other amusements are always in vogue. Deck chairs are provided without charge, and steamer rugs may be rented from the Purser at a nominal charge.

Each ship is equipped with wireless for the reception and sending of messages, and passengers are able to keep in touch with events of the world through the medium of the "wireless news" published aboard ship every morning.

SS. "Yukon." Length, 375 feet; displacement, 8250 tons.

[6

SS. "Northwestern." Length, 342 feet; displacement, 5450 tons.

SS. "Alaska." Length, 366 feet; displacement, 6551 tons.

SS. "Alameda." Length, 332 feet; displacement, 5000 tons.

7]

HERE are two pages of interior views of the liners pictured on the preceding pages. Comfort, a pleasant atmosphere and a spirit of informality are integral parts of every voyage to Alaska on this line. Passengers find this informality and luxury a distinctly restful feature.

Left—Social Hall of the S.S. "Aleutian".

Above—Observation Room and Social Hall of the S.S. "Yukon".

Every element of our service contributes to the complete enjoyment of the tourist. Absolute freedom of the ship and cordiality of the officers and crew assure the utmost in carefree vacation for every day of your trip.

Left—Lobby of the S.S. "Alaska".

WITH "THE ALASKA LINE"

THE spaciousness of the lounges and public rooms aboard the Alaska Steamship Company liners is a factor that always appeals to travelers. On voyages where one spends many days on the water, the opportunity to pass the time pleasurably in attractive surroundings adds immeasurably to the enjoyment of the trip.

Right—Social Hall of the S. S. "Northwestern."

Above—A bridge game on the S. S. "Aleutian."

The many windows in the lounges of these liners not only provide plenty of sunlight, but enable travelers to enjoy the constantly changing scenic panorama from all parts of the room.

Right—Social Hall of the S.S. "Alaska"

SAILING SHELTERED SEAS

NOT the least important part of any voyage is the meal service aboard ship, and in this respect the Alaska Steamship Company truly excels. A cuisine of the highest possible standard is always maintained, and the dining saloons are large, pleasant rooms where the choicest foods and fine service combine to make meal times highly popular.

Left—Dining Saloon of the S. S. "Alaska."

Above—Dining Saloon on the S. S. "Aleutian."

Afternoon tea on deck.

The Purser issues table seats.

[10

COMFORT-ABLE, pleasant accommodations contribute greatly to the enjoyment of a voyage on this route. Here are pictured typical staterooms.

Right—A standard first-class stateroom.

Below—Standard "C" deck stateroom with twin beds and pullman upper on the S.S. "Aleutian."

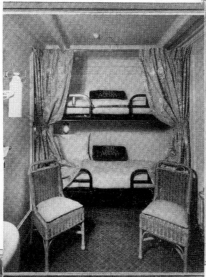

Above—De luxe stateroom with bed and pullman upper and bathroom on the S. S. "Alaska."

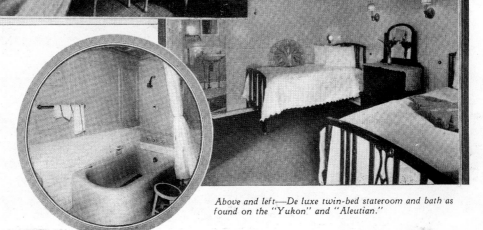

Above and left—De luxe twin-bed stateroom and bath as found on the "Yukon" and "Aleutian."

11]

SAILING SHELTERED SEAS

TAKU GLACIER, pictured above, is one of the highlights of the cruise between Petersburg and Juneau. In reality, there are two glaciers—one of the dead, or receding type, and the other of the live, or flowing type. The southeastern steamers approach very closely to the latter glacier and vibrations from the whistle usually cause large pieces of ice to break from the glacier's face and crash with a roar into the sea.

PETERSBURG, shown below, is located at the north end of Wrangell Narrows on Mitkof Island. It is the center of Alaska's shrimp fishing and packing industry, and also boasts salmon canneries and lumber mills.

WITH "THE ALASKA LINE"

JUNEAU, the capital of Alaska, is an important port in all Alaska Steamship Company itineraries. In reality, it is the "division point" for the southeastern and southwestern Alaska cruises. Our liners always remain in Juneau for several hours, giving passengers an opportunity to see the attractive business and residential districts, and the new Capitol building. The displays in the territorial museum located here are a never-failing source of interest to travelers.

A short distance from Juneau by automobile, over a delightful highway, are Auk Lake and Mendenhall Glacier, two scenic attractions of this territory. The city itself is pleasantly located at the foot of towering mountains, which are even now yielding the earth's rich minerals in abundance.

Across Gastineau Channel from the city is Douglas and Treadwell, formerly the locale of one of the world's greatest quartz gold mining plants. In Juneau itself is located the Alaska Juneau Gold Mining Company, now operating the largest quartz gold mine in the world. A lumber mill and large fishing fleet add prosperity to the city.

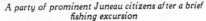
*A party of prominent Juneau citizens after a brief
fishing excursion*

13]

Homeward Bound !

Mentally relieved and carefree . . . physically rested and invigorated, the homeward-bound passenger looks back on his trip with mixed emotions.

Happily he recollects the days of pleasure aboard ship, with interesting companions to share the fun . . . the nights of romance, with a great, golden moon casting its ribbon-like reflection on smooth, sheltered seas . . . the thrills of motoring through flower-clad fields to great snowy peaks; winding through great canyons and across yawning chasms via railroad; sailing down wide, shimmering rivers by steamer . . . the awe-inspiring moments in the Russian church, at Columbia glacier, in Wrangell Narrows.

There are recollections of the magnificent Northern lights . . . quaint Indian villages with their weird totem poles, gaily colored baskets and robes . . . proud huskies, deer and mountain goat in abundance . . . glaciers that crumble into the sea with a resounding roar . . . the vast whiteness of snow-covered plateaus, and then the brilliant green of abundant foliage . . . the awe-inspiring beauty of majestic peaks that seem to tower almost to the clear blue heavens . . . a million-and-one other wonderful sights and sensations that will never be forgotten.

And yet a note of sadness creeps in as one realizes that the trip is nearing its conclusion. It is a happy sadness, though, for there is the knowledge that these experiences are even now becoming memories that will be cherished and fondled—memories that become so vivid, so compelling, that we find the same travelers, again and again, Sailing Sheltered Seas with "The Alaska Line."

The last Alaska Steamship vessel that Ben served on, the one he retired from after twenty years with Alaska Steam, was the *Yukon*. The *Yukon* was one of Alaska Steam's premier cruise ships, plying the Inside Passage.

The *Yukon* entered Alaska Steam service in January 1924. She was the sister ship of the *Aleutian* that was wrecked in 1929. She was originally built in 1899 at Philadelphia as the *Mexico* for the Ward Line. She was a twin-screw ship of 5,863 tons, 360 feet in length, and was powered by triple expansion steam piston engines of 5,000 horsepower.

On October 1, 1938 *Yukon* was traveling in a heavy fog off Jefferson Head, Puget Sound, bound for Alaska. The ship was an hour and a half out of Seattle. The cry was heard "SHIP AHEAD!" Ben's crew received orders to reverse engines and they did so, but it was too late and the *Yukon* collided head on with the steamer *Columbia*. The crew acted quickly and coolly, over the speaker the order was given for the passengers to report to the boat deck, the boats were swung out into position for lowering into the water, but none were actually lowered. This was not to be a repeat of the *S.S. Alaska* incident for Ben. The damage to both vessels was severe, but both vessels returned to port for repairs under their own power. The *Yukon* had 113 passengers on board and the *Columbia* 252. The ships collided with such force that the port side anchor and chain for the *Columbia* was imbedded in the smashed bow of *Yukon*. Most of the *Yukon's* passengers were transferred to the *Denali*. The *Yukon* was repaired and saw long service with Alaska Steam until she ended up a wreck in 1946, years after Ben had left Alaska Steam.

Ben was right back at it however, and he writes to his son from the ship November 13 "We sailed at 9AM Sat with sixty passengers and a good load of freight for this time of the year. We have had rain up to now and still raining, but a little warmer than in Seattle." "If all goes well we should arrive back the 24th Thanksgiving day and I guess you will be home."

S.S. Denali.   Puget Sound Maritime Historical Society

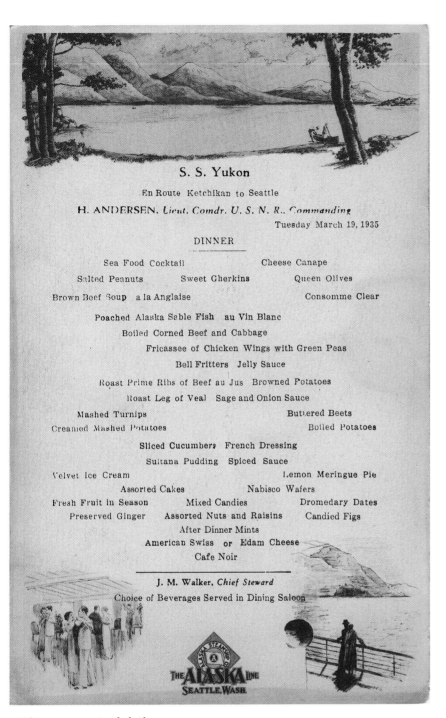

S. S. Yukon

En Route Ketchikan to Seattle

H. ANDERSEN, *Lieut. Comdr. U. S. N. R., Commanding*

Tuesday March 19, 1935

DINNER

Sea Food Cocktail   Cheese Canape

Salted Peanuts   Sweet Gherkins   Queen Olives

Brown Beef Soup a la Anglaise   Consomme Clear

Poached Alaska Sable Fish au Vin Blanc

Boiled Corned Beef and Cabbage

Fricassee of Chicken Wings with Green Peas

Bell Fritters Jelly Sauce

Roast Prime Ribs of Beef au Jus Browned Potatoes

Roast Leg of Veal Sage and Onion Sauce

Mashed Turnips   Buttered Beets

Creamed Mashed Potatoes   Boiled Potatoes

Sliced Cucumbers French Dressing

Sultana Pudding Spiced Sauce

Velvet Ice Cream   Lemon Meringue Pie

Assorted Cakes   Nabisco Wafers

Fresh Fruit in Season   Mixed Candies   Dromedary Dates

Preserved Ginger   Assorted Nuts and Raisins   Candied Figs

After Dinner Mints

American Swiss or Edam Cheese

Cafe Noir

J. M. Walker, *Chief Steward*

Choice of Beverages Served in Dining Saloon

THE ALASKA LINE

SEATTLE, WASH.

Above: *a typical daily menu.*

Right: *A "farewell" menu, front and back of four pages.*

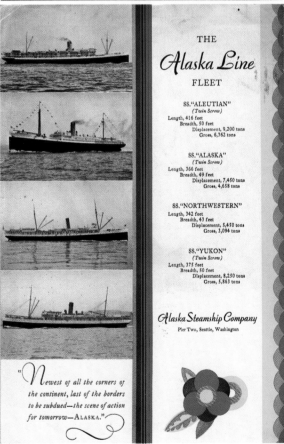

THE

Alaska Line

FLEET

SS. "ALEUTIAN"

(Twin Screw)

Length, 416 feet

Breadth, 50 feet

Displacement, 9,200 tons

Gross, 6,362 tons

SS. "ALASKA"

(Twin Screw)

Length, 366 feet

Breadth, 49 feet

Displacement, 7,450 tons

Gross, 4,658 tons

SS. "NORTHWESTERN"

Length, 342 feet

Breadth, 43 feet

Displacement, 5,450 tons

Gross, 3,094 tons

SS. "YUKON"

(Twin Screw)

Length, 375 feet

Breadth, 50 feet

Displacement, 8,250 tons

Gross, 5,863 tons

Alaska Steamship Company

Pier Two, Seattle, Washington

"*Newest of all the corners of*

the continent, last of the borders

to be subdued—the scene of action

for tomorrow—ALASKA."

The **S.S. Yukon,** *Ben's last Alaska Steam ship.*

Ben on the **Yukon.**

Ben in the engine room with his hand on the throttle, probably on the **Yukon.**

Alaska Steam had weathered the depression fairly well, but the Pacific Steamship Company and the Admiral Line had not. In 1933 Alaska Steam bought out the Alaska routes from Pacific Steam. In 1938 Alaska Steam absorbed what was left of the Admiral Line. Alaska had a fleet of eighteen ships in the years leading up to WWII. The future seemed bright, but, the specter of air travel loomed overhead.

Ben had had many challenges in his life, shipwrecks, and a life at sea, but he was prosperous. The Depression had not had an appreciable effect on this family. Ben's children had grown up with plenty, even during the Depression. But also during the 1930's was the disturbing news of the actions of the Empire of Japan in Mongolia and China, and that of Nazi Germany in Europe.

Ben was over sixty years old at this time, and the war clouds were brewing over the oceans. Ben retired from the Alaska Steamship Company July 6, 1941, having been a Chief Engineer for the company for nineteen years, and at his time of retirement, their top Chief. Ben applied to the Maritime Commission for a shore inspector position, and worked in California as a maritime inspector for a year.

World War II saw all of Alaska Steam's fleet taken over by Uncle Sam for war service in 1941. Several of their ships would be sunk during the war.

CHAPTER XI

Foreign Bound Lines

Up to World War II, steamships were the ultimate symbol of power and prestige. One name was to become synonymous with steamships—Robert Dollar. Robert Dollar was born 1844 in Scotland to a family of modest means. Robert worked in lumber camps from the time when he was a small boy. His family emigrated, choosing Canada when he was still a boy. He was an ambitious and sharp young man, and was managing a lumber camp by the time he was twenty-two years old. His family moved to Michigan in the 1880s. He was a sober, industrious, and frugal man. At age 55, Robert bought his first lumber mill on the west coast in 1893, and his first steamship in 1895 to haul his lumber.

Robert Dollar and his Dollar Steamship Company prospered in shipping over the next decades. A classic American entrepreneur, he saw the future of the Asian markets before many others, and actively promoted the trans-Pacific steamship trade. Robert was opposed to much of the union movement philosophies of his day, and was a key figure in breaking a dock strike at San Francisco in 1919. He had come a long way without any guarantees in life, and he didn't see why others wanted it differently. This of course made him none-too-favorable with some.

1907 saw economic depression. 1914 saw the advent of World War I. The United States was logistically unprepared at the beginning of the war, if it had to enter the war. The USA lacked the ships needed to carry off the huge movement necessary. There had already been a movement to get the U.S. government into the shipping business. In response, the United States Shipping Board was created by the Federal Shipping Act of 1916. Also known as the Alexander Act, it was sponsored by Representative Joshua Alexander (D) of Missouri. Its purpose was to establish a viable foreign Merchant Marine, to bring it back to its former glory, and it was actually established when the USA was still at peace.

When the USA got involved in the war in 1917, the game was a-foot and ships were needed. The government formed a corporation, the Emergency Fleet Corporation, and contracted to build merchant ships. This was a mixed government and private industry venture. The war ended before the shipbuilding program could really get going, but it was decided to build hundreds of the ships anyway. The ships were built on different contracts all over the country.

Many of them were built on an island in the Delaware River near Philadelphia called Hog Island. These ships became known as "Hog Islanders" and would come to symbolize the shipbuilding program. They used state of the art steam turbine propulsion, and were built from prefabricated sections, a radical new process.

A number of the government contract ships were built on Puget Sound and elsewhere in the Northwest, both steel cargo ships and wooden ships. The Skinner & Eddy yard in Seattle turned out dozens of steel steamships for the program.

The Emergency Fleet Corporation was just beginning its buildup of shipbuilding when the war ended. They continued building ships anyway, and this contributed to a postwar worldwide glut of ships, and became a source of tremendous waste. The oversupply was ruinous on shipyards. Many of the ships built were wooden ships that had absolutely no use after the war. The wooden ship shipyards went out of business altogether. The market was thrown asunder. There was a lot of controversy as to whether the government had any business being in the private shipbuilding industry at all.

The government program built three lines of high quality troop ships. One of the lines were Hog Islander's, the smallest. Since the war was over, the largest two lines were converted to passenger liners. The ships were built 1920-1921 and the first operators began running

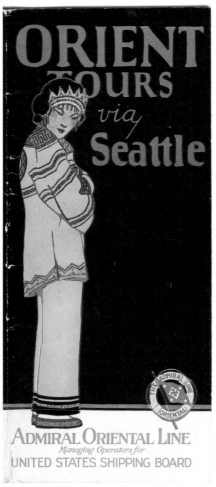

them in 1921. They were known as "502's" and "535's" for their length. Seven 502's were built and forty-one 535's. The 535's were 21,000 tons and were capable of 20 knots.

At first the shipping companies had to lease the government owned ships. The government was reluctant to sell its ships to private industry, they liked being in the shipping business. But, they eventually did sell to industry in the mid 1920s.

This was to be a new era in the world of international travel for pleasure. For the first time, ordinary but wealthy people could travel the world and partake of its wonders, simply for enjoyment and education. This was still the age of archeology; great discoveries were still being made. King Tut's tomb was discovered in 1922. It was a *National Geographic* world.

Admiral Oriental Line

One of the operators for the new government ships was a division of H.F. Alexander's Seattle based Pacific Steamship Company, the Admiral Oriental Line, which maintained a trans-Pacific service. This line was formed in

1917, and in 1921 was expanded with five of the new government ships. This was a separate division of the Pacific Steamship Company, which also ran the domestic coastal operation, the Admiral Line.

from SEATTLE *to*

YOKOHAMA :: KOBE :: SHANGHAI :: HONG KONG :: MANILA

THE SISTER SHIPS —

S. S. *President Grant*
S. S. *President Jefferson*
S. S. *President McKinley*
S. S. *President Madison*
S. S. *President Jackson*

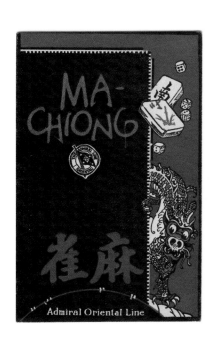

Left: *A booklet describing the Chinese game Ma-Chiong.*

Souvenir Passenger List from 1924, after the Dollar Company had taken over the line.

Going to the Orient

The Torii of Miyajima in the Inland Sea—
a glorious sight

Publishers' Photo Service

Publishers' Photo Service

Japan's sacred Fujiyama

A FEW YEARS AGO travel to the Orient was a pleasure only a very limited number of people could enjoy. Today thousands of men and women from every corner of the United States are reveling in the new and strange sights of the vast countries of the Orient, and thousands more are planning the trip.

They are planning to go now! Because never before in the history of ocean travel have advantages so combined to make the trip irresistible! Now Japan, China and the Philippines are nearer than ever before. No longer does the trip consume too much time, nor involve too great an expense. No longer does it entail the possibility of encountering travel discomfort or difficulty in a strange land.

If you are among the thousands of prospective travelers to the Orient, if you are going to materialize your dreams of the glorious East—it is for you to know what the new and magnificent United States Government ships have made possible for you.

The great fleet of the United States Government ships has set as its goal

A   D   M   I   R   A   L   O   R   I   E   N   T   A   L   L   I   N   E

Chinese farmer grinding corn with primitive hand implements.
Modern hurry seems unknown here

Publishers' Photo Service

The Great Wall of China—The largest engineering feat ever
completed. Built B.C. 230, it is 1500 miles long, averages 40
feet high and 20 feet thick

"perfection in the art of travel." Never before have efforts approached attainment so surely, so rapidly and with such wholly satisfying results.

The United States Government ships are operated by the Admiral Oriental Line, an organization whose vast machinery labors ceaselessly to provide super-service for its passengers. Its enviable reputation in the Pacific is based on the superlative record of its performance.

The ships sail from Seattle, Washington,

via Victoria, B. C., over the famous "Short Route." Seattle is easily reached by any one of four great railways. Sailing from this port has cut 1,230 miles from the trip! Now eleven short sailing days after America has become a wavering green line on the distant horizon, Fujiyama, Japan's sacred mountain, welcomes you to Yokohama and the Orient!

Sea Palaces—When you step on the gangplank that leads to your ship, you become a guest of the Admiral Oriental Line, whose care for your comfort and happiness does not cease until you step off the gangplank at your destination.

You will find the quarters which you have chosen of surpassing comfort and beauty. Your stateroom is unusually spacious, it is decorated in soft grays that

A   D   M   I   R   A   L   O   R   I   E   N   T   A   L   L   I   N   E

harmonize perfectly with the faultless taste displayed in the decorations of the entire ship.

The impressively simple Colonial style is used throughout. It is typical American, and replaces the gloom of the more formal style generally adhered to in large ocean liners with a genial and inviting atmosphere.

All the rooms are on the outside. All are equipped with hot and cold running water. Most rooms have private baths. There is a full-length mirror in your room too, a chiffonier, and large wardrobes. There are reading lamps and shaving lamps and thermos bottles. There are bed lights and twin beds instead of the old style

berths. All the rooms are equipped with electric radiators. A specially constructed blower and ventilating system forces fresh cool air throughout the room and passageways and insures an even temperature under all conditions.

And the food! The guests of the Admiral Oriental Line cannot restrain their enthusiasm when speaking of it. Here are chefs indeed. With the most modern equipment at their service, and employing an almost unlimited variety and abundance of the best foodstuffs obtainable, no wonder every meal seems the perfection of culinary art.

In the dining-saloon the mahogany tables are fitted

The American Consulate at Mukden, once a Chinese temple
Publishers' Photo Service

Publishers' Photo Service

Scene in the Pearl River. In these huddled sampans thousands are born, live and die

with movable chairs. The old style cushion swivel chair is unknown on these modern U. S. Government ships. The tables are arranged beneath a massive leaded glass dome which, together with the exquisite furnishings and brilliant lighting effects, recall a dining-room in a large metropolitan hotel.

Ample provision for your happiness and comfort has been made everywhere: there is the broad promenade deck, where a bracing wind whips color into your cheeks and a sparkle into your eyes; and there is a delightful glass-enclosed promenade deck on which you can walk or dance no matter what the weather does. The library of rare good books, is for your soberer mood.

You will find the charming tea room delightful for pleasant chatter with the other guests of the Admiral Oriental Line, when dusk and the evening sun paint the sky in riotous color. The orchestra, which in the evening provides irresistible dance music, is also notable for its artistic rendition of the classics.

A Stateroom with Bath on one of the "President" ships

The ships are mighty vessels, new and magnificent, of 21,000 tons displacement. Because they are oil-burning vessels they leave all decks free of the objectionable features of coal burners.

One of the fleet of famous "President" ships was recently exhibited to an industrial engineers' convention in New York as a vessel typifying the best construction of passenger ships and representing the most modern developments in safety.

Naval architects maintain that these liners are practically unsinkable. With their thirteen watertight compartments closed, it is said, the vessels can be cut in half and the sections remain afloat.

Modernity in the Orient—Today the well-informed know that travel in China and Japan is not a hazzard. The forbidden City, the Great Wall of China, and other local color all have helped to maintain this tradition many years after the reality has ceased. Today in China and Japan, side by side with the alien Oriental civilization,

A charming tea room done in wicker and
bright tapestries

Lower center—An inviting corner of the
writing room

flourish modern hotels
and railways, English-
speaking guides, etc.
Even that vast expanse
of China, Manchuria, most
recently penetrated, is accessible on commodious
modern trains, operated by the
South Manchurian Railway.

When first you land on the shores of
the Orient, your mind is crowded with
memories of a delightful ocean trip. Fresh
from the pleasant familiarity of American
diversions enjoyed in an American environment, you step upon alien shores at

Yokohama—five thou-
sand miles from home!
You step on land—
a bewildering confu-
sion of colors—red and
gold and green, vermillion
and orange and purple! Slight
figures hurrying by, yellow
skinned, almond eyed. A fascinating
sensation of unreality creeps over you.
These shadowy figures, the narrow crooked
streets with their tiny shops are not real!
You dreamed them years ago when travel
in the Orient was a dim hope you hardly
dared to cherish.

A   D   M   I   R   A   L   O   R   I   E   N   T   A   L   L   I   N   E

Great comfortable chairs, an open fire brightness and charm — such is the smoking-room on a "President" ship

Lower center—The Colonial motif in a suite on a "President" ship. Exquisite and complete in every detail

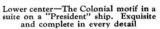

Before the ship lands at Yokohama, Kobe, Shanghai, Hong Kong and Manila, the ports of call of the Admiral Oriental Line, representatives of foreign branches of the Admiral Oriental Line board the ships prepared to answer all questions, to give all information desired, to secure competent guides, and to act in general as friendly advisers. The service of the Admiral Oriental Line needs no introduction to the seasoned traveler.

Now that it is offered on the new and sumptuous U. S. Government ships, the perfection in the art of travel, which is the Admiral Oriental Line's goal, seems well nigh attained.

If you are planning an Oriental trip, the Admiral Oriental Line cordially invites your inquiry regarding any phases of the trip on which you desire further information. Following are some of the salient points of value to the prospective traveler.

A D M I R A L   O R I E N T A L   L I N E

· The Trip of a Lifetime ·

— at little more cost than an ordinary vacation

THINK of the insignificant cost of these Orient tours today—the comfort, the pleasure, the magnificent Admiral Oriental liners that carry you.

Then think — in the background, as it were—of a certain day in the thirteenth century, and a certain home in Venice; after years of journeying, the father of Marco Polo has returned and embraces him. Gone before the child was born, he finds his bride is no more on this earth, his son a youth of fifteen years. Imagine, if you can, the struggle, the hardships, the costs, of that first journey of record to Cathay — fifteen years!

It was the spirit of Nicolo Polo that spurred the boy. Marco Polo became the greatest of all medieval travelers, and he it was who first published to the world the wonders of the Orient. His story reads even now like the tale of an extraordinary imagination, but no pen can outdo the actual things of this wonderland. China—Japan—Korea, the Philippines! You live in a perpetual panorama of things that thrill.

We are all travelers at heart. It is, with most of us, only a matter of ways and means. We all like to read of travel. We all would travel if we could. We feel the longing "to go" pull at our very heart strings. When we contemplate this—feel the impulse to see the world—it makes us remember that this same instinct is ages old and that it is an essential part of our progress and even existence. It is primitive within us.

Imagine Marco Polo seated before the great Khan Kublai, reciting his travels. Kublai was a man "full of high energy and intelligence." The young Venetian "was as a pitcher of cool water in the desert" to the thirsting mind of the great ruler, and he it was who sent Marco — who meanwhile studied all tongues of that world—on missions throughout his empire and beyond to bring back to him the accounts of peoples and things royal Kublai himself could not travel to see. If we could imagine it! — those colorful medieval Oriental scenes, the great ruler and the glittering entourage, all feasting on the stories of the great traveler! The great liners of the Admiral Oriental Line will carry you to the heart of our still strangely medieval Orient!

You, too, can be a Marco Polo, and thrill with and tell of amazing travel. You may see with your own eyes the marvels of that world—you will be captivated with it all even as the great Khan Kublai seven hundred years ago. And you may have this voyage there and back—a delightful journey by rail and sea—via Seattle by the Admiral Oriental Line —all for a reasonable cost; the cost, in fact, of little more than an ordinary vacation. It will prove a grand new chapter in your life, if you have not yet experienced it; a chapter that will prove rich with true pleasure.

Read about these different tours and the costs set forth in this folder. Write to us for additional information, or call upon your nearest ticket agent.

. . . a gorgeous festival of color! . . . for color is life in this ancient land of the Far East . . .

The estimated costs of the Tours shown herein include the following:

1 First-class steamer accommodations to the value of $300 to Yokohama, $346 to Shanghai and $375 to Hong Kong and Manila.

2 First-class railway accommodations.

3 Accommodations at the best hotels throughout the Orient. This includes bed-room, bath and meals.

4 Transfer charge between steamer and train, hotel, etc.

5 Heavy baggage may be left on board ship when making rail trips between the Oriental ports. Our Agents will arrange to have it placed in customs storage pending arrival.

6 Reservation of sleeping car accommodations and meals en route.

7 Sight-seeing as shown in the itinerary, either by rickshaw, sedan chair, motor car or carriage. In the more important places guides will be furnished. Guides pay and arrange entrance fees and incidental charges to museums, temples, etc.

8 Services of uniformed interpreters at the principal ports, who will meet the express trains upon arrival and departure and all Admiral Oriental Line steamers.

9 These estimates do not include any personal expenditures, tips, wines and liquors, laundry or the cost of excursions not provided in the itinerary. These "Orient Tours" are not sold as a "tour ticket." They are offered as suggestions for making a practical tour of the Far East within a limited length of time; making it possible to enjoy these trips —or any of your own planning—and making connections at our regular ports of call and with our schedules of sailing. Your ticket agent will gladly explain in detail.

Thru the YANGTSZE GORGES-
TOUR "E
—wonders of the world—included in this three-months tour of the ORIENT

THIS TOUR is planned for the traveler who wishes to make a thorough trip through the Orient and visit the places off the beaten path. It embodies a three weeks' tour of Japan, a leisurely jaunt through Korea, six days in Peking, two days in Hankow, excursion on the Yangtsze River to Nanking; six days in Shanghai and environs, Hongkong, Canton and Macao; Manila and return to Hongkong, Shanghai, Kobe and Yokohama. The trip through the Gorges is made in splendid specially constructed river steamers. It requires twelve days to make the trip from Hankow and return. There is nearly a daily service from Hankow to Ichang, where connections are made for the trip through the Gorges. This is one of the most interesting and picturesque trips in the world and takes one into the very Heart of China, terminating at the ancient city of Chungking.

. . . "shooting" the famous rapids through the Yangtsze gorges . . . the Chinese junk might be a bit too exciting, and we suggest you make this trip via a sturdy Dollar Line steamer . . .

1st Day—Sail from SEATTLE
  Via Short Route.
12th Day—Arrive YOKOHAMA
13th and 14th Days—Sightseeing in TOKYO *and*
  vicinity.
15th Day—To NIKKO
16th Day—In NIKKO
*17th Day—*NIKKO, AKABANE, IKEBUKURO,
  YOKOHAMA
18th Day—In YOKOHAMA
  Sightseeing.
*19th Day—*YOKOHAMA, KAMAKURA, OFUNA,
  KODZU
  Afternoon to Miyanoshita (Motor or electric car).
20th Day—In MIYANOSHITA
  Excursion to Lake Hakone.
21st Day—Leave MIYANOSHITA, DODZU
  Afternoon Nagoya.

*22nd Day—*NAGOYA, NARA
23rd Day—In NARA
  Sightseeing.
*24th Day—*NARA, KYOTO
25th and 26th Days—Sightseeing in vicinity,
  including LAKE BIWA
*27th Day—*KYOTO, OSAKA, KOBE
28th Day—In KOBE
*29th Day—*KOBE, MIYAJIMA

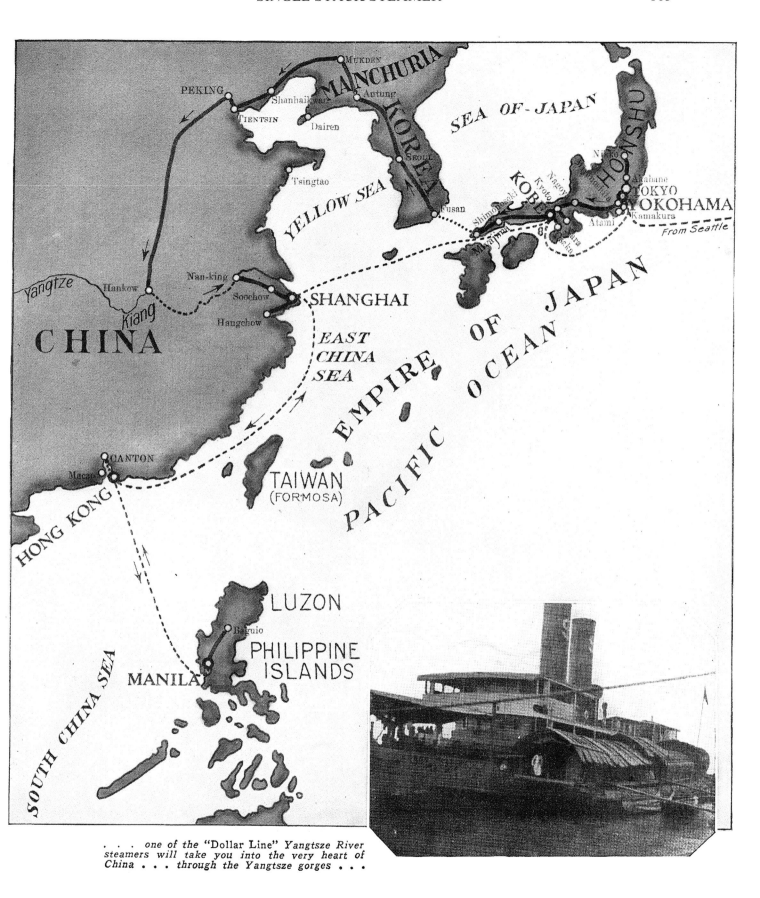

. . . one of the "Dollar Line" Yangtsze River
steamers will take you into the very heart of
China . . . through the Yangtsze gorges . . .

30th Day—MIYAJIMA, SHIMONOSEKI
31st Day—*Leave* SHIMONOSEKI
Arrive FUSAN
   7:00 P. M.
Leave FUSAN
   11:00 P. M.
32nd Day, A. M.—*Arrive* SEOUL
33rd Day—*In* SEOUL
34th Day—*Leave* SEOUL
   10:05 A. M.
Arrive ANTUNG
   9:30 P. M.
35th Day—MUKDEN
   Arrive 6:00 A. M., leave 10:15 A. M.
36th Day—SHANHAIKUAN
   Arrive 9:35 P. M., leave 10:00 P. M.
37th Day—TIENTSIN
   Arrive 6:35 A. M.
38th Day—*In* TIENTSIN
39th Day—*Leave* TIENTSIN
   7:00 A. M.
Arrive PEKING
   10:15 A. M.
40th to 43rd Days, Inclusive—*In* PEKING
46th Day—*Arrive* HANKOW
47th Day—*Leave* HANKOW
   By river steamer for trip through the Yangtsze
   Gorges. Return to Hankow. Total time for
   trip, 12 days.
60th Day—*On Yangtsze River en route* NANKING
61st Day—*Arrive* NANKING
62nd Day—*In* NANKING
   Leave afternoon train.
   Arrive Shanghai 10:00 P. M.
63rd to 66th Days—*In* SHANGHAI
67th Day—*Leave by steamer for* HONGKONG
69th Day—*Arrive* HONGKONG
   Excursion to Macao
70th Day—*Leave* HONGKONG
72nd Day—*Arrive* MANILA
73rd Day—*In* MANILA
   Excursion to Baguio
75th Day—*Sail from* MANILA
77th Day—*Arrive* HONGKONG
77th Day—*Leave* HONGKONG
   10:00 P M., en route Canton
78th Day—*Arrive* CANTON 6:30 A. M.
Leave CANTON 5:00 P. M.
Arrive HONGKONG Midnight
79th Day—*Sail from* HONGKONG
81st Day—*Arrive* SHANGHAI
82nd, 83rd and 84th Days—*In* SHANGHAI
   Trip through Native City; Willow Pattern Tea
   House, Loonghwa Pagoda, drive through Bubbling Well Road; visit to Siccawei Convent, etc.

85th Day, A. M.—*Leave Shanghai for* SOOCHOW
   Arrive Soochow early forenoon. Visit to Tiger
   Hill Pagoda and Native City; Leon Yoen Gar-
   dens, Great Pagoda and City Temple.
Leave SOOCHOW, *P. M.*
Arrive SHANGHAI
86th Day, A. M.—*Leave* SHANGHAI *for*
   HANGCHOW
   Arrive Hangchow afternoon.
87th, 88th and 89th Days—*In* HANGCHOW
   Excursion to Needle Pagoda, Tomb of Yao, the
   Upper Central and Lower Monasteries of India,
   Imperial Island, etc.
90th Day—*Return to* SHANGHAI
91st and 92nd Days—*In* SHANGHAI
93rd Day—*Leave* SHANGHAI
   En route Kobe—through Inland Sea of Japan.
95th Day—*Arrive* KOBE
96th Day—*Leave* KOBE
   Via steamer.
97th Day—*Arrive* YOKOHAMA
98th Day—*In* YOKOHAMA
99th Day—*Sail from* YOKOHAMA
   Via Admiral Oriental Line—"the Short Route."
110th Day—*Arrive* SEATTLE

*. . . you'll find the Orient a great
playground for your imagination . . .*

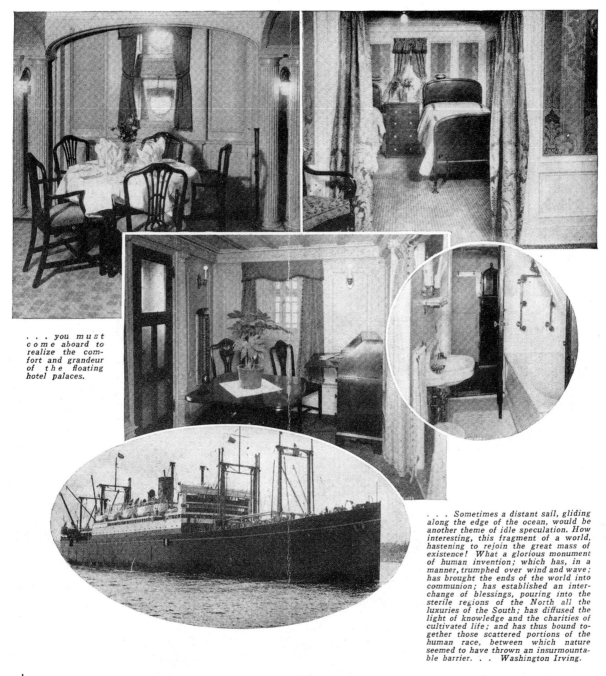

. . . *you must come aboard to realize the comfort and grandeur of the floating hotel palaces.*

. . . *Sometimes a distant sail, gliding along the edge of the ocean, would be another theme of idle speculation. How interesting, this fragment of a world, hastening to rejoin the great mass of existence! What a glorious monument of human invention; which has, in a manner, trumphed over wind and wave; has brought the ends of the world into communion; has established an interchange of blessings, pouring into the sterile regions of the North all the luxuries of the South; has diffused the light of knowledge and the charities of cultivated life; and has thus bound together those scattered portions of the human race, between which nature seemed to have thrown an insurmountable barrier. . . Washington Irving.*

• Admiral Oriental Line •
SUPERIOR SERVICE FEATURES

OU no sooner arrive at the ship's side than you wonder of what pleasant experience it reminds you. Here you are about to step on the deck of a glorious liner that will speed you over the crest of the world's mightiest ocean, and you already feel, somehow, that you are a guest in an old friend's home. No matter who you may be, you ask yourself, consciously or unconsciously, as it were, when, where, did something just as nice as this feeling of welcome come over you once before! Indeed, at the threshold of any Admiral Oriental liner you are the welcome guest! It is all wonderful; but, over and above all the thrill of it, you feel the cheer and the heart-comfort of a welcome to a real home.

It is the great free Spirit of the Pacific. These men who command and man this ship truly realize they are your hosts, and as they open the door, so to speak, the glow of a fireside is there, and welcomes you with its warmth. And soon you find that guest meets guest on this ship with that same fine spirit. It permeates! It is contagious! There is a subtle something that says: You are at home, please!

Well — perhaps it is, after all, the Spirit of Rest!

And you may indeed rest on an Admiral Oriental liner. "What a wonderful stateroom!" you exclaim —the air is as fresh as roses! Remember, we are in Seattle—white crags of the mighty Cascades to the East, and to the West the gorgeous emeralds of the Olympics. An empire of mountain giants all about you, and, supergiant of all this towering wonderland, is Mount Rainier. Interesting, too, you think, that a great mountain should be named after a man of the sea—Naval Lieutenant Rainier, of nearly a hundred years ago. These mountains, veritably, have a mortgage on the sky that domes this Empire City. Remember that nowhere in the world is there such a panorama of mountain magnificence to be seen from the deck of a ship. Fierce fires and dynamic blasts raged here thousands of years back!—they are inexorably peaceful now, and truly they seem to be benignant and to join in the home-welcome to the stranger!

Now you cannot miss your host. The spirit is everywhere here. You are delighted with the ample width of your room; your quarters are very beautiful — exquisite lines in the architecture, restful grays in the coloring; and you did not at all realize there would be all this comfortable furniture here!

. . . you'll find many "cozy corners" aboard these great liners . . . and the enjoyable hours will seem too short! . . .

But why not there be? These great ships of the Admiral Oriental Line are superb in their furnishings and equipment. And spacious staterooms—twice the size of ordinary steamship accommodations! You can see a true master mind designed these ships of the Admiral Oriental Line, and they are most modern in every respect. Like everything else—sculpture, painting, architecture, the garden—it is the super-mind behind that has accomplished the modern improvements. It is evident that here a truly great mind carried out his ideas of what perfect, wholesome, comfortable travel on the high seas should be! In truth, the perfection of these ships, their exquisite appointments, have been the inspiration to the entire creed of providing the most delightful tours the history of navigation has known, which has been enthusiastically adopted by the officers of the Admiral Oriental Line.

All the rooms of the ships to which we invite you to be our guest across the Pacific and through the wonderful Orient, have a very important feature —namely, they are all outside rooms and open to wide interior corridors. There is thus no doubt in your mind—your room, you are completely assured, is an outside room! Here again, the master designer of these ships has been wide awake to the principles of advanced modern travel. Over and over again travelers on the Admiral Oriental liners have commented on this splendid modern feature. And it means so much to your comfort!

But, wherever we go, wherever we look, we find the same comfort, the same charm, as if you were in some grand, well-designed country mansion. Many of the rooms have a private bath or shower adjoining. You have a chiffonier, a large wardrobe, and hot and cold running water. Reading lamps and shaving lamps, thermos bottles, electric radiators; evenly tempered, pure, fresh air gently fanning through your stateroom! Another innovation—the rooms have real twin beds; beds—not the old-style berths of the older ships.

Almost every detail of these magnificent modern liners is perfected—and remember, all the Admiral Oriental ships are creations from the one concept of the design that here must be the utmost refinement in ocean travel. The graceful Colonial style! No hotel ashore provides you with more luxurious ease,

in the dining room, the social hall and throughout. Observe the deep davenports, the comfortable chairs, the settees, the fireplaces! You wander into the library, and you find here is another nook with a wonderful array of fine volumes that you will enjoy. The writing room!—still another place to wander, to retire alone with your thoughts! The social hall and smoking room, its draperies, its finely conceived wall decorations! Then the tea room and palm garden—it is all that the cunning of "the mind that knew" could devise. So different, to repeat! Such variety of pleasant and comfortable surroundings.

The dining saloon is high above the water line, and above is the massive glass dome — it is all superb. And when we think of dining, we must not forget the orchestra, always present at the right moment! You love music, of course. You love it in its purity, and you feel it in your veins when it races away from the academic and touches a little primitive strain in you! These musicians are artists. They will play you Beethoven. They will play you Strauss, Mendelssohn, Bach, Wagner, Victor Herbert! Sousa! Old Black Joe, Darling Nellie Gray, the Old Oaken Bucket, Suwanee Ribber! Barney Google! Or any diversified program. You may waltz or fox trot! The orchestras of the Admiral Oriental Liners are entertainers you will never forget.

If we forget all else, one thing would suffice. That one thing is the dining service. Chefs who know. Chefs who are provided with everything in food supplies, and in equipment. The electric bake oven has a capacity of 1000 loaves a day. There are electric pastry ovens and electric grills where savory meats are broiled to perfection. There are refrigerators where the best of everything that can be provided in food, in fresh vegetables, in meats and game and fish. There is the wonderful arrangement by which the purest, finest water in the world is stored for both the outbound and homebound passage—the same wonderful mountain water which tumbles down from the snow plateaus of the Cascade mountains and makes Seattle the healthiest city in America—there is no finer water anywhere than the Cedar River water supply of this metropolis. Whatever praise is given by the guests of the

Admiral Oriental Line to all its other many perfections, no guest has ever forgotten to remember the most exquisite cuisine.

You have only to look at the pictures here to appreciate the appointments. To repeat—superb! When we think of the older ships, the comparison is obvious. The Admiral Oriental Line ships have the finest of upholstered rattan furniture on the decks—supreme comfort, which is a very great desideratum of the enjoyment of the outdoor aspect, of the little affairs, the moments of reading and quiet, which is so rich a part of the voyage Deck games, of course —shuffle board, always exciting; indoor golf; tennis; quoits! Motion picture programs, too — the splendid releases!

But we would write a volume before completing the story! And, after all, well, the days go too fast! You live in the thrill of the day — day by day — and you live in the thrill of the fairyland you are journeying to!

. . . the cuisine of these U. S. Government liners is unsurpassed . . . you'll find this feature of our service a constant delight . . .

Detailed information and literature descriptive of this fast American Trans-Pacific service will be gladly furnished by your local railroad or tourist agent or any of the Admiral Oriental Line agencies listed below. They will plan your trip and make advance reservations for you.

• ADMIRAL ORIENTAL LINE •

Managing Operators for
UNITED STATES SHIPPING BOARD

D. J. HANSCOM, General Passenger Agent, Headquarters, L. C. Smith Building, Seattle, U. S. A.

Agents

New York City, 32 Broadway	*San Francisco,* 653 Market St.	*Yokohama,* 41 Yamashita Cho
Boston, 177 State St.	*San Francisco,* Robert Dollar Bldg.	*Kobe,* No. 7-A Kaigan Dori
Philadelphia, 101 Bourse Bldg.	*Oakland,* 1451 Franklin St.	*Shanghai,* 29 Nanking Road
Chicago, 112 W. Adams St.	*Oakland,* 1325 Broadway	*Shanghai,* 3 Canton Road
Detroit, Dime Bank Bldg.	*Berkeley,* 2121 Shattuck Ave.	*Hongkong,* No. 4 Des Voeux Rd.
Seattle, 408 L. C. Smith Bldg.	*Los Angeles,* 501 So. Spring St.	*Manila,* 24 Calle David
Tacoma, 1111 Pacific Bldg.	*Los Angeles,* Mortgage Guarantee Bldg.	*Singapore,* Hongkong Bank Chambers
Vancouver, B. C., 605 Hastings St., W.	*Long Beach,* 124 W. Ocean Ave.	*Tientsin,* Robert Dollar Bldg.
Vancouver, B. C., Board of Trade Bldg.	*San Diego,* 201 Broadway	*Hankow,* Robert Dollar Bldg.
Victoria, B. C., 901 Government St.	*London,* 14 Regent St., SWI.	*Dairen,* 48 Echigo Cho
Portland, Ore., 101 Third St.	*Paris,* 11 bis Rue Scribe	*Vladivostok,* 21 Aleutskaya
	Genoa, Coe and Clerici	

or any tourist or railway agent

page 21

***

DOLLAR STEAMSHIP LINE

Robert Dollar was ever vigilant to acquire his own Asiatic fleet. One of the lines he gobbled up was the Admiral Oriental Line. Dollar acquired the line in 1922 and ran it under its name until the end of 1926, then changed it to the American Mail Line and continued to run the line from Seattle, garnering a reputation for world-class service.

In 1923 Dollar purchased all seven of the 502's from the Shipping Board. In 1924 the Dollar line began a regular around-the-world service with the seven government ships. The President Liners, as they were called, stopped at 21 ports in 14 countries around the world. This was a regular service and it was quite revolutionary and popular. On a round the world Dollar Line trip, you could layover at a port and get the next ship making its way around the globe. It was a new and unprecedented American service. As part of their operation, the Dollar Line held a U.S. Mail contract.

In 1925 Dollar acquired the assets of the Pacific Mail Steamship Company of San Francisco, a line that had been around since the California Gold Rush, which had been operating a fleet of 535's for the Shipping Board.

The Dollar Steamship Company had through acquisitions become the dominant Pacific Ocean passenger and freight line, and had grown large and was very profitable in the 1920s. Through the rest of the roaring twenties the company added more president ships to the line. Robert Dollar had become an international celebrity. He was a hero in China, an admired and respected businessman, and philanthropist. His face graced the cover of *Time* magazine.

The company borrowed money from the government to build two first class passenger liners that were to haul mail on government contracts. Both the *S.S. President Hoover* and *S.S. President Coolidge* were delivered to the Dollar Line in 1931. These were the largest American built passenger liners at the time, and the Dollar Steamship Company was the largest U.S. steamship line. Robert Dollar died in 1932, and his sons took the helm.

In the late 1930s the company still had its two major divisions, the Dollar Steamship Lines and The American Mail Line. The Dollar Steamship Line was the big-ticket Pacific Rim operator. It was still based out of San Francisco. The American Mail Line was a Seattle based company.

Round *the* World Guide
DOLLAR STEAMSHIP LINE

"The Sunshine Belt to the Orient"

SEE THE ORIENT

Every Saturday a magnificent President Liner departs from San Francisco for the Orient and Round the World. It calls at Honolulu, Japan, China, the Philippines, Malaya, Ceylon, India, Egypt, Italy, France, Boston, New York, Havana, Panama and Los Angeles.

On fortnightly schedules, President Liners sail from Boston and New York for the Orient and Round the World via Havana, Panama and California.

Large comfortable accommodations. A world-famous cuisine. Personal service.

Full information from any ticket agent or

604 Fifth Avenue, New York City
Robert Dollar Building, San Francisco, California

DOLLAR
STEAMSHIP LINE

STATEROOMS are all outside rooms, furnished with taste and distinction. They have wide comfortable beds. The majority of staterooms have private baths. Unusually well-lighted and well-ventilated, and equipped with electric fans, PRESIDENT LINER staterooms are adapted to comfortable travel in all climes. Suites de luxe are available for those desiring extra comforts.

Above right:
1926 magazine ad

Left: *From 1928 American Mail Line schedule*

Right: *Postcard*

Facing page:
Full page magazine ad, 1928

Following page:
Full page magazine ad, 1929

ROUND THE WORLD
(Passengers and Express Freight)
from SEATTLE *via* VICTORIA, B. C.
and from
LOS ANGELES AND SAN FRANCISCO
VIA HONOLULU
to
Yokohama, Kobe, Shanghai, Hong Kong, Manila, Singapore, Penang, Colombo, Suez, Port Said, Alexandria, Naples, Genoa, Marseilles, Boston, New York, Havana, Cristobal (Panama Canal), Balboa, and return to Pacific Coast.

ORIENT~ROUND THE WORLD
SUNSHINE BELT VIA HONOLULU.

FLEET
PRESIDENT CLEVELAND	PRESIDENT PIERCE	PRESIDENT MONROE
PRESIDENT LINCOLN	PRESIDENT HARRISON	PRESIDENT HAYES
PRESIDENT WILSON	PRESIDENT GARFIELD	PRESIDENT ADAMS
PRESIDENT TAFT	PRESIDENT VAN BUREN	PRESIDENT POLK

DOLLAR STEAMSHIP LINE

Glorious Playgrounds
Round the World — the one finest
trip of a lifetime

Japan casts her spell upon you from the moment your ship enters Yokohama harbor. For behind this great city, rising to the sky is mighty Fujiyama, sacred mountain.

Then you enter the life of this gay and joyous people. Japan is a land of festivals and a land of progressiveness as well.

The lure of China is the lure of the ancient East. See her temples, her people. Stop here in quaint bazars for ivories, laces and jade; for silks, batiks and rare embroideries.

On we go to Manila, reminiscent of old Spain. Malaya, Ceylon and India beckon to new adventures, as interesting as those behind us, but wholly different.

Round the World to Egypt, to Italy and France.

Palatial President Liners to take you in complete comfort. All rooms are outside. Beds, not berths. Spacious decks. A swimming pool. Public rooms large and luxuriously appointed. A dining service unexcelled, world travelers tell us. Optional stopovers.

A Dollar Liner sails every week from Los Angeles and San Francisco for the Orient via Honolulu and Round the World. Fortnightly sailings from Boston and New York for the Orient via Havana, Panama and California. See the Pacific Coast.

An American Mail Liner sails every fourteen days from Seattle and Victoria to Japan, China and Manila.

Fortnightly sailings from Naples, Genoa and Marseilles for New York and Boston.

For complete information communicate with
ticket or tourist agent or

Dollar ⚓ Steamship Line
American Mail ⚓ Line

25 BROADWAY, NEW YORK, N.Y.; 32 BROADWAY, NEW YORK, N.Y.; 604 FIFTH AVE., NEW YORK, N.Y.; 101 BOURSE BLDG., PHILADELPHIA, PA.; 1018 BESSEMER BLDG., PITTSBURGH, PA.; 177 STATE ST., BOSTON, MASS.; 514 W. SIXTH ST., LOS ANGELES, CALIF.; 110 SOUTH DEARBORN ST., CHICAGO, ILL.; DIME BANK BUILDING, DETROIT; 21 PIAZZA DEL POPOLO, ROME, ITALY; 11 BIS RUE SCRIBE, PARIS, FRANCE; 22 BILLITER ST., E. C. 3, LONDON; ROBERT DOLLAR BUILDING, SAN FRANCISCO; 4TH AT UNIVERSITY, SEATTLE, WASH.

Plan days  in Java
to learn the lure of this tropic isle

From SINGAPORE it is but a step across to the Dutch East Indies, which have fittingly been described as "a necklace of emeralds strung along the equator." Long, slender Java, swarming with more than thirty million picturesque peoples of the East, is a world in itself. Besides its vast plantations of sugar, coffee, indigo, rubber, it presents tropical scenes rarely surpassed. Yet Java is well governed and easily traveled, with splendid roads and some 3500 miles of railways, divided into two native principalities, yet all under the security of Holland.

Batavia, canal-filled as any city of Holland proper, is far-famed for its exotic air. Buitenzorg, the summer capital, not far away yet higher up, has a botanical garden justly renowned to the ends of the earth. Then there is Djokjakarta, whose ruler boasted two hundred wives and hundreds of children at last inventory, where tiger baiting is a favorite sport, to say nothing of a race meeting every spring to which Europeans come from everywhere in that corner of the globe.

And no journey to the East would be complete without a glimpse of Borobudur, greatest of Hindu temples. Picture to yourself a structure that is really a hill rising a hundred and fifty feet above the plain, the lower terrace five hundred feet long, with statues, exemplifying Hindu art at its height, so numerous that stood side by side they would reach for three miles; base reliefs compared with which any in Europe seem the mere scratchings of the cave men...

And on the east, opposite the unforgettable city of Sourabaya, lies the peerless island of Bali, where the Hindu worship which Mohammedanism has driven out of Java proper still persists. Troops of Malay comedians whom even sophisticated travelers find the most laugh-provoking on any stage...

Harry A. Franck

WORLD TRAVELER AND AUTHOR OF "A VAGABOND JOURNEY AROUND THE WORLD," "WANDERING IN NORTHERN CHINA," "EAST OF SIAM."

You go as you please Round the World under the advantages offered by this unique steamship service. Stop where you wish, for as long as you like, within the two year limit of your ticket. Your fare, including meals and accommodations aboard ship, as low as $1250 Round the World.

Every week a palatial President Liner sails from Los Angeles and San Francisco for Honolulu, Japan, China, Manila, and thence on fortnightly schedules to Malaya—Java 36 hours away—Ceylon, Egypt, Italy, France, New York and Boston.

Fortnightly sailing from Boston and New York via Havana and Panama to California and Round the World.

Every two weeks a similar liner sails from Seattle and Victoria, B.C. for Japan, China, Manila and Round the World.

Magnificent liners, they offer outside rooms with beds, not berths. Spacious decks. A swimming pool. Luxurious public rooms. A world-famous cuisine.

COMPLETE INFORMATION FROM ANY STEAMSHIP OR TOURIST AGENT

AMERICAN MAIL LINE
AND
DOLLAR STEAMSHIP LINE

Down the Highway of the World

American Mail Line to the Orient and Round the World

CHAPTER XII

The Dollar Line and the New Deal

During the Depression, the left-leaning President Roosevelt and government decided that they wanted America to be a worldwide maritime powerhouse. In 1936 congress passed the Merchant Marine Act, and one of the provisions of this act was the formation of the Merchant Marine Commission to replace the Shipping Board, and which was to promote the industry in a number of ways, and regulate training. The companies operating under the American Merchant Marine were to be provided with operating subsidies, so they could better compete with foreign interests, it was thought. Joseph P. Kennedy was the first head of the commission. A major part of the New Deal, this was all-out socialism of an industry in the United States.

Roosevelt loved ships, the greatest symbol of power and prestige of the day. The government's stated purpose of the act was to promote the industry, but by passing the act, the government sought to control the industry. The government was stating that it did not trust private industry.

As one of the first items on the Maritime Commission's agenda, it investigated the ailing Dollar Steamship Company.

Like most American companies, the Dollar Company had a tough time making money in the Depression years of the 1930s. There was, of course, the effects of the tight purse strings caused by the Depression. Then there were damaging strikes. The war in China with Japan was causing disruptions. The company suffered some mishaps, and the loss of two of its ships, one of which was the *President Hoover*, which ran aground. To the disgruntlement of some, in spite of losses, the Dollar sons continued to make large personal salaries. By 1937 the company owed more than its assets. The Maritime Commission and Joseph Kennedy decided the company was headed for insolvency.

In 1938 the Dollar family made a deal with the government for a "bailout," and gave the government the assets of the company in return for canceling its debt. The government called its company the American President Lines. The flagship of the line was still the passenger liner *S.S. President Coolidge*. The American President Lines and American Mail Line were separated at this time.

S.S. President Coolidge *in Dollar Line livery. Flagship of the Pacific Ocean.*

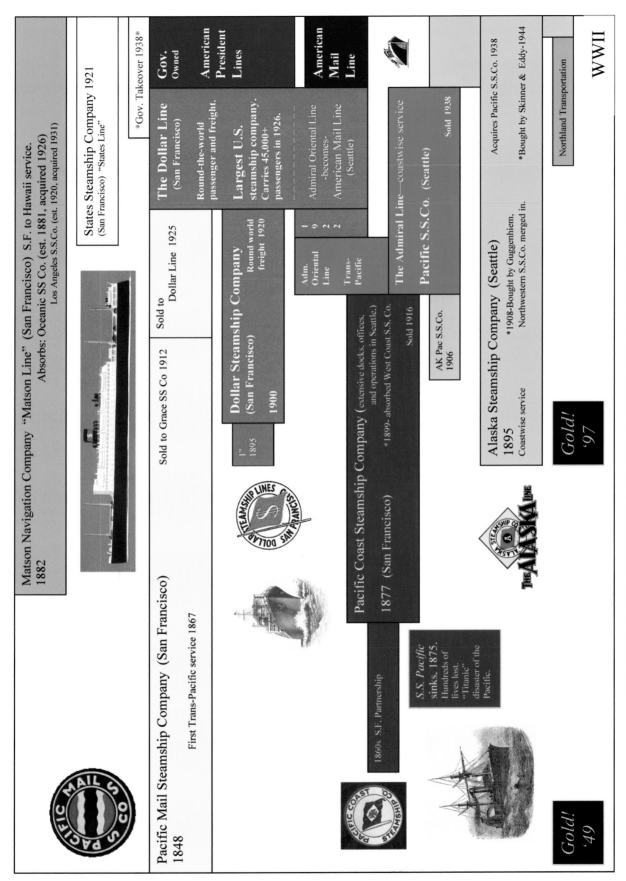

Matson Navigation Company "Matson Line" (San Francisco) S.F. to Hawaii service.
1882
Absorbs: Oceanic SS Co. (est. 1881, acquired 1926)
Los Angeles S.S.Co. (est. 1920, acquired 1931)

States Steamship Company 1921
(San Francisco) "States Line"

Gov. Takeover 1938

The Dollar Line
(San Francisco)

Round-the-world
passenger and freight.

Largest U.S.
steamship company.
Carries 45,000+
passengers in 1926.

Admiral Oriental Line
-becomes-
American Mail Line
(Seattle)

Gov.
Owned

American President
Lines

American
Mail
Line

Pacific Mail Steamship Company (San Francisco)
1848

First Trans-Pacific service 1867

Sold to Grace SS Co 1912

Sold to
Dollar Line 1925

Dollar Steamship Company
(San Francisco)

1st
1895

1900

Round world
freight 1920

Adm.
Oriental
Line

Trans-
Pacific

1
9
2
2

The Admiral Line—coastwise service

Pacific S.S.Co. (Seattle)

Sold 1938

AK Pac S.S.Co.
1906

Pacific Coast Steamship Company (extensive docks, offices,
and operations in Seattle.)
1877 (San Francisco)

*1899- absorbed West Coast S.S. Co.

Sold 1916

1860s S.F. Partnership

S.S. Pacific
sinks, 1875.
Hundreds of
lives lost.
"Titanic"
disaster of the
Pacific.

Alaska Steamship Company (Seattle)
1895

Coastwise service

*1908-Bought by Guggenhiem,
Northwestern S.S.Co. merged in.

Acquires Pacific S.S.Co. 1938

*Bought by Skinner & Eddy-1944

Northland Transportation

WWII

Gold!
'97

Gold!
'49

PRINCIPAL U.S. WEST COAST STEAMSHIP COMPANIES 1848-WWII

Of course, if the government had not bailed out the line, one of two things would likely have happened: the line would have made a recovery, or, it would have failed and its assets would have been absorbed by other steamship lines. Perhaps the government reasoned that the Dollar Line was too big to fail?

The American President Lines was not returned to private ownership until 1952, and then only after a lawsuit initiated by the Dollar family. Despite the lawsuit, the Dollar family never regained the company.

Another goal of the Merchant Marine Act was the construction of a fleet of ships to be leased to private industry, which could be used by the government in times of war. The government had built the "Hog Islander" ships following WW I, but these were aging and in need of replacement.

The ships were to be built in private shipyards under government contract. They were modern turbo-electric powered designs. The ships were built to standard designs, and were given designations like C1, C2, C3, and C4, which were successively larger cargo ships, and tankers such as the T2 series. Only a few ships were built before World War II started, but, once the war began they were built at a dizzying pace.

When WWII came along, steam reciprocating engine powered Liberty ships(even at this time out of date) and later more advanced turbo-electric Victory ships were built in large

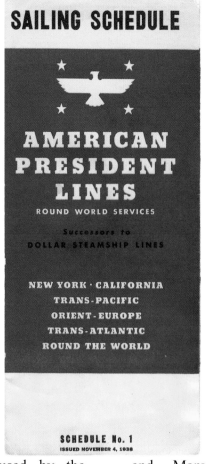

SAILING SCHEDULE

AMERICAN PRESIDENT LINES

ROUND WORLD SERVICES

Successors to
DOLLAR STEAMSHIP LINES

NEW YORK · CALIFORNIA
TRANS-PACIFIC
ORIENT-EUROPE
TRANS-ATLANTIC
ROUND THE WORLD

SCHEDULE No. 1
ISSUED NOVEMBER 4, 1938

numbers to fill the wartime needs.

Eighteen shipyards were built to build Liberty ships. The Liberty's were built in sub-assemblies at remote factories. Then the various sections were assembled at the actual shipyard. This was a revolutionary process, and the result was that well over 2700 Liberty's were built in a few years. This was an unprecedented shipbuilding program in all of history. Liberty ships were built during the war in a matter of weeks, and even in a matter of days in some cases. The Victory ships were a late war outgrowth of the Liberty ship program, and were built with the advanced turbo-electric propulsion system. A further 531 Victory's were built by war's end. Many of the MARCOM ships were built in the Pacific Northwest.

C1's were smaller and varied in size from 338' to 412'. 408 were built. The C2's were 459', and displaced 13,910 tons laden. 173 were built between 1939 and 1945. The C2 would prove to be a favorite. The C3's were 492', 18,215 tons, and 465 were built between 1939 and 1947. The Navy liked these in WWII and transformed many into escort carriers and tenders. The C4's were 522' and displaced 22,449 tons laden. 75 were built 1942-1945. Several of these were 15,000 ton hospital ships.

So, completely aside from the Navy, the government was in the steamship line business, and in the ship building business.

CHAPTER XIII

A King's Pointer, Class of '42

In the Merchant Marine, an officer was a licensed mariner. License=officer. To get the license one had to pass very difficult examinations. One could go to a state nautical school to get the necessary experience and knowledge to pass the tests, if one came from a family with the means. State nautical schools had their own ships and cadets actually got real "sea" experience at these schools. About 25% of replacement Merchant Marine officers got their licenses this way. Or, one could "work their way up through the hawsepipe" like Adolf Loken had in the earlier part of our story. By the 1930s a majority of Merchant Marine officers got their license this way.

The various Merchant Marine Acts of the United States and the formation of sailor's unions had improved the conditions of the American sailor dramatically since the late nineteenth century. But, this made the American sailor a little more expensive than his foreign competition in many cases. Some outspoken critics of the unions claimed they were run by communists. To be a communist before WWII did not carry the same stigma as after WWII. The communist label within the unions would prove a touchy subject following WWII.

In the 1930's it had been charged that many seamen in the industry were somewhat lacking in knowledge and skill, that the training process was erratic, and therefore a proactive approach to raise standards was determined to be required. In 1938 the U.S. Merchant Marine Cadet Corps was formed, which eventually became the U.S. Merchant Marine Academy at King's Point, New York. In the early program, cadets were to spend three years at sea working and studying in a structured program, and one year in a formal school. Then the cadet would qualify to be able to take the exam from the Bureau of Marine Inspection and Navigation, a division of the Department of Commerce, and get their license.

This was an excellent training program and produced a generation of superb licensed mariners. The class of '42 would be the most famous class of this institution's history. They saw the brunt of action in World War II.

"United States Merchant Marine Cadet Corps, 1942"

The teenage Charles.

Charles Harrison Parker, Sr., son of Ben Parker, known as "Charlie" to his friends—of whom were many—started out as a rambunctious and care free young man in the as yet un-populated areas of south Seattle.

Though naturally intelligent, Charles did not apply himself in school as well as his parents would have liked. Like most high school boys, Charles wanted a car and to have fun. His father writes to him from his ship in August of 1937.

> The reason I didn't take much interest in the auto is that I want you to assume some responsibility and look after one thing yourself, in fact I don't care if you ever get it, as I am about fed up with junk heaps. Charles boy if you don't give up the kind of boys that you chose to run with, they will get you down and keep you there…
>
> It doesn't take much money to have good healthy fun. I will always be dad and pal if you will let me, and I know you will. You have a loving Mother and Sister that would do anything for you if you will only meet them half way. As soon as you see the folly and bunk of chasing around with the wrong sort, you will set your course and go ahead in the right way, and you will want to!

Ben further states that Charles should "go in for the kind of fun that will build you up in body and mind, and there is lots of good wholesome sport. I admire you for cutting wood and selling it, and that will harden you up."

Since his father had spent a life at sea on merchant vessels, it was decided that Charles might do well to follow his father's footsteps.

After high school Charles went to the Puget Sound Naval Academy, which was then at Winslow on Bainbridge Island from August-September 1938 to June 14, 1939. The now inactive Fort Ward on Bainbridge Island was used for this school as well. Charles got generally high marks at the naval school, except in navigation, in which he was usually near failing. He must have felt that navigation was not going to be very important to him in his life.

After the academy Charles went to the University of Washington. He did not do well here. He did not see much point in attending his classes and so was a failing student. This of course did not please his parents. His father writes in November 1939 "Well, you seem about as haywire as ever and I hope you will settle down and study, and forget about the kid stuff. I won't give you any advice as we have done enough of that, so it is up to you to make good." He was a bright lad however, his

Charles in his academy days. He is seated at far right.

In front of **S.S. President Coolidge** *with his mother*.

Charles, Ben.

A proud moment.

future wife recalls that he could remember anything and did not have to study much.

Through some combination of mom and dad's interest, and Charles' bright mind, Charles was arranged an appointment to the Merchant Marine Commission. The Maritime

Commission had set very high scholastic standards. In 1940 Charles had to take a test, and was one of a couple dozen out of many thousands to be selected. This was to signal the beginning of Charles' adult life. From here on out the skies would be clearer for him. Charles went to the U.S. Merchant Marine Academy, which is at King's Point, New York, but during the war was also being conducted on San Francisco Bay and New Orleans. Charles attended at San Francisco and Treasure Island.

Charles was on the American President Lines ship, *S.S. President Coolidge*, as an Engineer Cadet out of San Francisco beginning August of 1940. The *President Coolidge* was a 654', 22,000 ton, twin-screw turbo-electric liner. It was an ideal school ship for a group of young cadets. Turbo-electric propulsion involved steam turbines, which drove huge generators. The generators in turn drove giant electric motors, on the *Coolidge* they would have been two stories high and together produced 26,500 shaft horsepower, driving the ship up to 20 knots. The steam turbines spun at very high speeds, and required reduction gears to drive the generators. The interior of the steam turbines resembled the compressor section of a modern jet engine, and was the forerunner of them. The ship had the same type of boilers as the reciprocating engine ships, and had twelve of them. The engineering spaces would have been several stories high, and a factory-sized maze of machinery, wiring, plumbing, catwalks, nooks, and crannies. There were control stations with dozens of dials and indicators, levers and valve wheels.

President Coolidge would depart from San Francisco and sail to Honolulu, Yokohama and Kobe in Japan, Hong Kong, and Manila. Then, back to Hong Kong, Kobe, Yokohama, Honolulu, San Francisco, and finally Los Angeles.

In the structured military style life of the Merchant Marine Academy, Charles found his place in life and soon excelled in his studies. It seemed to be the natural calling for him. From here on out, he would work hard to become a marine officer. Charles impressed his superiors while on the *Coolidge*. In a letter, a superior boasted that Charles was a "damn good man."

Charles sailed on the *President Coolidge* until May of 1941. During this time he spent some of his time ashore in school. From July to October 1941 Charlie was on the Hog Islander freighter *S.S. Independence Hall*. From this point forward all Charlie would know is cargo ships and tankers. After the war started, the cadets were graduated years ahead of time to join the war effort. Charlie graduated King's Point in the class of '42 and got his license as Third Assistant Engineer May 8, 1942. Both the *President Coolidge* and *Independence Hall* would be lost in WWII.

S.S. President Coolidge.

Photo from collection of Charles Parker, Sr.

Menus from Coolidge, 1941, reflecting the various locals and cultures visited by the line.

A dinner at the "Sky Room" in Manila, 1941. Charles is second from left. Charles soon realized that the life of a mariner was for him.

S. S. PRESIDENT COOLIDGE

Dinner

Appetizers
Fresh Crabflake Cocktail with Lemon
Green and Ripe Olives   Garden Rose Radishes
Pickled English Walnuts   Stuffed Eggs Romanoff   Dutch Tid Bits
Smoked Oysters on Croutons   Little Pigs in Blankets

Soup
Cream of Tomatoes, Americaine   Consomme Arco Iris
Chilled Essence of Celery en Tasse

Fish
Poached Alaska King Salmon with Eggs and Chives or Butter Sauce

Entrees
Glazed Smoked Ham Burgundy Sauce, Spinach, Candied Sweet Potatoes
Boiled Ox Tongue with Risotto, Piedmontaise
Fresh Globe Artichokes with Hollandaise or Melted Butter

Roasts
Roast California Tom Turkey, New England Stuffing, Cranberry Sauce
Roast Hind Quarter of Lamb, Natural Gravy, Mint Jelly

Grill
To Order From Our Charcoal Broiler » » Allow 10 Minutes
Broiled Filet Mignon Steak with Frozen Bearnaise, Hoteliere

Vegetables   Carrots and Peas in Butter   Summer Squash in Cream
Boiled Patna Rice

Potatoes   Snowflake   Baked Yakima in Jacket

Cold Buffet   Choice of Assorted Cold Cuts Served with Potato Salad

Salads   Heart of Romaine   Fruit Chantilly

Dressings   French   Thousand Island   Mayonnaise   Caruso   Roquefort

Desserts   Ice Cream   Jell-O   Cookies
Devil Food Layer Cake   Raspberry Sundae

Cheese   Domestic Swiss   Pineapple   Danefield Blue

Saltina Soda and Toasted Bents Wafer Crackers

Fresh Fruit in Season
Demi Tasse

En Route to Manila   -   J. J. Presser, Chief Steward   -   Sunday, Sept. 14, 1941

"En Route to Manila" "Sunday, Sept. 14, 1941"   *Charles and classmate.*

President Coolidge *in the evening hour.*   Photo from collection of Charles Parker, Sr.

Hong Kong.

CHAPTER XIV

Campaign in the Aleutians

In 1942 America was focused on North Africa in the European theater of war, and in the islands of the South Pacific. Little did almost anyone know, was that the Japanese had invaded islands in the Aleutians—U.S. home territory. Both Ben Parker and his son Charles would find themselves in this unknown theater of war.

After graduating from the Cadet Corps on May 8, 1942, Charlie found himself on the Army transport ship *U.S.A.T. Delarof* May 19 as her 3rd Assistant Engineer.

In June 1942 the Japanese invaded the Aleutian Islands Kiska and Attu. At the time hardly anyone knew about it in the States. The *Delarof* was quietly sent to evacuate Aleut islanders. Charles writes home of his experiences.

Sorry that I have not written before but have been so busy taking on oil and fixing up things that have not had time. We broke our rocker arm and had to make a repair job to get back and are working on that now. We went aground up north and had quite a time getting off—that is what put the strain on the engine so that it broke…The chief and 1st are swell to work for and he does a lot of explaining to me about things that I don't understand but now I am on the plant pretty well. We took off a lot of natives from the Pribloff Islands and had 500 of them on board. We stopped in Ketchikan to get enough oil to get back as we gave most of our oil to the Navy up there and both my oiler and fireman got drunk and I had quite a time taking the ship out. It is quite an experience being on the throttle yourself and am used to it now.

A month later Charlie writes again.

Just a line to let you know that we got back in Seattle and are okay. This trip we went up the inside passage to the Icy Straits where we anchored for a couple of days waiting for a convoy to form. The old Victoria was in it and she sure has nice lines. This ship is getting on my nerves and anyway I don't like the Army Transport Service at all but have had some good experience here. In Seward all of the gang got drunk and nobody stood a watch and I had a terrible time. These ships seem to get the worst crews on them. The Aleutian came in and Mr. Kelly said to say hello to you and he said that if I hadn't got on the Delarof that I could have come on the Aleutian. Also saw a fellow by the name of Tracy in the Purser's department that said to say hello. Mr. George Decker who is the Pilot on here also gives you his regards.

Had a lot of trouble with the feed pump and the packing in the generators—we repack them about once every two weeks. They use anchorite packing on here and I don't think it is much good. Have three 15 KW generators going all of the time.

The Chief's name on here is Owens from Frisco and the 1st's name is Schwngen from Seattle…My fireman is 16 years old and was just made a fireman in Seward due to the other fireman getting drunk And losing his "status" and has been seasick for a couple of days and I had to do all of his work but he is doing all right now.

In January 1943, the *Delarof* was sent to the Aleutian isle of Amchitka as part of an assault landing group that was to take the island, in order to build an airfield. The January 12 assault went unchecked. The only casualty was a navy destroyer that went aground. Less than two weeks later the Japanese started bombing the airfield. Nonetheless, the airfield was operational in February.

One of Charlie's war stories survives. Charlie had been up on deck watching the battle action. A Jap dive-bomber was over the ship. The plane nosed over and snarled towards the nearly helpless ship. The tracers from the triple-A whizzed through the air. Charlie looked over the side just as the bomb struck a glancing blow just below the water line! The bomb was a dud and didn't explode, else that would have been the end of young Charlie. This story might possibly have happened later at Leyte Gulf in 1944, but it most likely happed in the Aleutian campaign.

The Japanese were driven out of the Aleutians by August of 1943. Charlie finished with the *Delarof* March 31, 1943, after the Amchitka operation.

Ben Parker was called out of retirement for the Aleutian operation. He sailed on the new Portland, Oregon built Liberty Ship *S.S. Cushman K Davis,* being operated by the Navy. Ben was technically working for Alaska Steam on these trips, however, and paid by Alaska Steam. He wrote three logs on these trips. This must have been kept secret for many years, as none of the family members had any recollection of Ben's WW II service. With the Depression right behind them, Ben is often appalled at the waste of the military.

While Ben was on this Alaska mission, he came into the possession of an English translation of a diary that belonged to a Japanese officer who had died in the battle for Attu, which took place from May 11th to the 30th of 1943. It tells a powerful story.

YEAR 1943
THIS IS COPIED FROM THE DIARY OF NEBU TATSUQUCHI, ACTING MEDICAL OFFICER, NORTHERN 5216 DETACHMENT.

MAY 12   0155
Carrier base plane flew over, fired at it. Air raids carried out frequently until 1000. Heard land noise. It is navy gun firing. Preparing for battle, equipment & etc.

Information: American transports, about 41, began landing at Hakkai Misaki. 20 boats landed at Massacre Bay. It seems that they are going to unload heavy equipment. Days activity: Air raid, navy gun firing, landing of U.S. forces.

MAY 13—BATTLE
The U.S. forces landed at Shiba Dai and Massacre Bay. The enemy has advanced to the bottom of Misumi Yama from Shiba Sai. Have engaged them. On the other hand Massacre Bay is defended by only one platoon. But upon the unexpected attack, the AA machine cannon was destroyed and we have withdrawn. In the night attack we captured 20 enemy rifles.

There is tremendous mountain artillery gun firing. Approximately 15 patients came into the field

hospital. The field hospital is attached to Arai Engineer Unit.

MAY 14—BATTLE
Our 2 submarines from Kiska assisting us have greatly damaged enemy ships. 1st Lt. Suyuki died by shots from rifle. Continuous flow of wounded to field hospital. In the evening, the U.S. forces used gas, but no damage was done on account of strong wind. Enemy strength must be a division. Our desperate defense is holding up well.

MAY 15
Continuous flow of casualties to our field hospital caused by fierce bombardment of enemy land and naval forces. The enemy has a great number of Negroes and Indians. The West Arms units have withdrawn to near Shitagata-Dai. In the raid I was ordered to West Arms but it was called off. Just laid down from fatigue in barracks.

Facial expression of soldiers back from West Arm is tense. They all went back to the front line soon.

MAY 16
If Shitagata-Dai is occupied by evening, the fate of East Arm is decided, so we burnt documents and prepared to destroy the patients. At that moment

there was on order from headquarters of sectors unit. Proceed to Chichagof Harbor by way of Umanose at 0100 in the morning. Patients from Ind. Inf. were lost so accompanied the patients. There was an air raid, so took refuge in the former field hospital cave. The guns of a Lockheed spit fire and flew past our cave.

MAY 17

At night, about 1800, under cover of darkness I left the cave. The stretcher went over the muddy roads and steep hills of no man's land. No matter how far or how much we went, we didn't get to the pass. Was rather irritated in the fog, sleep, dream, and wake up again. Same thing over again. The patient on the stretcher who does not move, is frostbitten.

After all the effort, met sector commander, Volnrl Yansaki. The pass is a straight line without width, and a steep line towards Chichagof Harbor. Sitting on the butt and lifting the foot, I slide very smoothly and change direction with the sword. Slide down in about 20 minutes. After that arrived Chichagof harbor after straggling. The time expended 9 hours for all this without leaving patients. Opened new field hospital.

Walking is now extremely difficult from left knee rheumatism which reoccurred on the pass.

The results of our Navy, the submarine, battleship, cruisers 3, destroyer, air-borne troops, six transports—by the favorable turn since the Battle of East Arms. Reserves came back, off shore of Shiba-Dai. Six destroyers are guarding one transport.

MAY 18

The Yeneguwa Detachment abandoned East and West Arms. About 60 wounded came to field hospital. I had to care for all of them myself all through the night. Heard that the enemy carried out a landing in Chichagof Harbor. Everybody did combat preparations and waited. Had two grenades ready. 2nd Lt. Omiro left for the front line on Hokuchin-Yama. Said farewell. At night a patient came in who engaged a friendly unit by mistake, and received a wound on the wrist. The countersign is Isshi Hoke.

MAY 19

At night there was a phone call from sector unit headquarters. In some spots of the beach are friendly float type planes waiting. Went into Attu Village Church. Felt like someone's home, some blankets were scattered around. Was told to translate a field order presumed to have been dropped by enemy officer in Massacre Bay which was in the possession of Captain Robert J. Edwards, Adj of Col. Smith. Got tired and went to sleep. 1st Lt. Ujiie is in charge of translation.

MAY 20

The hard fighting of our 303rd, Bn. in Massacre Bay is fierce and it is to our advantage. Have captured enemy weapons and used that to fight. Mowed 10 enemy coming in under fog. Five of our men and one medical NCO died. Heard enemy, pilots faces can be seen around Umanose. The enemy naval gun firing near our hospital is fierce. Drops around 20 meters away.

MAY 21

Was strafed when amputating a patient's arm. It is my first since moving over to Chichagof Harbor that I went in an air raid shelter. Enemy plane is a Martin. Nurcusness of Owia, commanding officer is severe and he has said his last words to his NCO's and officers that he will die tomorrow, gave all his articles away. Hasty chap, this fellow.

The officers of the front are doing a fine job. Everyone who heard this became desperate and things became disorderly.

MAY 22

0600 air raid again. Strafing killed one medical man. Medical man Okayaki wounded in right thigh, fractured arm. During the night, a mortar shell came awful close.

MAY 23

Seventeen friendly medium naval bombers destroyed a cruiser off shore. By naval gun fire a hit was scored on the pillar pole of tents for patients, and the tent gave in, two died instantly.

From 0200 to 1600 stayed in fox hole. Days rations: igo, 1.5lbs. Nothing else. Everybody looked around for food and stole everything they could find.

MAY 24

It rained sleet and extremely cold. Stayed at Misumi barracks alone. A great amount of shells were dropping from naval gun firing, and rocks and mud flew all around the roof, and falls in a fox hole about five yards away. Hayaska, a medical man, died instantly, by penetration of shrapnel through the heart.

MAY 25

Naval gun firing, aerial bombardment, trench warfare. The worst is yet to come. The enemy is constructing their positions. Battalion Commander died. At Umanose they cannot fully accommodate all patients. It has been said that at Massacre Bay District, the road to sector unit headquarters is isolated. Am suffering from diarrhea and feel dizzy.

(*A note is inserted here stating:* Would add here that the U.S. forces did not use gas. They used smoke bombs which the Japs took for gas.)

MAY 26
By naval gun firing it felt like Misumi barracks blew up and things shook up tremendously. Consciousness became vague. One tent burned down by a hit from incendiary bombs. Strafing planes hit the rest room. Two hits from a 50 cal shell, one stopped in the ceiling and the other penetrated my room. Looks like an awful mess from the sand and pebbles that came down from the roof. Hirose 1st Lt. of the medical corps is also wounded. There was a ceremony of Granting of Imperial Edict. The last line of Umanose was broken through. No hope for reinforcements. Will die for the cause of Imperial Edict.

MAY 27
Diarrhea continuous, pain is severe. Took everything from pills, opium, and morphine then slept pretty well. Strafing by planes, roof broke through. There is less than 1000 left from more than 2000 troops.

Wounded from coast defense unit field hospital headquarters. The rest are on the front line.

MAY 28
The remaining rations are for only two days. There is a sound of trench mortars, also AA guns. Our artillery has been completely destroyed. The company on the bottom of Attu Fuji has been completely destroyed except one. Rations for about two days.

I wonder if Commander Yenigaws and some of the men are still living. Other companies have been completely annihilated except for one or two. 303rd Bn. has been defeated. Yenegawa Bn. is still holding Umanose.

Continuous cases of suicide. Half of the sector unit headquarters was blown away. Heard that they gave 400 shots of morphine to severely wounded and killed them. Ate half fried thistle. It is the first time I

have eaten something fresh in six months. It is a delicacy.

Order from sector commander to move field hospital to island. It was called off.

MAY 29
Today at 2000 we assembled in front of headquarters. The field hospital took part too. The last assault is to be carried out. All patients in the hospital were made to commit suicide. Only 33 years of living and I am to die. I have no regrets. Banzai to the Emperor. I am grateful I have kept the peace in my soul, which Edict bestowed upon me.

At 1800 took care of all patients with grenades.

Good bye Toeke, my beloved wife who has loved me to the last. Until we meet again, grant you God-Speed. Misokin, who just became four years old will grow up unharmed. I feel sorry for you Tokiko born Feb. of this year and gone without seeing your father. Well be good Matsue(brother) be good Koehon, Sukechon, Masechon, Mittichon, good bye.

The number participating in the attack is a little over 1000 to take enemy artillery positions. It seems the enemy is expecting an all out attack tomorrow.

The end of the diary.

LIFE FACTS
March 6, 1929 graduated from Keryi medical school of Herashima. 1929 graduated from Frazer English ACD. Sept 15, 1929 to May 22, 1932 Pacific Union College Medical Dept, Agwin Calif. Sept 1, 1933 to June 1937 College of Medical Evangelist, received college medical license Sept 8, 1938. Jan 10, 1941 transferred to 1st Imperial Guard Inf. Reg. Jan 13, 1941 ordered to officer's candidate, promoted to PFC. Med. Dept. July 1 promoted to Superior Private Med. Corps. July 20 ordered as officer's candidate. Aug 1 promoted to Corporal. Sept 1 entered Army Medical School. Graduated Oct 24. Acting officer since December.

The Japanese forces on Attu Banzai-charged the American forces on May 30, 1943, and nearly all of them were killed. The following is a voyage log of Benjamin Parker detailing his experiences in the Aleutian campaign, summer 1943. Ben's story follows on in the aftermath of the Attu battle, and as American forces are preparing for more actions. The story wanders through both the excitement of war, and relentless tedium.

SS CUSHMAN K DAVIS. VOYAGE 2 FROM DUTCH HARBOR TO ATTU

Left Dutch Harbor 2 pm Mon July 26. Convoyed by a PC boat, there was the *SS Lamont*[6], Capt Coops, and one other ship.

TUES JULY 27
There was fog last night which made going rather tough, but had to keep going the same speed. The weather today is pretty good.

WED JULY 28
A little fog last night. Arrived Adak 9 am and there is lots of ships of various kinds in the harbor including the *George Flavel* & the Navy Transport *Heywood* that I overhauled at the LA shipyard.

Lots of invasion boats of all kinds and planes flying overhead. Raining hard tonight with poor visibility. Good food but spoiled by the cooks.

THURS JULY 29 my birthday.
7AM. Just got up, and it seems to be clearing up, but a strong wind is blowing. Last night was sure a real blackout.

10 PM. Another day of laying around. Eight more ships arrived today, making about 35 in the harbor.

Was talking with an Army captain who is going to Attu with us, and he said they are bombing Kiska from here with heavy bombers. They take a load from this air field, go drop them, then go back to Amchitka and get another load, go drop them, then back to this air field. It is hard to get good weather for bombing. When they took Attu they used green troops from Calif. instead of using seasoned troops at Dutch Harbor. There was lots of sickness and deaths caused from exposure.

FRI JULY 30
At 5PM a number of bombers came in from a raid on Kiska. Three destroyers just went out.

11PM. Left Adak 10pm. We are the only ship leaving for Attu with a PC boat convoying.

SAT JULY 31
10 AM. Blowing, raining, and it seems like winter. Poor visibility. The little boat ahead of us must be having a rough time.

The Army captain's name is Sperry, and he is going to the island named Shemya where they are going to build an air base. I am giving the magazines to him as he says that the men that are there are isolated and will be glad to get them, and very few ships call there.

4PM. The weather is getting better.

11PM. Still daylight, calmed down some, quite

---

[6] Italics of ship's names added by author

cool. There were 2000 Japs on Attu and only seven prisoners taken.

SUNDAY AUG 1
7AM. Sea calm, cold, can't see far. Temperature of sea 50, of atmosphere 52. 10:30AM, running along Attu island. Raining, poor visibility.

One of our subs just went by, also a PC boat. The wireless man heard a call from a ship last night saying torpedoed, position 51 degrees north, 155 degrees west. 11am, anchored in Massacre Bay, waiting to dock.

5PM. We are at the dock and it is pouring rain with thunder, lightning, and fog. There is great activity, soldiers and plenty of trucks. The colored troops do the longshore work. They are starting to unload. Had turkey for lunch. Talking with a soldier, he said the going was tough when they landed here, and that the Japs killed all the prisoners they took, and in turn we killed all the Japs, many of the Japs commited suicide rather than be taken. There are a few of them left in the hills now. This place is named Camp Earl in memory of the first officer to fall in battle. The Army and Navy have accomplished lots in regards to building docks, roads, and buildings.

I was told that there is a Jap task force around these parts consisting of ten transports and about twenty naval craft.

MONDAY AUG 2   Attu
7PM. After breakfast one of the MP's took me for a ride in a Jeep. We went up the valley and around Engineers Hill, then over to another valley. I saw the fox holes that our troops dug when driving the Japs out, and where lots of Japs are buried. They just dumped them in trenches and covered them up. This camp is sure spread out over a large area. It must have been a tough job getting at the Japs as most of them were up on the mountains where they could shoot down at our boys. Heard some shooting across the valley and saw men running and at times lay down, the MP thought they were after some stray Japs.

After supper I took a walk to the cemetary. It is over near the foot of the mountain and named Little Falls cemetary after two little falls that flow down the mountain. I counted 428 graves and several of them had wreaths of wild flowers on them. Quite a number of officers were killed. An aviator had a blade of a propeller on his grave. The boys are living in tents, and talk about sandy mud, there is oceans of it and wet, and they say that when it dries out, which is seldom, the dust is terrible. One tent is named the Boar's Nest. There are equipment and materiel dumped all over the place, gasoline, diesel oil, coal, ammunition, machinery, and lots of other gear. What men I have talked with seem to be in good spirits.

We brought up quite a lot of whiskey for the medical corps but I think the officers will get their share. The men are willing to pay any price for a pint of whiskey. They make something to drink out of raisins, potato peelings, and anything else they can get hold of. I think those that want it should be given a couple of shots a day in a place like this. Rained most all day.

TUESDAY AUG 3
10PM and still daylight. Got up 7am and it was raining some but cleared up before noon and the sun has been shining and things have dried up some.

After supper I took a walk up on the hill and talked to an MP and he said some of our boys were sure mutilated when they were killed. Some of them were married and have children. I have heard so much about the battle that I am getting tired of it. They are dumping good coal over a bank and the greater part of it will be lost.

WEDNESDAY AUG 4 Unloading at Attu.
Got up 7AM. The weather not so good. The first and I went as far as we could go on the road, down in a valley and near a lake. There is a camp of soldiers near the lake. Went over on the mountain side and there was clothing that belonged to some Jap soldiers scattered around so I cut off some buttons.

Lots of fox holes. On a knoll where we had some machine guns there was lots of rifle and machine gun ammunition laying around. Such a waste, and it sure runs into money for the taxpayers. There was a cold wind blowing in the valley. Got back in time as it started raining hard and it still keeps up. Some of the boys are anxious to get out of here, and I don't blame them.

THURSDAY AUG 5
8:30PM. Raining hard this morning but cleared up this afternoon. The tug boat *Brooklyn* came along side this morning and I know the fellow who is Chief of her. He used to oil for me on the *Old Vic* years ago. I went over on her this morning and talked some, and he gave me an army coat and some candy. Have been typing some today. Have a cold from being out in the cold wind yesterday. Strong wind last night and some barges and small boats blew ashore.

Will call it a day.

FRIDAY AUG 6
8AM. Got up at seven o'clock and had breakfast. Heavy fog. An amphibian tractor went by, they can run on land or water.

7PM. Pumped 500 BBL's fuel oil to the U.S.A.T. tug Brooklyn. The third asst told me that yesterday the Red Cross sent a wire home for him, free of charge. So this afternoon the gunnery officer and myself went up and I sent a message to Gen.

We passed by the commanding general and chief of staff's quarters and they are located in a good place, on a ridge overlooking a valley and lake and well protected. When getting back to the dock, the Coast and Geodetic Survey boat (*Explorer*) was along side for water. A man spoke to me as I went by and he used to be on the *Minnesota* with me. He is Navigation Officer on the *Explorer*. They are surveying close to Kiska and he thinks there will be something doing around there before long.

10PM. My friend's name is Mr. Wiedlick and he was just over to see me and we talked a while.

SAT AUG 7
10PM. There has been all kinds of weather today, wind, fog, rain, and sunshine. Took a walk over to Navy Town. Got back at noon.

The troop ship *John Floyd* got in from Adak with the 37th Infantry and she was sure loaded. Fresh water today so we have enough to go home.

Colonel Nichols said there was 105,000 tons of cargo unloaded here during the month of July and they are getting ready to handle 150,000 a month. The second asst and a couple of others went souvenir hunting, and the second got a couple of gold filled teeth from a dead Jap, but I don't think it proper to do it.

SUNDAY AUG 8   Attu
10PM. This morning I saw a fellow who used to be on the *Yukon*, his name is Glen Walley. He is Navigating Officer on the gun boat *Charleston*, they were doing some shooting during the battle for Attu and came near being blasted by torpedo bombers. Sergeant Dobuvocky of the MP took me for another Jeep ride to Sarana Valley and as far thru Navy Town as we could go. Saw a lot of P.B.Y. bombers. Am getting tired of laying here and wish we were on our way. Today has been a fine day and the dust is flying behind the Jeeps and trucks. They say Attu will be the largest Army base in Alaska.

MONDAY AUG 9   Attu
9AM. Got up at seven and took a look around. This is a beautiful morning. While at breakfast I heard an officer speak about the Second Foot winning the Battle of Attu. I asked what he meant by the Second Foot and it is the Second Infantry, which has been in existence since the Revolutionary War, and has seen lots of action.

Frank Marsh, Chief of the tug *Brooklyn* is going

out with us.

Temp of sea water 47 degrees, of atmosphere about 80 in the sun. The *John Floyd* sailed at 2PM.

It has been so clear today that you could see Aggatu Island, about 80 miles away. No one is on it.

The points of attack on Attu island were from Holtz Bay(Chichagof Harbor) and Massacre Bay.

TUESDAY AUG 10
3PM. We are all ready to leave. Have some Army men and three invasion boats aboard for Adak.

Today's weather: Cloudy with showers. Will be glad to get under way.

7PM. Just left Attu with two other ships and small destroyer as escort. Four ships came before we left. Didn't eat any supper, Don't feel so good.

9PM. Planes flying overhead. The sunset is very pretty over Attu Island, we can also see Chemya, also Aggatu. The ships ahead are not very fast and we are only making about eight knots. Sea smooth. A little cold out. Will black out my ports and go to bed.

WEDNESDAY AUG 11   At Sea
Up at 7AM. The sun was up and looked like a ball of fire.

9AM. It is cloudy now, smooth sea, temp of sea 50, of atmosphere 60. At eight thirty could see a convoy of six ships going the other way. We now have three convoy boats with us. About 1am this morning on of the convoy boats sent up a white flare which meant submarine, the gun crew was called to their stations. The third mate said he thought he heard a depth charge go off. We are about off Kiska. Speed about 9 knots.

The ships ahead of us are the James Griffiths and the American Star. Bill Peel's son is Chief of the Griffiths.

10pm. It turned out to be a fine day, sea like a mill pond and temp 80.

THURS AUG 12   Adak
12:30PM. Just had lunch. Arrived here 10am. There is quite an armada in the harbor. Battle ships, cruisers, destroyers, transports, Liberty ships, and what not. The transports are loaded with troops, and it looks there will be something doing at Kiska before long. Cloudy and cool today.

10PM. Some of the fighting ships have gone, and lots of the other ships are flashing signals, so I guess they will be going. We are waiting for orders to leave, but will lay down in the meantime. It is cold out.

FRIDAY AUG 13   Under Way
10PM. Left Adak 5PM. This morning when I got up some more of the [Navy] had gone including three

battleships and some troop ships. The men on the troopships must be restless and like a bunch of cattle being led to slaughter. They are supposed to start in the Big Show on the 15th. We have aboard a Major in the Canadian Provost and eleven of his men. They brought up 50 prisoners to put with a Canadian Regiment, they had deserted and other offences. The Major is a very fine man and he said he never saw such waste as there is in the American Army, and I know it. We have the same bunch in the convoy with a tanker added. There are Liberty ships laying at Adak loaded with all kinds of material for Kiska when they take the place. Not such a bad day. Am glad to be headed homeward. Will blackout and then to bed.

SAT AUG 14   At Sea
8PM. We have been plugging along slow but sure. Cloudy and a raw wind. Rolling a little. I heard while at Attu that we are bombing the island of Paramushiru at times. Some seem to think that we are to keep going towards Japan. We are traveling two abreast now. Tempt of sea 50 degrees.

S.S. Northwestern, *formerly of the Alaska Steamship Company, after being bombed at Dutch harbor.*

SUNDAY AUG 15   At Sea
2PM. This morning when I got up it was cold and blowing hard and we rolled a lot last night. Arrived Dutch Harbor 10am, only a few ships in the harbor. I could see the old *Northwestern* laying over near the beach with only her hull and stack showing, but still she had steam in her boilers. They say that she is going to be towed back to the states, I feel sorry for her.

Sailed from Dutch Harbor 1pm and headed for

Seattle. Getting to Dutch Harbor is like getting back to civilization again.

Tempt of sea 46.

11PM. Fair wind, smooth sea, moon looks pretty.

MONDAY AUG 16

10AM. Sun shinning and fair wind. Was talking to a Mr. Wright, who was first asst on the tug *Brooklyn* at Attu, and he left on account of her being in such bad shape. He also worked on the Alcan Highway to Alaska and had charge of the first consignment of freight to go over the highway, and I saw his papers stating so. There were 26 trucks and only 3 Nielson Huts for cargo, and it took them 47 days from Dawson Creek to White Horse. He said it is an awful road and never can be made anything. Millions of dollars wasted. Wrecked machinery and trucks all along the way. It is about 900 miles from Dawson Creek to White Horse. People don't know what is being done with their money.

Got up at six and did a little patching and washing, also worked on my log.

10PM. Fair wind and sea all day. Sea 51.

TUESDAY AUG 17

7AM. Cloudy this morning and misty, smooth sea. Tempt of sea 52 degrees.

WED AUG 18   At Sea

10AM. Tempt of sea 55 degrees. Fair wind still holds. Making around 13 knots.

1PM. Just had gun and boat drill. These ships could put up a pretty good fight.

11PM. Met a freighter northbound, fair wind and sea. Tempt of sea 57 degrees. Is hot in the engine room.

THURS AUG 19

8AM. Up at 7. Tempt of sea 58, cloudy. Last midnight position, 53'-15"N 137' 31"W.

FRI AUG 20

6:30AM. Sun up, rainbow & smooth sea.

9AM. Tempt of sea 60 degrees.

6PM. It's been cold & rainy all afternoon.

8PM. Blowing hard, clouds & fog, seems like winter, don't like it.

11PM. Passed Swiftshore Buoy 10:30, sea 50.

SAT AUG 21

6AM. Going up the Straits of San Juan de Fuca. Fog, running slow. Cold.

6:10AM. Stopped at Port Angeles for boarding officer. 6:30 on the way to Seattle.

After arriving in Seattle, Ben has a week and a half to spend with his wife ashore while the *Cushman K Davis* is reloaded. The ship is back underway, headed north to the Bering Sea and Alaska on the 30th of August. They spend a month at Adak, and then shove off for Attu September 28, 1943.

SS CUSHMAN K DAVIS. VOYAGE 3

MONDAY AUG 30

1PM. We left the dock at 12:30 and are now adjusting compasses, didn't get a chance to call up home as we expected to go any time. Had some soup for lunch and it was real tasty. Left Seattle 3:15PM.

10PM. Went below to see how the new third Asst was making out, and he is o.k. as he has been on several of these jobs. Had hash and egg for supper and then took a nap as I didn't get much sleep last night. We have 12 enlisted men and 5 army officers as passengers. Very dark out.

AUG 31 Tuesday

7AM. A strong wind off the stbd bow and the sun is shining. Will eat breakfast.

10PM. Had fire and boat drill at 4pm. Cloudy most all day with some rain. A heavy head swell and we are pitching some. Will turn in.

Wed Sept 1st

10PM. Just came up from the engine room, was talking to the third asst and he is rather a nice young man. Got up 6:30 this morning and only had about an hour's nap this afternoon, so will hit the hay. Been a pretty good day, but the wind seems to be howling now.

Thurs Sept 2

9AM. Wind still blowing and heavy sea.

9:30PM. Still blowing hard and heavy sea. Every one seems to have hibernated in their rooms so think I will crawl into bed.

Fri Sept 3

7PM. —The Second Asst called me at 2am this morning to look at a leaky Boiler Tube. I had to cut the boiler out and we are running on one boiler as the rest of the tubes look bad. I told the Capt we would have to go into Kodiak and get the boiler repaired as we are on the way there. Haven't eaten much today as things seem to worry me more than they used to. The weather has moderated as regards to wind, but is raining and very dismal out. Will see if I can get a little sleep.

Sat Sept 4
11PM. We are anchored off Kodiak. Arrived here 10pm. Wind been blowing all day. Don't feel so good on account of boiler. Will sleep a little if I can. Where we anchored is named Monashka Bay.

Sun Sept 5
Arrived at the dock in Womans Bay 10am and went to work on the Boiler. Not getting any sleep.

Mon Sept 6
10AM. Still plugging along on the boiler.

Tues Sept 7
Womans Bay is the Naval Base near Kodiak. Left Kodiak 7am. Been a nice day and all is ok (knock on wood) and I hope we won't have any more trouble. Twelve midnight so will retire.

Wed Sept 8
6PM. This morning at 6am they started popping away with one of the port AA guns and woke all hands up. I was awake but didn't get up to see what it was all about as one may as well be bombed in bed as up on deck. They were shooting at a tank that was floating near the ship. Haven't eaten much since breakfast, only fruit as these cooks have turned out to be as bad as the others were.
    The weather was fine this morning but now it is raining and blowing so cold. Had the Cadet cut some pieces off the damaged boiler tubes so I can have them to show when I arrive Seattle. Will turn in early.

Thurs Sept 9
12 Noon. We are hove to in a heavy gale of wind and very heavy seas looking for a man who washed overboard off another Liberty ship. We can see the ship ahead. I don't think there is much chance for the man in this weather.
    1PM. Proceeded on our way.
    3PM. We got close to Dutch Harbor and they signaled us to keep out. Have a hard time turning around in the heavy seas.
    10PM. We are hove to and running slow in a gale and heavy seas.

Fri Sept 10th
10PM. Arrived Dutch Harbor 10am and anchored. Not many ships in the harbor. They say the wind was blowing 80 miles an hour. Washed some clothes. Don't feel and too good. Mailed a letter to Gen.

Sat Sept 11th
6PM. Left Dutch Harbor 3pm and now outside bucking into a gale and heavy seas. We have a PC boat convoying us. Ahead is the *Humoconda*, next the *Thomas Condon* and then us. There is new snow on the mountain tops. I think a man is nuts to keep running up here in the winter. They didn't get the man that fell overboard off the *Condon*(that was the ship) and it's a hard way to go. He was a navy man and was washed off the stern when she took a sea over. Saw a large Seal swimming around and the heavy seas didn't bother it any.

Sun Sept 12
10PM. Wind quieted down, also sea. Not such a bad day but looks like a southeaster is in the making. Fire and boat drill 4pm. Still thinking about Boilers.

Mon Sept 13
9AM. Adak Island in sight. Showers & cool.
    11PM. Arrived at the dock in Adak 3pm. Quite a few navy ships in the harbor and a few merchant ships. Doing some work on one of the boilers. Raining quite hard. They are discharging some of the deck load.

Tues Sept 14   Adak
10PM. We moved away from the dock at 9 o'clock this morning and anchored in the bay and here we are and it is blowing a gale.

Wed Sept 15
11PM. Well, here we are anchored in Adak Harbor, gale still blowing and raining hard. Last night we drug anchor some and had to steam slow ahead. Had to shift to another anchorage.

Thurs Sept 16   Adak
10PM. Another day of laying around and it is very tiresome. Been raining all day but not blowing quite so hard. Am glad that Charles[7] is not running up here this winter as it is much more cheerful where the sun shines.

Fri Sept 17   Adak
Had a boat drill and lowered the Stbd boats and sent the men out in them to get a little practice, and the bums need it. I think most people are morons the

---

[7] Benjamin Parker's son

way they act. The wind has changed to the northwest and no telling how hard it will blow. We don't know a thing about when we will leave here and don't think any one cares. Will crawl up on the shelf again as it is ten o'clock.

Sat Sept 18   Adak
10PM. Have just been talking to the third asst and he is not to bad. Tonight we had corn beef hash for supper and it was just a mushie mess and the rolls were like a dough ball, so I left the table without eating anything. These Cooks are the worse then we ever had. Weather not to bad or not to good. Looks as though we will lay here for a while. I don't see what they want with so many ships on this run and not be able to handle them. I had to get after the crew and officers about using so much fresh water as they have been using 24 gallons per man per day.

Sunday Sept 19th   Adak
11AM. It is blowing a gale from the southwest and quite cold. Have just been listening to religious services over WXLB on the northern road to victory. There was fine singing and speaking. A Lieut. in the Northern Air Command who used to be a missionary in Japan spoke and he was very good. They sang some of the old hymns and there were some good voices among them. The radio man has a speaker in our mess room. There seems to be a lot of men who have religious beliefs. Will see what there is for lunch.

10PM. Four ships came in this afternoon, three of them Libertys. I don't see why they have so many ships up in this country at one time just to lay around to be unloaded. Still blowing a gale and if there were any trees to blow down, they sure would be down. Men are getting restless. To bed.

Mon Sept 20
7PM. Some time last night the wind changed to the north and has been blowing hard all day and still is and is cold. There are 24 ships of all description in the harbor and I have been looking them over with our glasses and they are all right and one can see a small object quite a distance. The Army Camp is scattered all over the hills and I can see tents, huts and winding roads with our glasses. It is hard to get the Asst engineers interested in anything in the engine room that does not involve overtime. I have had enough of ships and the sea under present conditions.

10PM. Was down in the engine room talking to the third. Some of the men are playing poker, but they always play for high stakes. Will retire.

Tues Sept 21   Adak

11PM. The wind has made several changes today but went back to the north this evening and is blowing a gale now. Wrote and mailed a letter to Gen and wish I was home with her as I am sure lonesome. Was below talking to the third asst and the oiler and fireman, they seem to be better company then some of the rest and the right sort of conversation. This is my bath night but don't feel like it now. The first asst is the big drawback in the engine room, the rest are ok. Have finished reading Micah Clarke again. Have been laying at anchor, just one week as of this morning. Now to bed.

Wed Sept 22
8PM. Well, it cleared up this afternoon and the sun came out and there was a pretty sunset and there's nothing like the good old sun. Three Cruisers came in today, also four other ships among them. The Denali of Alaska Steam was one and she went in to the dock.

Having them do some painting in the engine room as it will brighten up things and make the men feel better as most of the engine rooms I have been in look to gloomy. I am going to take a bath and go to bed early because if the weather is good tomorrow I will try and get in and get a hair trim. Chilly out.

I was told that the Capt of the Denali has his son as first mate and yet Mr. Murphy wouldn't let me take Charles, and I don't feel to good about it.

Thurs Sept 23   Adak
10PM. Well, the Capt., Mate, Purser, and myself went ashore this morning and got back at five o'clock. The weather was good and calm so we took the ship's boat. I wanted to get a hair trim and got one at the navy barber shop, cost 25 cents. I went and saw Westcott, chief of the Denali and on the way back went aboard the McKenzie and the Meeks and I saw the Chiefs on them, Davis and Gorenson, and I saw Kalem and he wants to get back on this ship. Rather a bother going ashore in a small boat as it is quite a distance but was a little change. They have had trouble with the boilers on some of the other ships. About 7 pm one the steam pipes to the forward winches cracked and I am having them make some clamps to put around it. The Meeks left for Seattle and wished it was us. Will lay down a little while and get up later and see how they made out with the clamps.

Fri Sept 24   Adak
3PM. I sure used my head when I went ashore yesterday as it is blowing and quite rough in the harbor. Sent the winch pipe ashore to be repaired. The last two nights I haven't slept at all good and last night I dreamt but can't remember the dream only I

woke up with a start when I thought Charles called "Daddy, Daddy," and I didn't feel any too good. Some of the men on the other ships expressed themselves as sorry that Charles had to get with Gloomy Gus the Chief of the *Lancaster*.

10PM. It's raining out now and wind gone down. There are only eleven ships in the outer harbor now. I don't see why in the world they want to spend so much money in overtime loading these ships in Seattle and then have them lay around up here like we are. Will go to roost.

Sat Sept 25
All kinds of weather today with a little sunshine. Three Liberty ships came in. Just looked around today to see what I could growl about as one feels like it. Its now eleven o'clock so will to bed and read a little, am reading the story of Alaska by Andrews.

Sun Sept 26   Adak
10PM. Was just down in the engine room for two hours talking to the third and I rather like him as he seems to want to learn and is a little interested in what I tell him and he was telling me about the

offshore ship and what awful crews they get and I hope Charles gets a good gang. It has been a stormy, foggy and gloomy day and I have felt rather out of sorts and down and don't want to be around people. Am eating a few raisins. One of the ships that used to run around the world for the American President Line is in the harbor anchored. Will go to bed hoping tomorrow we start going some place.

Mon Sept 27
9PM. Another day gone by and is still blowing. Well, at least we heard a little good news saying we may get out tomorrow and I hope so.

Tues Sept 28
9PM. Well at last we are on the way and what a relief. We left Adak at 3pm with two convoy boats and the Liberty ships *Greenup* and *Alguin*.

Wed Sept 28   At Sea
It hasn't been such a bad day, a little head wind and choppy sea. Everything going pretty good below. Will take a look in the engine room and then retire.

After Ben and the *Cushman K Davis* arrive at Attu, it takes a month before they can get their ship unloaded and out of there, during which time they experience an air raid and heavy seas.

Thurs Sept 30
9AM. It is a clear crisp morning and the sun is shining and we can see Attu about 15 miles off, can also see Aggatu and Chemya, just looks like a speck.

9:30. Its clouded up now and cold wind.

11AM. We have just anchored in Massacre Bay—Attu Island.

10PM. We moved into the dock at 5pm and are unloading some tractors and other gear. I went over and saw Mr. Randall who is chief of the *Greenup* and it seems like all the ships are having trouble with the boilers. Had a leak in one of the tubes in the auxiliary condenser. Filling the fresh water tanks up. Raining some. Wrote to Gen.

Fri Oct 1   Attu
10AM. Got up 6:30 and washed a suite of underwear and pair of socks. Still raining. I am keeping the ship at the dock so I can blow the boilers down and put fresh water in them.

9PM. Went over on the *Christopher Greenup* and talked to Randall for a little while. All kinds of weather today and it looks rather foreboding out now. Gave the magazines to a young MP that I met at the head of the dock. Am glad that I have a room so I can be by myself when I want to. Will go to bed and read.

Sat Oct 2
10PM. After lunch the cargo security officer got a jeep and took me up to the PX (post exchange) and I bought some items and then came back to the ship. We got orders and moved away from the dock at 3:30pm so here we are anchored again, for how long no one knows. We have had all kinds of weather today and it is raining hard now. The third asst and an old fireman named Butler walked over to Chichagof Harbor to get some souvenirs and the old man was all in when they got back about ten o'clock and soaking wet and they said never again. The *John Floyd* got in from Chemya so she will have to be unloaded first and the *Wylola*, *Diamond Cement*, *American Star*, and *Cushman K Davis*. They say that all of the cargo will have to be unloaded to lighters and towed to Chemya 37 miles away. I don't see how they are ever going to do it with the bad weather setting in.

Sun Oct 3   At anchor Massacre Bay
10AM. I could hear the wind howling through the night and this morning when I got up at 7 o'clock the Mountains were covered with snow about half way down and looks like winter is setting in. have just been below looking around.

10:30PM. Wrote some to Gen and walked up and down on the after hatch, read, went below a few times. Rain, wind and cold. Will retire.

Monday Oct 4

9AM. Got up at 7 had breakfast and went below and looked in the Stbds boiler to see how the tubes are and they are OK. Cloudy this morning but no wind.

9PM. The Maine arrived with cargo for Chemya. Wrote some to Gen. Looked in the Stbd boiler. Cloudy, no wind.

Tues Oct 5

9PM. Another Liberty ship came in today, the *Recolaag* with a load for Chemya, what a joke. Wrote some to Gen., also a letter to Murphy. Not such a bad day only a few squalls at times. Will go below, then to bed.

Wed Oct 6

7PM. Well, we are on the way again. Got orders at 5pm to get ready and go with the eastbound convoy, no one knows why but there must be something doing regarding the Japs as planes have been on the go all day and they are on an alert ashore. I suppose they don't want so many ships in the harbor if there is a bombing as there might be quite a loss. There are two small convoy boats and one that looks like a light cruiser, then there is the *American Star*. *Maine*, *Cushman K Davis* and *Ole E Rolvaag* and we are all in line going we don't know where. This morning I saw the tug boat *Moran* towing a loaded lighter towards Chemya and a little while ago she passed us towing it back again and seemed in a hurry. One can never tell whether you are coming or going or what is going to happen up in this neck of the woods. Weather good so far today.

Thurs Oct 7

7PM. The weather had been cloudy and cool today and we have been plugging slowly along as the leading boat hasn't much speed. Just a little while ago another ship joined us with her escort, it looks like a transport, so we now have four naval vessels and five merchant ships. The leading naval ship is named the *Beaver*. No one knows where we are going or what for and it gets the Capt kind of sore and he says he is nothing but a conductor, but they don't mean much to the Navy. Was in the engine room all morning looking after stopping a leak in the Aux Condenser. Laid down a while this afternoon but didn't sleep any. Things are pretty quite while at sea as those punks in the Gunnery crew have to stand watches and all others stay in their rooms. Will play a few games of solitaire before I go to bed as I will have to do something to help pass the time.

Two of the mess boys, one who looked after our rooms, and the one who worked on the galley went ashore yesterday and were left at ATTU and I feel sorry for them as they were not at all bad, and one was quite young and the first time away from home, and he was they say pretty home sick.

Friday Oct 8th

9AM. Cold wind and cloudy. We were heading east but at 8:30 we all turned round and now heading west and not any of us know what it is all about. Will work on my log.

9:30PM. Had some sunshine today and a very pretty rainbow about five o'clock. Have the Cadet checking non-expendable equipment and it will be quite a job for him and Charles had to do it on the *Coolidge*. Walked for about two hours on the lumber pile. Wind coming from the north and feels rather nippy. Had brains and scramble eggs for supper and they were not to bad. Worked on my log a little after supper. Feel a little like a cold so will go the shelf.

Sat Oct 9

7AM. Have just been up on deck and it is still dark and Venus was shining out bright between clouds. Seems to be blowing up some. Feel a cold all through.

8:45AM. Just saw the sun come up from back of some clouds and was very pretty. Right now the wind has died down and smooth sea. Had breakfast, will go back on deck.

10AM. Squally out now and I was in a hail storm. I want to keep hardened up so I can hop right into a job ashore. Washed clothes. Will go below.

4PM. We can see Attu – Aggatu – and Shemya and it is blowing hard.

10PM. We are back at anchor in Massacre Bay, arrived here 6:30. The *Maine* & *American Star* went to the dock and I think we will all unload here. Don't feel so good so will turn in. Bum weather out.

Sun Oct 10

1PM. Got up 7am, but it stays dark until after eight o'clock as our time is back three hours from Seattle time. After breakfast I washed out a pair of jeans and wiped up the deck in my bed room as our room boy hasn't got aboard and we don't know where the two of them are. Went back aft and stood around the trash burner. Weather changeable this morning but real nice out now and the sun is shining.

9PM. The Gunnery Officer was ashore and came back with very pleasant news that it would be about a month before we would go to the dock as there would be four or five ships ahead of us.

Sun Oct 10

The deck gang painted out the passageways today and our rooms are full of paint smell and hard on the eyes, so think I will go to bed and put out the light so I can open the port. Sunset at 7:30pm. Don't feel any too happy.

Mon Oct 11
8:30PM. The weather today has not been so bad through the day but boy it is miserable, raining and cold. Last night I got so cold, so today got another blanket from the Steward so I can have the ports open and get all the fresh air I can. The *Greenup*, *Diamond Cement* and another ship came back and they had gone all the way to Adak. They will go to the dock ahead of us. The news is that we won't get to the dock before the last of the month. The tobacco that I got is not much good, as it is moldy and dried out and had to throw some away. Quite a few planes leave in the morning and back in the evening.

Am reading some of the Outline of History. The Capt. don't feel so good, had to leave the table at supper. Will start eating some Garlic as my heart beats a little too fast. Will turn in soon. Another rainbow today.

Tues Oct 12
9PM. Raining all day and blowing hard from the southeast. When I went to the supper table no one was saying a word and all heads hung down so when I got through I got up and beat it, remarking what a sociable gang, but I suppose everyone is feeling this enforced idleness. Was below all morning showing the third and cadet how to find the tools and do a job and they seem to want to learn. Some of the men received letters today, but not me. Saw two tugs towing lighters headed, I think, for Shemya. Will read a little, eat some garlic, and then to bed.

Wed Oct 13
11:30PM. Worked below all morning. After lunch the Capt. Gunnery Officer and myself went ashore in the ship's boat and I went aboard the *Greenup* and gave Randall a letter to Murphy and asked him to call Gen up. Had my blood pressure taken by the navy doctor and he said it is too high and he said not to worry and watch my eating which I do. Got back at four o'clock. At 7:45pm there was a Jap air raid and everything was blasting away and we got ready in a hurry and pulled out of the bay with the other ships but were ordered back so here we are anchored again. Not so pleasant. Will go to bed now.

Thurs Oct 14
9:30PM. Today has been a fine day only the wind has been blowing hard. Planes have been buzzing around all day and still are. A Sub went out and

other naval craft also. Saw a tug coming back with a loaded lighter and I suppose from Chemya and it must be tough to land anything there. Missed my bath yesterday but will take it before I go to bed.

They say the Japs didn't do any damage but it was just luck as plenty of bombs were falling at the head of the bay, and some down this way. Lots of wild shooting from the ships. The last one of our planes landed at 11pm.

Fri Oct 15
10PM. Been raining and blowing most of today and I don't care how long the weather holds this way. Took my bath after lunch. Three Cruisers and three Destroyers came in at one o'clock and went out again at 7pm also the *Maine* and *Christopher Greenup* left and wished it was us. All the gunnery officers on these cargo ships were ordered not to shoot unless by orders from ashore, unless attacked by dive bombers. Most of the heavy bombers attack at about 20,000 Ft and these 20MM guns are only good for 3000ft and the guns ashore are 90MM and good for 20,000 ft, and with so much going on it confuses the ones ashore. To bed.

Sat Oct 16
9PM. Weather changeable today but looked a little to good near sunset as we don't want the weather to good now. A passenger ship came in this morning and went to the navy dock. Had the gang in the engine room practice trying on the gas mask so they will know how if we have to use it. Just been poking around all day, don't feel any too lively tonight so will go to bed.

Sunday Oct 17
1:30PM. Was below this morning regulating the fires also a navy man was over to see about my giving a destroyer some fuel oil. Last night it snowed some and half way down the mountains are covered. It is nice day so far. They lost some more lighters at Chemya. Wish I were home.

9PM. No rest this afternoon as there were two alerts and a case of getting the engine ready each time. Ships at the dock had to move away each time and then go back again. Lots of planes up and all ships ready. Blowing hard and raining tonight. The Steward had to get some stores from the Army and he had some corn beef hash and I hope they don't spoil it. Think I will sleep tonight.

Mon Oct 18
9:30PM. We moved to the dock at 7:30pm and they have started to unload, and are all hands happy. Have the water hose out as that is one of the first things we do. Was just talking to a colored longshore

boss and he said he saw them knock the engine off one of the Jap bombers, he also said that there was a dog fight over Aggatu Island yesterday. They are sure on their toes around here now. Tokyo said they lost five planes. Some received letters today and some didn't and I was one that didn't. Fine weather up to 4pm then it clouded over with a low ceiling. Will take a look around, then to bed.

Tues Oct 19
6PM. Got up at 7 and after breakfast I took a letter to the ATS hut and mailed it to Gen, then took a walk to the top of the hill and looked down and saw where they are piling the Chemya freight, and there is a pile of it. Then I went out to where they dump the coal and there must be thousands of tons, then came back to the ship. This afternoon the Capt and I went over to the *William T Sherman* and I saw Egaas and several others that I know. She arrived this morning and is laying at navy town, the *Lamont* also got in and I heard that Coops is not on her. Major Peterson took us over in a Jeep and back again and the mud sure flew. Its been raining all day. Wars sure cost money, this is small I think compared with Europe or the south seas, but it sure looks big when one looks around. Haven't made much progress with the unloading as they are shy of trucks, to many boats in. Egaas said that his wife wants to get some land outside of the city. Am going to bed early.

Wed Oct 20
7PM. Last night it blowed a gale and the rain came down in torrents, but not so much wind or rain today. The *American Star*, *Diamond Cement* and *Iola* left at 5pm. The Capt heard from the chief of the *Lamont* that the Coops got off our place the 28th of Sept and that was a little good news. The *Rolvaag* came in to the other dock and she is loaded with bombs and gasoline, not so good for her to be so close. Last night when I opened my port, I thought it was hooked good, but when I looked out, the port light and dead light dropped on my head so I have a black eye and cut cheek, but will live through it. The deck load is off and they have started in the holes and working all hatches and have plenty of trucks so the unloading should speed up. Ironed some shirts.

Thurs Oct 21
7PM. After breakfast I walked over to the other pier and went aboard an invasion barge that they are loading for Chemya and they are some large affair, 317 FT long and lots of room to put things in. They can open the bow and trucks and tanks can go in and out. I walked along the beach going over and I picked up some lemons and apples that had floated up on the beach, so I will eat a lemon in the morning.

When I got back, the Capt was starting out for navy town to get a hair cut so I joined him and when going up the dock Major Peterson came along with a Jeep and picked us up and drove out near the lake where they are piling Chemya freight, and what a place, everything on can think of is piled out there. He then drove up the valley and showed us where thousands of barrels of gasoline, diesel and stove oil are stored. Then we went to the barber and I got a good hair cut, then I walked back to the ship alone. Egaas came over for a little while. Today has been fine but has clouded up and looks like fog. Three more ships came in and are laying out near the point. My eye is sure black. I had a good steak for supper, the first I have eaten this trip. We are near out of butter. The cargo is going out pretty good as we are getting most of the trucks. Will read some.

Fri Oct 22
10PM. Today has been bad, there has been wind, rain, and fog. Mailed a letter to Gen and they said it would go out this afternoon but I don't see how with this weather. Just poking around looking at the cargo, and go below at times. I heard that a little boat was lost with all hands. Will go to bed and read.

Sat Oct 23
1PM. What a country, this morning it was blowing a southeast gale when I got up and at eleven o'clock all ships had to move away from the dock as the swells were too heavy and we would damage the pier. Then I had a little trouble below with the Aux Condenser. Will have to go below and look at some valves.

11PM. Wind died down so we came back to the dock at 7pm. Went aboard the *Ole E Rolvaag* and met the chief & capt and some of the rest and a right nice bunch but didn't stay long. Another Liberty ship came in, the *Jack London* and that makes seven ships in the bay. Will go to bed but don't feel like sleeping.

Sunday Oct 24
10AM. Got up at seven, had breakfast, took bath and shaved, changed clothes ad wound clock, so I am all set. Cloudy this morning with a little drizzle. Cargo going pretty good.

6PM. Went down to supper but didn't eat any as wasn't hungry. I heard that the Quartermasters Dept burnt up a lot of brand new clothing and shoes but wouldn't issure them to the men. Most of the men up here think this war is only a racket. These colored men are unloading four of the holds and get army pay which is about $50 a month, the deck dept unload the other and make about $30 per day and work twelve hours the same as the troops. Most of the men are only thinking of the day when they will leave here. I don't see how the human race stand for what they do without rebelling against the ones that cause it. I also heard that some men on these ships sell whiskey to the soldiers at $50 per quart and I think they should be shot. I can hear the colored troops kidding each other and they seem to be the most cheerful on the island.

10PM. Been sitting in the mess room listening to some towboat capt talk.

An Aviator was aboard this afternoon who has flown over Paramushiru(Jap island) in a reconnaissance plane, said they saw lots of Russian ships in the harbor and wonder if Russia is selling Japan things she gets from us. Cold out tonight. Will hit the hay.

Mon Oct 25
3PM. This morning when I got up what is left of the moon was shining, also the stars, a little while latter it was hailing, then sunshine, now it is half snow and rain. The mountains are covered with snow which fell during the night. Two of the Liberty ships that were laying in the bay are at the other dock. This morning I went around the winches to see how they are working.

8PM. Its snowing hard and everything covered and also cold. I see there is another Liberty ship in and anchored in the bay. Will go to bed early as the noise made me lose a lot of sleep last night.

Tues Oct 26
9PM. This morning everything was covered with snow and there was snow squalls up to noon, then it cleared up and the sun came out but it still stays cold. Stars are out now. No one likes clear weather around sunset as that is the best time for an air raid. Have been out on deck most all day and feel rather tired so will go to bed. The cargo is very nearly out.

Wed Oct 27
11:45PM. This has been to tough a day to do any writing now, will wait till morning.

Thrus Oct 28
9AM. The wind has swung around to the northwest and blowing a gale. Didn't sleep much last night as we rolled quite hard.

Yesterday was one H—of a day. A strong southeast gale came yesterday morning and lasted until this morning. I had trouble with the water barge and got wet getting things straightened out, and then it was one thing after another until we moved away from the dock at 6pm. In getting away we rammed a schooner, and a time turning around. When we got anchored, she started to drag so the skipper hove the anchors up and then couldn't handle her in such a

wind so we drifted down the bay again nearly running down some small boats that had depth charges on them, and they say the men on them were screaming for us to keep away. We rammed the schooner again and struck something with the propeller and we sure had two narrow escapes from going ashore.

The *Rolvaag* went on the beach and three other small boats and the small ones are smashed up, but they got the *Rolvaag* off with a number of tugs and she is anchored back of us. Theses Liberty ships are sure unmanageable when light and I don't want any part of them. Will look around.

10PM. Been busy all day at different jobs and feel very tired. There's been lots of worry around this place. There was about 60 tons of sacked coal dumped over the side that was left in the deep tanks. Will see if I can sleep.

Fri Oct 29
3PM. This morning the wind had changed after blowing a gale all last night and has been blowing hard today with snow squalls. Have been filling water in #4 & 5 holds for ballast. AT LAST we have orders to sail at 4pm and I am glad. Will have to get anything that will move secured as they say these crates can roll when light.

7PM. Attu is fading away in the distance and that's the last I will see of it, we have been there one month and I feel sorry for the rest of them that have to lay there waiting. The sun was out till just a little while ago, but now it has clouded over. Rolling a little but its better than being in that bay not knowing when the ship was going to drag her anchors. We are the only ship going to Adak and have one convoy boat. Will go to bed early as the last few night have been bad.

Sat Oct 30
9AM. Last night we did some rolling but not to bad. The wind seems too strong. Just did some wash. Will work some on the log. The patrol boat we have with us makes us run zig-zag courses.

10PM. Have just been below to see how she is going as the engine is racing some as there are heavy seas running. About noon the wind started getting stronger and now we are in a southeast gale and the old ship trembles all over. Rained a lot today. Will read some and then to bed.

Sun Oct 31
4:30PM. Adak—Arrived here 3pm after a day of rolling around. It was blowing out at sea but its sure terrible in this harbor. Took bath this morning and washed clothes. Ships here waiting to go to Attu and I pity them. Attu to Adak 422 miles.

Mon Nov 1

Didn't get a chance to do any more on this log last night as she was rolling too hard. When we got to Adak they told us we were going to leave right away, then said anchor for the night, then at 7:30 they signaled out to get underway and join the convoy of three other ships that were leaving. It was dark then and the Capt came near running down a Tanker and a small navy boat. When we got outside it was sure boiling and we have been rolling about 35 degrees all night with no sleep. Everything that could move did so and our storeroom is a mess. Not much cooking going on.

10AM. The weather seems a little better but still blowing hard. Got away from the other ships during the night so we ARE on our own. Engines racing.

10PM. Wind not so strong, sea a little smoother so I think all hands will get a little more sleep, so will see how I make out.

Tues Nov 2

11AM. At 10am we passed Bogoslof Island on our port side, and the story is that it sunk and came up again, we can also see Umnak Island. Some swell from the port quarter and engines race some, not much wind. Have been back to the steering engine doing some adjusting. Feel a little better as I get nearer home.

6:30PM. Arrived Dutch Harbor 3pm and left at 4:30. The convoy that we were supposed to be in arrived an hour ahead of us. There were two Liberty ships on the way out when we were going in and one left while we were there, then us, and one more to leave after us. Everything had snow on it around Dutch Harbor and cold and reminded me of the last trip to Nome. It sure looks gloomy out tonight. No mail for anyone at D.H. and suppose it was at Adak. The Cruisers that came down to Attu were laying at D.H. and a long way from any trouble. We are going out by way of Unimak Pass. Will do some log work and go to bed soon. Adak to Dutch Harbor 420 miles.

Wed Nov 3   At Sea

10PM. What a change from being in the Bering Sea. Today has been not to bad, sunshine and cloudy at times and the sun had a little warmth which makes one feel altogether different. Had fire and boat drill. The *Garrison*, a Liberty ship, passed us at 3 o'clock but our propeller is damaged or she wouldn't have done it. A little moonlight tonight. Clock goes ahead a ½ hour so will turn in.

Thurs Nov 4   At Sea

10AM. Got up at 6:30 and shaved and went on deck but it was dark. We only have dried eggs now and they are not so good. Was down #1 hold showing them a job to do. Wind from the northwest and not very strong. Cloudy now.

10PM. We are south of Kodiak Island and it is cold out tonight. Had a strong northwest wind up to 8 o'clock but now it has died down a lot, but some sea running. Had turkey for lunch and I tried some but it was NG. Pumped out #1 deep tanks so as to bring her down by the stern some. Will retire. Clock goes ahead one hour.

Fri Nov 5   At Sea

9:30AM. They only set the clock ahead a ½ hour last night so I got up at 6:30 instead of 7. I woke up at 1am hungry so got up and had some nuts and a few prunes. I also dreamt of eating. Fair wind and sea and cloudy. Had dried eggs and army butter for breakfast and don't think I would want them for a steady diet. Ship rolled a lot last night.

10PM. Weather about the same with a little less sea running. Been reading some and will go to bed as the clock will go ahead one hour for sure.

Sat Nov 6   At Sea

7PM. Well, its just been another day and nothing much to say.

Cloudy all day, not much wind but a heavy swell and the old ship rolls around like a tub. The first asst sure chisels any overtime but I won't say anything now as I don't want him to quit as he will be the only engineer left as the second and third are going up and get their licenses raised. Will have a cup of cocoa after a while.

Mon Nov 7   At Sea

7PM. Last night no one got any sleep as the ship rolled so hard and has been the same all day. It did let up a little around five o'clock but seems to be starting in again. Was catching up with a ship but it got out of sight in the haze. When a choppy sea hits these ships, they tremble all over. Feel out of sorts tonight.

Mon Nov 8   At Sea

7AM. Woke up thinking about what a lot of no good punks there are going to sea, and the third that I thought might be alright turned out to be just another no good Wop. Still rolling around. Will eat.

7PM. Ship has been rolling, pitching, and pounding and some rain. The seas seem to have gone down some (we just started in to roll hard) and thick fog has set in. Feel nervous and the grub is NG. Forgot to mention that there is 11 civilian and 13 soldier passengers aboard and they sleep in what we term the dog houses.

They are blowing the whistle but are not supposed to, but there might be some other ships around and none of the ships burn any running lights. Looks like a little sleep tonight.

Tues Nov 9th   At Sea
11:45PM. Smooth sea today and cloudy. Have been busy pumping tanks and making up shop orders. No more butter and about all out of everything. Passed Cape Flattery 11:25

Wed Nov 10
4AM. Stopped at Port Angeles for orders and will leave in a few minutes.

   9AM. Will arrive pier B army dock so will close the log after a very bad trip. Dutch Harbor to Seattle 1775 mile.

                              ***

```
        SS CUSHMAN K DAVIS
      VOY #1
    NORTHBOUND , PORTLAND TO
    NUSHAGAK IN BRISTOL BAY,
    ALASKA.
       DISTANCE RUN 2814 MILES,
           "   BY REV,S 2746 MILE,S
    # OF REV,S 1011675
       AVERAGE SPEED 12
    SLIP % 2.4 NEG
    RUNNING TIME 9DAYS 18 HOURS
    18 MINS

    PORTLAND TO SEATTLE 364   MILES
    SEATTLE TO PT, WELLS  14    "
       "       BELLINGHAM 78    "
       "       AKUTAN    1810   "
    AKUTAN TO NAKNEK    392    "
    NAKNEK TO NUSHAGAK   64    "

    NUSHAGAK TO AKUTAN  394    "
    AKUTAN TO FALSE PASS 129    "
    FALSE PASS TO KING COVE 46  "
    KING COVE TO SQUAW HARBOR 88 "
    SQUAW HARBOR TO CHIGNIK  120 "
    CHIGNIK TO KODIAK      255   "
    KODIAK " BELLINGHAM  1292  "
                      NAUTICAL
                      MILES
```

    This was the final voyage of Benjamin Parker's career. The old man of the sea was callin' 'er quits. He would spend the rest of his days in safe harbor. From now on Charlie would carry on the family sea-going tradition. When Charlie made it home for brief stints in 1943, he made the most of his time. There was a certain girl…

CHAPTER XV

On to Victory!

For Charlie, a "Danish"

In the early forties Charlie met his future wife Wilhelmina Anna Brandt, daughter of Frederick Jorgensen Brandt and Anna Marie, both Scandinavians. Charlie's attraction to Willie was natural as she was a tall, blond, beautiful young girl. Charlie's father Ben was pleased with Willie and was always nice to her, but Genevieve had a mother-in-law's jealousy for her only boy. Genevieve thought that Willie was a little too fancy for her boy, but Charlie seemed happy all right.

Willie's father Frederick Brandt was a scrappy farm lad from the Danish isle of Moen. He was in America to stay, but he was very proud of his homeland. He had come to Seattle with near nothing, and had grown rich in construction and real estate management. Fred was all about money, and he was a hard man to work for. He built houses and businesses all over Seattle. Willie had six brothers and sisters. Fred had achieved the kind of success a farm boy from old Denmark could dream of.

Charlie and Willie were married in May of 1943 and began a life together in West Seattle. In their early years Charlie could be a little critical of Willie, later in their life it would be the opposite.

During the rest of the war years the young couple went to California a lot because of Charlie's duties. They liked San Francisco and Charlie even wanted to move there, but Willie wanted to stay close to family. Willie had six brothers and sisters in the Seattle area and never lacked for social opportunities. This generation would be noted for parties and entertaining, both with family and friends. Willie was a proper and socially disciplined young girl, however, and entertaining in those days was a little milder and more formal than today, though still jovial. The 1930's and 40's were noted for alcohol consumption and cigarette smoking, but Willie would never partake much of either of these her whole life. Charlie on the other hand, would partake and then some. Charles went to sea and Willie was a housewife with an occasional part

Charles and Willie on the right. This shot was taken in July of 1943, two months after they were married.

time job. Willie eventually found that the life of a mariner's wife could be lonely at times.

While Ben was in the Bering Sea getting ready to go to Attu, Charlie shipped out on the *Northwind* on May 28, 1943 being promoted to 2nd Assistant Engineer. The *Northwind* was an armed diesel-electric icebreaker, built for the Coast Guard in 1942, but being operated by the Navy. This trip only lasted until July 22.

A couple of weeks later Charlie shipped out on the Liberty Ship *S.S. Samuel Lancaster*. The keel of the *Samuel Lancaster* had been laid just weeks before, on July 14. She was launched August 3, 1943, and Charlie was assigned to her on the 7th of August. These were the frantic days of the Atlantic convoys and their terrible losses to the U-boat Wolf-packs. American merchant shipping losses in 1942 and 1943 were staggering. This trip lasted until just before Christmas that year. On top of that, the Chief of the *Lancaster* was a tough old curmudgeon nick-named "Gloomy Gus." 1943 was the longest

year of Charlie's life.

In the Atlantic Charlie saw his ship and the ships around him fired upon by torpedoes from the German U-boats. Charlie told his grandson that his ships had torpedoes launched at them more than once. Fortunately they all missed, but that has got to be a character building experience. Charlie related that ships nearby his in their convoy were not so lucky and fell prey to the U-boats. It is very easy to believe that Charlie saw some of his fellow merchant mariners meet their end in the icy North Atlantic. His ship likely picked up survivors at least once.

The telegraph from the bridge was labeled with STOP, SLOW AHEAD, HALF AHEAD, FULL AHEAD, ASTERN, and "Finished With Engine." Several decks down, the black gang was ever wary that if a torpedo struck its mark amidships, they would be *Finished*—With Engine.

There is a movie "Action in the North

Atlantic," staring Humphrey Bogart which depicts the Merchant Marine service in WWII. It is a propaganda film, made in 1943, but it is very good. It gives you a bit of the feel of the times. There is even a character in the film named "Ensign Parker," a young cadet studying to be a Merchant Marine officer. A fictitious character, this Parker is a deck officer. However, this movie was made when Charlie was going to sea in the convoys and it must have been quite an ego boost at the time. Unfortunately, the Parker in the movie dies at the end.

Charlie was a man of his times. Much like the characters played by actor John Wayne, such as in the movie "The Sea Chase," both a little bit of a scoundrel and hero, with a good heart.

January and February 1944 Charlie went to turbo-electric school at Treasure Island Naval Station in San Francisco bay. Charlie was to have a long-term love affair with San Francisco. He would sail out of the City by the Bay many, many times. He even wanted to move there at one time, he liked the Sausalito area, but Willie wouldn't have anything to do with it. Probably a good choice, but even today the Sausalito area is very nice. In those days San Francisco was a very romantic city indeed, that was the city's golden era.

Charlie finished turbo-electric school February 19, 1944; and was promptly returned to war. His next ship was the *U.S.S. Pequot*

Hill, a seven-month old T2-SE-A1 tanker, 523' in length and 21,880 tons laden, with turbo-electric power of 6000 shaft horsepower.

The famous Liberty class ships of the first part of World War II, employing the outdated, even at the time, triple expansion steam piston engines, were being superceded by the Victory's early in 1944. Charlie said that the Liberty ships were very primitive ships. Later in life, while reflecting about the war period, Charlie reminisced that he was proud of his Victory-class ship, however, being steam turbine powered and state of the art in 1944. Charlie writes home April 5, 1944.

Well, am at anchor on this wagon and this trip shouldn't be to long although we are not doing anything at present. Haven't had any major troubles as yet and it has run along o.k. Will be glad to get back however. Find out the dope on those Victory ships—maybe the Alaska S.S. will get a couple of them. Got a pretty good sun tan but have sweat it all out down here. This fireroom is sure hot and noisy with those big forced blowers roaring away and as far as noise is concerned an up and down has them beat a mile. According to the 1st however the up and downs are a thing of the past but I still think that they will be running them after the war.

The "up and downs" Charlie refers to are reciprocating piston engines. Victory ships were used extensively after the war for commercial shipping. Charlie would make a career out of the turbo-electric VC2 "Victory" and the similarly powered and highly commercially viable C2 and C3 ships.

A couple of months later Charlie writes again "Just a line to say I'm o.k. and expect this trip to be a little bit longer than I expected." He gives some particulars about the boiler tests, fuel oil heaters and the evaporator. He hasn't been feeling very well "Wish this tub would ramble back to the U.S. so I could pile off of it. Sure get tired of steaming all over the ocean." Then Charlie writes in early September.

Just another hasty note to tell you I am ok but "fading" fast as was just informed we had another trip to make which is bad. I won't get home until the last of Oct. and maybe Nov. now. It has also been very hot the last couple of days and that always makes me feel lousy.

The cleaning the boilers got didn't seem to help them any and it still takes a lot of air pressure to force through the air heaters which are plugged up. The soot blowers don't do a very good job any more and both safety valves on the superheaters have given us trouble.

This is supposed to be our last haul however so can look forward to going to the States after it is over and I suppose we will end up on the East Coast. Well, I don't care so long as there is a dock there where I can get away from this thing.

In the Pacific Charlie participated in the battle for Leyte Gulf, which took place in late October of 1944. This was the huge D-Day style invasion of the Philippine Islands headed by General Macarthur. The force consisted of 738 ships and smaller craft carrying 200,000 men and their equipment. This was the Seventh Fleet commanded by Vice Admiral Kincaid. Most of the vessels were landing craft, but there was a battle fleet present including six battle ships resurrected from Pearl Harbor. Also part of the operation was Admiral Halsey's Third Fleet, which represented the bulk of the U.S. naval power. Charlie's ship served in direct support of this invasion, his fleet-oiler was to help the armada keep gassed-up.

This operation turned out to be the last big naval battle with the Japanese in WWII. The Japanese had divided their fleet in two. One fleet was supposed to lure the majority of the American naval forces, the Third Fleet

commanded by Admiral Halsey, away from Leyte Gulf while the other Japanese fleet, which was itself divided in two, was supposed to destroy the American invasion force with a pincer movement from two sides. The Japanese almost met with some success. The actions took place between October 23-26 and were actually 5 battles. Charlie no doubt had heard that the Japs were coming sometime on the 23rd. The first two actions took place that day on the other side of the Philippines. The Japanese force sent to destroy the American invasion armada was divided into two groups, as stated earlier. The southern force, consisting of battleships, cruisers, and destroyers was coming up to Leyte Gulf through Suriago Strait on the night of the 24th. They met the old battlewagons, the ones that had been at Pearl Harbor, of the Seventh Fleet in the middle of the night off the southern end of Leyte and a devastating naval battle ensued. Charlie looked out over at the giant flashes and explosions as the Jap southern force was almost annihilated under the stars of the night sky.

There was a center Japanese force also coming to destroy the invasion force, and it was much more powerful than the one the Seventh fleet destroyed in the early morning. Admiral Halsey and his Third fleet were supposed to be guarding the San Bernardino Strait waiting for them, but he had taken the bait and was in pursuit of the Jap decoy force heading north away from Leyte. Admiral Halsey's fleet, however, dealt the Japanese decoy force of four aircraft carriers and other ships harsh blows.

The Japanese center force caught the invasion force defended by only destroyers, and small aircraft carriers. This, the battle off Samar, was almost a great disaster for the U.S. forces, and actually the objective of the Japanese planners. Ships like Charlie's tanker were the juicy targets they were after. However, the U.S. Navy attacked with ferocity, and used smoke to cover themselves, and the Japanese were duped into thinking there was a larger U.S. force, perhaps elements of the Third Fleet. They were also heavily attacked from the air. They withdrew, and the relatively lightly guarded invasion force was spared a worse fate. The Japanese sunk three destroyers and one escort carrier.

Charlie enjoying one of a sailor's favorite pastimes in his cabin. Charlie was a man of his times. A lot like the characters played by actor John Wayne, such as in the movie **The Sea Chase.** *Charlie even had the same slanted smile as the actor. And Charlie might even be described as a little like Humphrey Bogart in the old movie* **Action In The North Atlantic.** *Yes, like any good sailor he was a bit of a scoundrel, but a man admired by men. And, he had charm.*

In the whole of the battle at Leyte Gulf and at sea, the Japanese lost three battleships, four aircraft carriers, nine cruisers, destroyers and other ships, totaling 26. The great Imperial Japanese Navy would no longer be a threat. This was the largest naval battle in history, and it was the last great naval battle in history.

Charlie's networking efforts paid off and December 21, 1944 Charlie shipped out on *S.S Kodiak Victory,* which was registered to the Alaska Steamship Company, headed out of Portland coastwise to San Francisco. From there they made a foreign trip, which lasted until the end of March . Easy money by this point in the war. Charlie was now promoted to 1st Assistant Engineer, his career was moving at break-neck speed. In just a couple of years he had become First Assistant Engineer on a turbine powered ship, life was good.

The American Mail Line and APL

The Seattle based American Mail Line had been a part of the Dollar Steamship Company and therefore had close ties with American President Lines. When the government took over Dollar Steam and transferred its assets to APL, American Mail was separated for a time.

In April 1945 Charlie was given the Chief Engineer job on the Victory-class ship *Furman Victory*, which he sailed on under the flag of the American Mail Line. He was her first Chief, and she was his first Chief's job. At twenty-four years old, it has been said that Charlie was the youngest Chief Engineer in the history of the M.E.B.A. union.

The keel of the *Furman Victory* had been laid down January 23, 1945. The ship was a VC2-S-AP3, which was an up-engine model from the more widely produced 6000 shaft horsepower VC2-S-AP2. The faster AP3 had 8,500 hp. The ship was delivered on the 19th of April, and Charlie was listed as her Chief Engineer on the 20th. His discharge book states that they were on a foreign trip, which lasted until just before Christmas, December 12, 1945. By then, the war was long over, and Charlie's peacetime sea-going career had begun. Christmas 1945 was a time for rejoicing.

Charlie earned the Merchant Marine Combat Bar, and the ribbons for the Pacific Combat Zone, and Atlantic Combat Zone.

Furman Victory was transferred to American President Lines June of 1946. Charlie continued as Chief on her for APL through February 1948, on the round-the-world route via the Panama and Suez canals, and departing from San Francisco, Los Angeles, and New York. *Furman Victory* steamed through the Pacific, South Pacific, Indian Ocean, the Red Sea and the Suez Canal, Mediterranean, and back across the Atlantic to the U.S. east coast and Caribbean to do it all again.

Charlie and Willie in 1945. Charles jr. was born November 1944.

The VC2-S-AP3 Victory ship **Furman Victory,** *Charlie's first chief's job. Note the wartime gun tubs and fast deploying life rafts.*

The Victory ships were the successors to the famous "Liberty" ships of World War II. They were a more advanced design however, using steam turbo-electric power, and were used more extensively after the war. This model had a C3 engine of 8,500 shaft horsepower, 2,500 more than the "standard" model. The reciprocating engines of the Liberty ships had only 2,500 SHP.

The steam turbine was actually invented in 1897, but it wasn't until the 1920s that it was perfected and came into wider use. The steam turbine had blades similar to those that would later be in a jet engine. In fact it was the precursor to the jet engine compressor.

Following page: *In the engine room on* **Furman Victory.** *Two turbines provide power for one shaft. The two high-speed steam turbines powered a giant electric generator via a reduction gearbox. The generated electricity drove a single giant electric motor that actually powered the ship. This electric drive was very flexible. The steam generating boilers of the ship were the same as in the old triple-expansion reciprocating engine days, but by now the coal-fired boilers had long since been supplanted by the more user-friendly oil-fired boilers. Boiler steam pressures became ever higher as the technology advanced.*

Charles with his father, Ben, in front of **Furman Victory.**

Charles with his mother, Genevieve.

CHAPTER XVI

Post War Prosperity

Charlie sailed for the American President Lines on *Furman Victory* until February 1948, then transferred to the American Mail line, who he sailed for until summer 1956. He alternated between Chief Engineer and First Assistant Engineer, but the money rolled in either way. The Parkers were to take a full measure of the post WWII prosperity. They would live the "happy days" of the 1950s.

In November 1944, Charlie and Willie had a son, Charles Jr., known as "Rusty" for the color of his hair. A few years later, they had a daughter, Annie. These two would occupy most of Willie's early years of marriage. With Charles gone most of the time, the children got the majority of their mother's attention.

Willie occupied herself with her children as a housewife in the 1940s & 50s. The family purchased a nice home in West Seattle, at that time it had a view of the city. Willie had several family members in the local area to keep busy with, and the Parker house was a social one. Willie had attended the Lutheran Church as a girl, but in adult life seldom attended.

Willie traveled with her father to the old country many times, and absorbed much of Danish culture, her whole family was very proud of their Danish heritage. Willie was active in the Scandinavian culture here in the Seattle area. Willie, like her sisters, was a long-time, and very active, member of the Danish Sisterhood in Seattle. Charlie had his own way of appreciating the Dane's organization, and would sometimes humorously call it "the box-head joint." Charlie had a good time with the Dane's however, and was even President of the Danish Brotherhood. On the whole, the old Scandinavians were a pretty good lot and the author as a young boy enjoyed being in their company.

In the first years after the war America struggled with recession while returning to a peacetime economy. The breakneck speed of production was slowed to a crawl, or cancelled altogether. Many of the Liberty ships built during the war were laid up. In Detroit, tanks ceased rolling off the assembly lines and auto production resumed. Typewriter companies, who had been making rifles, went back to typewriters, and etc. Back to business as usual. Same for America's unions, back to business as usual. Labor unrest promptly resumed post war.

The Parker family would have to endure challenges in the years immediately following the war also. Ben Parker had lived an interesting, if not hard, life. He had his early childhood troubles, with his natural parents dying young. Later he was to survive shipwrecks on the high seas. And after five decades of his sea going career, finally retiring to his Seattle home, he suffered a stroke in 1947 which rendered him partially paralyzed and unable to walk. Ben was working on a ladder outside at home, and fell on a fence. Ben lived for four years in a Marine Hospital during which his wife and children visited often. To make matters much worse, Ben's daughter Esther tragically succumbed to a stress related death in March of 1951, only forty-three years old. Ben finally died just ten days from his seventy-second birthday, Thursday, July 19,

S.S. Furman Victory *in post war APL livery sailing the globetrotting round-the-world route.*   CHP photo

"We can not list here all the ports of call on all the routes of the Cargoliners. However, here are most of the ports which you might possibly visit in the course of leisurely Cargoliner cruises: New York, Panama Canal, Los Angeles, San Francisco, Honolulu, Guam, Yokohama, Kobe, Nagoya, Otaru, Shimazu, Okinawa, Hong Kong, Manila, Iloilo, Cebu (and other Philippine outports), Sourabaya, Jakarta, Belawan, Singapore, Port Swettenham, Penang, Colombo, Cochin, Bombay, Karachi, Suez, Port Said, Alexandria, Naples, Leghorn, Genoa, Marseille."

"Just which of these ports you will see, or what others not mentioned in this list, will depend, of course, on what trip you take and how far you go."

Going through the Gatun Locks, Panama Canal.

"I can see why you don't get upset at the misspelled words in your letters."

AMERICAN MAIL LINE

Pacific Traders Short Route

SEATTLE	SAN FRANCISCO	PORTLAND
CHICAGO	NEW YORK	WASHINGTON, D. C.
VANCOUVER, B. C.	TACOMA	LOS ANGELES
LONGVIEW, WASH.	DETROIT	WINDSOR, ONT.

OCTOBER 1955	NOVEMBER 1955	DECEMBER 1955

"We'd be simply lost without our graphs."

AMERICAN MAIL LINE

PACIFIC TRADERS SHORT ROUTE

JUNE 1956	JULY 1956	AUGUST 1956

AMERICAN PRESIDENT LINES

311 CALIFORNIA STREET • SAN FRANCISCO, 4, CALIFORNIA, U. S. A.

Trans-Pacific Service • Round-World Service

October 9, 1951

Mr. Charles H. Parker
Chief Engineer, SS CANADA MAIL
American Mail Line
740 Stuart Building
Seattle, Washington

Dear Mr. Parker:

We have been informed by Mr. E. C. Morris of our Manila office that you rendered invaluable personal assistance to him in connection with certain replacement parts urgently needed in order to permit our SS PRESIDENT PIERCE to promptly continue her voyage.

Mr. Morris further informs us that you are the same Mr. Charles Parker who served as cadet in the SS PRESIDENT COOLIDGE from August 1940 to May 1941, and as Chief Engineer of the SS FURMAN VICTORY in our operation from June 1946 to February 1948. It is our pleasure to have our relationship renewed, even though in this instance it was while you were employed elsewhere. We do want you to know that we are highly appreciative of your fine assistance in this recent episode at Manila and trust that we will be able to reciprocate in some manner in due course of time.

By copies of this letter we are apprising Mr. Morris and our Assistant Operating Manager-Engineering, Mr. E. E. Mann, of our appreciation. At Mr. Morris's request we are not apprising your present employer, which appears to have been your desire.

Again, many thanks.

Sincerely yours,

O. W. Pearson
Vice President - Operations

TCC:fs

cc ECMorris, Manila
   EEMann, SF

The **American Mail,** *a C3.*

1951. These turn of events of course were not easy for Geneva, but she is said to have taken them as well as could be expected and remained cheerful, still attending her fiftieth high school reunion in Wichita. Geneva raised Esther's son James.

Willie's mother died in 1948, and her father a few years later in 1951. Her father had a large estate, a large family, and money had always been what Brandt was all about. A scandal ensued over the estate. These were the family's challenges at this time. But, once the 50s got going, there was no looking back.

At the end of World War II, the government began selling the wartime built Maritime Commission ships to private industry. They also

PACIFIC NORTHWEST TO THE ORIENT

JAPAN · CHINA · PHILIPPINES · MALAYA · N.E.I. · INDIA
AMERICAN MAIL LINE

FARES
and
General Information

FARE SHEET No. 4
Issued June, 1949
Subject to change without notice

sold ships to the American Mail Line and the American President Lines that the government owned. Especially valued were the C2s and C3s. Besides cargo, these ships also could carry a dozen passengers in first class comfort.

Ships that Charlie sailed on for American Mail were the C3 *American Mail* for most of 1948, the C2 *Java Mail* in '49, and the C3 *Canada Mail* from 1950 to 1956. In 1954 the American Mail Line was re-acquired by American President Lines, which was corporate owned again.

During Charlie's sailing career, he sailed to virtually every country in the world that had a seaport. The Mediterranean, Atlantic, Pacific, Indian Ocean, Caribbean, etc., he had tramped around to them all. He said of Italy, he had

Charles Parker.

never seen pizza on a menu, back in the day.

He sailed to exotic places like Rangoon in Burma, and Calcutta in India. In Bombay he said that you had to keep your hand over your beer to keep the bugs out of your glass. One time in India he consulted a palm reader, and she gave Charlie the grim advice that his life was going to end at fifty-eight years of age. This Charlie is said to have taken fairly seriously and it apparently always troubled him.

For American Mail he sailed to the Japanese ports of call at Yokohama, Kobe, and Nagoya. A regular stop was Hong Kong. In the South Pacific, Charlie visited ports of call in the Philippines at Manila, Cebu and Iloilo. On the Malaysian Peninsula at Singapore, Port Swettenham, and Panang. In Micronesia, the regular stops were fabled Indonesian islands of Java and Sumatra, respectively the ports of Djakarta and Medan. Sailing the Indian Ocean, Charlie visited the Punjab at the Indian ports of Calcutta and Madras, and at the island of Sri Lanka at Colombo.

Like those before him, Charlie was a mariner through and through. He loved ships and his job. He used to tell his grandson that he could tell how many knots the ship was making from his bunk in his stateroom, by the screw

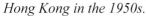
Hong Kong in the 1950s.

(propeller) vibrations transmitting through the ship. Even at home, he never went downstairs, he went "below." He did not go to the bathroom, he went to the "head." He did not decide that it was time to leave, rather that it was time to "shove off."

Like in previous generations, Charlie's being away all the time caused tensions at home and Charlie took a shore job for a few years, to be near the children as they were growing up. In 1956 Charlie took a shore job for an insurance company inspecting boilers.

Objects from C.H. Parker collection. Photos of objects by the author.

The **Rusty Ann.**

On Puget Sound

The sea going nature was natural to the Parkers, and the home life was no different. Charlie bought a boat in 1956, which he named the *Willey*, a twenty-two foot outboard boat that he swore burned way to much gas. Charlie had the *Willey* built in Japan, by a German, and then shipped back home. The next boat, acquired in 1957, was called the *Rusty Ann* and was a twenty-eight footer built by Grandy of Seattle in 1928. The third Parker vessel was the *Charmaine*, a thirty-two footer with gracefully beautiful lines. The northwest lends itself to yachting, with the extents of Puget Sound and the San Juan Islands farther north. The favorite and usual destination was Hood Canal.

Now we will entertain a sea story of a smaller nature, a Puget Sound sea story. It was spring break in 1958 and Charlie had brought his son and a couple of his cousins out to Blake Island on the *Rusty Ann* for a three-day adventure. The three little troopers were Rusty, Sandy, and Johnny. After Charlie had dropped off the boys, the weather had turned very much for the worse. Gusts up to sixty-five miles an hour, and Charlie began to worry about the well being of the little adventurers. They were camped on the east side of Blake Is. near the little cove there. The wind had downed their tent, and their attempts at building a fire had not gone well either.

It was late in the day when Charlie arrived on the scene in the *Rusty Ann*, amid the very choppy seas. He attempted to anchor in the little bay on the east side of Blake Is. Rusty made it out to the *Rusty Ann*. The anchor was now stowed. It was the usual practice on those slow, old boats to tow their dinghies behind them on a line. The *Rusty Ann* was drifting toward the nearby rocky shore, and she was attempting to go astern to keep some water under her keel. In the confusion, the towline for the dingy was caught up in the propeller, and now the *Rusty Ann* was definitely in a tight spot, drifting precariously towards the steep, rocky, shore. Charlie found himself in a most disagreeable situation, and thinking quickly, decided there was only one thing to do. He took off his shoes, grabbed a handy knife, put it between his teeth like in an old pirate movie, and dove in the numbing water to free up the propeller. Charlie cut the line from the propeller, got back in the boat, and motored *Rusty Ann* to safety just in time to avert a disaster.

After recovering the dingy, and getting the remaining members of the shore party on board, the decision was made to anchor on the northwest side of the Island. Well, the tide was going out and Charlie thought that he might have anchored to close to shore, so the order was given to weigh anchor. They ran the boat over the anchor to get it free of the bottom. Rusty was busy with the anchor line on the foredeck, but couldn't haul the line in; something was caught on the anchor. They motored out a bit into the bay, but the anchor wouldn't free itself, and the bow was starting to dip down under the weight of the strain. Charlie gave the order to little Rusty; "ah...to hell with it—cut the line." Rusty cut through one strand of the anchor line and the other two strands snapped under the tremendous weight alone. It turns out that old sailing ships had been burned and sunk off that part of the Island in the previous years, and that *Rusty Ann's* anchor line had snagged a spar or something.

Now it's three in the morning, no anchor, and in those days no dock to tie up to, so they had to make for home in the moonlit night. Not an attractive option in the days before small boats had navigational aids; but they made it home all right to the Riverside marina, feeling they had all been through quite an adventure. ■

Willie became a travel agent at the dawn of the jet age in the late 50s. Passenger travel to Europe now became really affordable to the masses. This picture was taken at a ceremony to mark Scandinavian Airline's first jet service from Europe to Seattle. This was a very significant event, and several dignitaries were present, including two senators and the Governor. Willie was there to represent the Danish contingent, she's on the right. Willie and Charlie went to Denmark on this maiden flight with the senators. Until well after the first half of the twentieth century, Scandinavian influence, art and culture could be felt throughout the entire region. Not a few businesses would represent this as well(i.e. "Scan" Travel, Viking...etc.).

The Parkers were to share full measure in the post World War II era prosperity. Charlie's job paid extremely well. The family lived in a nice house at 3057 36th Ave S.W. in West Seattle.

Young Rusty grew up completely spoiled. In 1959 he entered West Seattle High School. This was the *Beach Boys* era and Rusty lived as in a *Beach Boys* song. Letterman's jackets, hot rods, drag racing down the boulevards, speeding tickets, girls, drive-ins, Alki Beach, and parties on the custom built family yacht *Charmaine,* a sleek and fast thirty-two footer. *The Spud* fish-and-chips at Alki Beach was always a Parker family favorite. These were the last few years of innocence in post war America, the last few years of fun and games.

Charlie and Willie endeavored to invest wisely and made several real estate purchases, plus the property they both inherited. Later on in Charlie's retirement, these properties would be his occupation, in addition to inspecting boilers. In the early sixties Charlie traded the *Charmaine* for some investment property. He never bought another boat again. He had learned that often quoted definition of a boat: "a hole in the water into which one pours money." Instead, the family opted to build a weekend cabin on their beloved Hood Canal. From here on out, the Parker's were only interested in things that made money, not consumed it. Becoming a millionaire was an objective of Charlie.

There were plenty of friends and relatives to entertain. Parties were common, this generation loved to get together. Willie always had her Danish Sisterhood. With the coming of the jet age Willie found herself making trips to Europe and elsewhere every year. Many times Charlie would go also. The late fifties and sixties were the glamour age of air travel.

After raising her children through the 40s and 50s, Willie took a job at *Where to Go?* Travel Service in 1959 during the dawn of the jet age to learn the travel agent business. Willie was thirty-nine years of age. At first Willie worked for very little just to learn the business. In the early years of the jet age, the airlines were ultra fashionable, and a very hip business to be in. Save for Hollywood, no business was more chic. And Willie was all about money, like her father.

The inter-modal freight era.

In the fifties the subsidies to the maritime industry were taken away, and the industry would have to pull its own weight. The ship was loosing its prominence as the ultimate symbol of prestige to the airplane. To compound the problem, the airlines were now subsidized. Some of the weaker segments started to fail. The Alaska Steamship Company discontinued passenger service in 1954, continuing with freight service only. The company ran a fleet of EC-S-C1 Liberty ships. Alaska Steam was one of the pioneers of the new containerized "intermodal" freight system.

The main reason for Alaska Steam giving up passenger service was skyrocketing labor costs. The unions were continually making demands. The union standards were just as much, or more, an issue as labor rate. The company continually got less and less for its labor dollar; two people to do the job of one, etc., and that is not to mention the numerous strikes.

In 1954 two women took a holiday north to Alaska on the old *S.S. Alaska*, Gwen Mallory and Iris Short. They wrote a book, *Two Towels and an Orange,* about their little excursion the next year. Little did they know that this was the last year of Alaska Steam service. By this time the Alaska steam fleet was old and dilapidated,

the legacy of the war, and the labor movement was having strikes continually.

The book starts out in Seattle where the ladies board and are finding their way and getting acquainted with the ship. The *Alaska* had been built with an eye to cargo hauling, and passenger space was a bit squeezed.

> "What a small lounge! Where will they put all the people?"
> "Well, I can't find any place."
> "We'll just have to take refuge in the bar."
> "Ah, refuge, did you say? To heck with refuge! I'll take a Manhattan.
> "Hm-m, I'll take a coke—high."
> As we became refreshed, we readily became acclimated to the nautical atmosphere.
> When we went back to our stateroom, we still had no bathtowels. Well, we could return to the bar and ask the friendly waiter.
> "Press the button by your bunk," he said, "and tell the boy you're dirty as hell and have to have some bathtowels."
> So we staggered to our stateroom. I pushed the button—nothing happened. I pushed it twice. Still nothing happened, but the third time—ah! A cross, black geni appeared and grudgingly grumbled, "Whadda-yuh-all want?"
> We gave him the words as instructed. Right there we lost faith in the waiter, for the words did not work like a charm. He told us he didn't do such chores—they were the work of the room stewards who were all off shift. Finally, after much explaining, begging and coaxing, on our part, he appeared with a big supply of two bath towels.
> We were becoming educated fast to unionized labor. A man who brings an orange to a stateroom is not supposed to bring two towels. We never did find out on what shift each of these specialists worked.

A long era had passed. For the most part, the airlines were taking over passenger travel. The airlines were coming on strong in the fifties, and were clearly the way of the future. When all was said and done, people just wanted to get to their destination as soon as possible. For the same reasons, the passenger trains suffered the same fate. With the then new superhighways, Americans would rather drive, or fly. When Charlie had to travel to get to a ship's sailing, he flew there on a plane.

The shipping industry would have to gain

Photos from author's collection.

Seattle-based Alaska Steamship Company was one of the early pioneers of the inter-modal freight system.

In the inter-modal system, containers are loaded at the point of origin, and not reopened until arriving at their intended final destination. Trucks, trains, and large cranes do the lion's share of the work.

Containerization is a great labor saving system in the freight business. It eliminated a lot of longshoreman jobs, a group of workers who had historically been prone to labor strikes. In addition, when cargo had been loaded piece-by-piece every segment of a voyage, cargo was inevitably "lost" in transit. The container went a long way to curtail this. Containerized freight moves much faster, cheaper, and more reliably than the old way. This makes the cost of all imported goods much less than otherwise would be.

The post-war Alaska Steam freight business was home-ported at a larger and more modern Pier 42.

Alaska Steam made use of the slow reciprocating engine powered Liberty ships, unlike Seattle based American Mail Line, which made use of the larger turbine powered C3's.

Alaska Steam would not succeed in this endeavor, however, and a man named Malcom McLean would form Sea-land Service to take the inter-modal concept to the extreme and be wildly successful.

Today all sea-born freight carriers use this method.

efficiency. The cost of all goods moved over the oceans by the ship conveyance includes the cost of manufacture of the commodity, plus the costs of the shipping, and tariffs.

In the maritime shipping business there were of course the construction and maintenance costs of the ships, born by the shipping companies, and costs for port facilities born by the cities and the shipping companies.

The basic operational costs of the shipping were divided into two parts: The operation of the ships, i.e. fuel and crew, and the loading and unloading cost of the cargo, which was very significant.

In the glory days of the steamship, a port city had large docks, or "wharves," lined up on its waterfront. The city of Seattle still has many of these today. The dock had a large building on it that constituted a warehouse, passenger terminal, and offices. Freight was brought to the warehouse by truck or train. The ship, tied up next to the wharf, had large cranes on it over its cargo holds. The cranes were large enough to swing out over the wharf. Freight such as barrels, and pallets with stacks of various commodities tied down with nets were moved out from the warehouse to the dockside, where they were then loaded piece by piece to fill the ship's holds. This process required an army of workers called longshoremen. It was a tedious and laborious task, which required many days for each cycle, loading or downloading. While the ships were being loaded, the sailors would carouse the town. A lot of the freight might be sold or traded in close proximity of the waterfront. This was the action of a port city. But the small nature of a waterfront made it something of a choke point for this movement.

The longshoremen had formed powerful unions, and were prone to go on strike frequently. The longshoremen were often accused of helping themselves to some of the ship's cargo. In addition to the already tedious task of loading and unloading the ships, these factors contributed to a higher cost, than otherwise might be, of shipping anything by the sea-born conveyance. These costs would ultimately and inevitably be passed on to the end consumer.

There was an extremely ambitious North Carolina farm boy turned trucker named Malcom McLean, who had formed his own business in the struggling years of the Depression. He had become very successful, and had become the owner of the Pan Atlantic Steamship Company, which had a fleet of C2s, in the 50s. His dream idea had been to come up with a system to drive the trailers of the trucks directly onto the ships, eliminating the need for all the cargo handling, which amounted to a lion's share of the shipping labor cost, and consumed a huge amount of shipping time. By the early 60s his dream was coming to fruition. The "inter-modal container system" in which freight was loaded into a container at its source, then trucked to the train or ship, and loaded onto that medium, then shipped to final destination without ever being handled again. This company was known as Sea-Land Service. This system eliminated a lot of longshore handling labor traditionally used in bulk loading the ships. The unions of course were furious, they wanted to keep things the way they had always been. Port cities were affected also as the port infrastructure streamlined and shrunk. In Seattle the freight handling went from downtown waterfront piers where it had always been, to a container terminal at the south end of Eliot Bay.

The container ships became specialized to their task and very large. Many of the popular C2s were converted to this specialized task. And when the larger C4s became available in the sixties, they were a natural choice for a container ship.

The cranes on the ships were removed, and the containers were loaded by land-based cranes. This inter-modal container system revolutionized shipping efficiency, it was a major game changer. The container ships were made very large to handle the volume, and a fewer quantity of ships were required to handle a given tonnage of cargo containers. With fewer ships, this of course meant fewer seamen were required for a given tonnage of cargo. Some people didn't like this. Of course, with an increase in efficiency, more cargo can be moved. Over time, that is what happened. More cargo was moved, a lot more. And it moved a lot faster.

In 1961 Charlie sought a commission in the U.S. Navy reserve, but was rejected for some kind of physical standards problem, possibly his asthma.

Shore jobs didn't pay enough, so in 1961 Charlie went back to work for the American Mail Line as a 1st Assistant Engineer on the *Java Mail*. In 1963 Charlie had worked his way back up to Chief Engineer on the *Java Mail,* but then he left the American Mail Line. This was a tough year for him. His son had gotten married to a very young teenage girl, who was pregnant, and life at home was in turmoil.

This was a tough year for America as well, the year President John F. Kennedy was assassinated, son of the first head of the Maritime Commission, Joseph Kennedy.

Charlie worked as a 2nd and 3rd Assistant on a few trips the rest of '63 through the summer of '64.

In the late fifties, many C4 ships that had been kept in the Reserve Fleet were struck from the register, and in the mid-sixties they started to be purchased by the shipping companies.

In June of 1964 Charlie got on with Sea-Land, and shipped out on the *S.S. Anchorage* as a 1st Assistant. The *S.S. Anchorage* was a C4 that had been enlarged and modified to carry containers. The *Anchorage* made its name by bringing regular year round service to Alaska through the ice. Sea-Land's container ships made their mark supplying the Viet Nam conflict and proving the viability of the inter-modal container system.

Charlie was 1st Assistant on the *Anchorage* through to the end of 1965, then he became

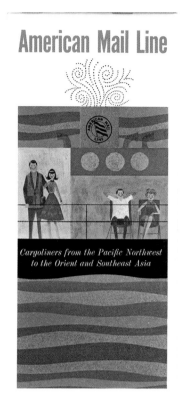

American Mail Line

Cargoliners from the Pacific Northwest to the Orient and Southeast Asia

Chief Engineer again through 1967, when Charlie became a business agent for the M.E.B.A. union.

While Charlie was business agent for the union, he led the only walkout by the Washington State ferryboat engineers that ever took place, in 1969. His son Charles jr. remembered a day when his pops said, "come on, lets go downtown." When they got down to the Coleman Dock, Chuck learned of their mission.

Charlie was a popular business agent, and when he ran for office in the union, everyone that he talked to said they voted for him. But, the other guy won the office. Charlie had the opinion that the election was dirty, and that the union had put "their man" in.

Wilhelmina and Scan Travel, Ltd.

Through the 1960s airline travel exploded. U.S. and European airlines grew by leaps and bounds. Affordable travel for the masses had arrived.

After working as an agent for many years, Willie struck out on her own and formed *Scan Travel, Ltd.* Located at 5th and Union, it didn't take Willie long to make the downtown travel agency a success.

As the name implies, at first the business specialized in tours and travel to the Scandinavian countries. This worked well in Seattle because like Willie, there were many Scandinavians in the area that still had close ties with the homeland of their fathers.

Willie's nature suited her well for business. This was no cookie baking, dinghy old lady. Quite the contrary she was sharp minded, frugal with most things, opinionated, quick to judge, stern woman. If she were cross with you, she would often quickly let you know, and very plainly. She lived a healthy lifestyle, and always had a clear head. She loved her grandchildren, and liked to have them at the Scan Travel office to run errands.

The American Mail ship **Java Mail,** *a C2.*
Puget Sound Maritime Historical Society

The Sea-Land Service ship **Anchorage,** *a C4.*   Puget Sound Maritime Historical Society

By contrast, Charlie was a belly-laughing, rollicking sailor, and could be the life of the party—he was larger than life, but his moral compass was called into question from time to time. He drank a lot, especially at parties—and there were lots of parties. For example, one time when in a social setting he was talking about travels in the far east, with his wife present, he paused, waxed poetic, and with a glassy twinkle in his eye, reflected "I've never seen so many beautiful women in one place, at one time, as in Shanghai…" Willie was often not pleased with him. In later years she thought of him as a slob. You could even say she hammered him often "—CHARLES ?!," in the tone of "what *are* you doing Charles?" She had been attracted to him because he was the "bad boy," but now it wasn't as much fun anymore. In a later generation they might have even been divorced. They always did things together, however, until the end. Charlie always respected his wife. He had vices, but he also had a heart, and a capacity to love, and be sympathetic of people's feelings.

He had character. This was no base, foul-mouthed sailor. He could correct your grammar, "that's whom, not who." If he really loathed

someone, the worst epitaph that he would put on them was "shit-bum." You were really, really bad if you were a shit-bum. But mostly if he were dressing someone down it would be with formal language, and loathsome tone of voice. He could always put on a formal demeanor when the occasion called for it.

He could also have a voracious temper on rare occasions. And at that point—the argument was always over. One time when asking his son Rusty for help on something, Rusty refused. Charlie lost his temper, and with a furious boom, he exclaimed "IF *YOU* WANT SOMETHING, IT'S A HORSE OF A DIFFERENT COLOR— ISN'T IT!!!" All Rusty could do was walk away. That's about as foul of language you'd ever hear—around family, at least.

The End of an Era

In July 1969 Charlie was back at sea, working for Sea-Land again, on a C4 that had been converted to a container ship, the *S.S. Philadelphia.* He was Chief Engineer now and would remain so the rest of his career.

S.S. Rose City *on the Duwamish.*   Puget Sound Maritime Historical Society

July 29 to November 2, 1969 Charlie took part in the shipyard overhaul and conversion of the *Anchorage* to the *Rose City*. This was done at Todd Shipyards in Seattle. The shipyard sea trial report states that the "S.S. Rose City – C4-M3/J1 – is the result of a conversion by Todd Shipyards Corporation of the former C4-S-B2 'Anchorage' to a jumboized container ship by severing and joining the C4 stern to a newly constructed 'J1' forebody." The *Rose City* would be 695' in length, 78' beam, with a 30' draft, and capable of holding 622 containers, 64 of them refrigerated. She had 9,000 shaft horsepower. After the *Rose City* put to sea, Charlie sailed on her in and out of San Francisco through April 1970. At that time he shipped out on the old C2 *S.S. Warrior,* then back on the *Philadelphia*, making coastwise trips on the west coast.

In the mid-seventies, Charlie gave up the sea for good. From the summer of 1971 Charlie had been working on the *S.S. Warrior* making coastwise trips up and down the east coast, New York to Jacksonville, Florida. On March 9, 1974, the *Warrior* set out on a foreign trip.

Charlie could be a bit of a hot head once in a while. He is known to have had a ferocious temper occasionally. His last voyage turned out to be an example of this. He was on the *Warrior* in the middle of the Atlantic Ocean, anchored at Hort in the Azores. He got into an argument with the captain. Charlie wouldn't budge; and as he was of retirement age he told the captain what he could do—and took to shore in one of the boats never to come back. This is how Charlie himself told the story. His discharge book documents his leaving the ship at Hort, March 18, 1974, the last entry of his sea career.

Following Charlie's sea going career, he obtained a state boiler inspector license. He was awarded state boiler inspector commission 4369-W in April 1974 and worked as a boiler and machinery inspector for the Chubb insurance company. Charlie liked to take his grandson along when he went all over Seattle inspecting boilers in various buildings around town, and telling little Chris sea stories. Charlie got his grandson into the engine rooms of a few old ships, like the old *Princess Marguerite*. Charlie was a President of the Washington State branch of the National Boiler Inspectors Association. Charlie worked as an insurance inspector pretty

*The Canadian **Princess Marguerite** at Victoria, British Columbia. She was the last of the old Pacific Northwest steamships on a regularly scheduled service. She spent her final days on the Victoria to Seattle run.*

much for the fun of it. His other retirement job was managing several real estate holdings over west and south Seattle, including an apartment building on California Ave in west Seattle.

Charlie worked for Chubb a few years until he got cancer in 1978. His cancer was attributed in large part to his career long exposure to the asbestos in the engine rooms, which was used as insulation on the myriad steam pipes and etc. Mesothelioma as a result of working on the old steamships would become a huge issue. He died a month before his fifty-ninth birthday, April 19, 1979. After Charlie was cremated, his ashes were spread over the ocean in sailors' tradition.

In the 1970s the age of the steamship was passing. Diesel engine powered "motor-ships" were taking over the tanker and container ship fleets. The Maritime Commission ships like the venerable C2s and C3s built in the 40s were being broken up, one by one. By 1980 the C4's began to go the same way. These ships were broken up in foreign shipyards—to skirt the mesothelioma issue?

As Charlie's career was ending, so to was the entire American Merchant Marine. The passenger ships were long gone, and the container ships and tankers were moving overseas. It was the end of an era. The passing of the Merchant Marine was in part eclipsed by the meteoric rise of the airlines, and the fact that ships were still coming in and out of the harbors, albeit in fewer and fewer numbers. But the ships were being registered in foreign ports, and had foreign crews. The very thing the Maritime Commission and Joseph Kennedy in 1936 had sought to prevent.

In the 1970s, Charlie's job paid wages that an airline pilot would have compared *his* too, and Charlie only had to go to sea six months of the year.

The Alaska Steamship Company, long since hauling freight only, and having its Liberty ships converted to accommodate the latest method of containerization, gave up the ghost in 1971. As Alaska Steam closed its doors for good, after almost 80 years, the main reason given was the continual union demands and union standards.

After Alaska Steam folded up…the company that Charlie's father Ben had worked for—the company that had been such a part of the Seattle waterfront in the twentieth century—Charlie had begun to ponder on the subject of unions. He had been a staunch union supporter all his life, worked for the union—had he been wrong?

Charlie sat with his grandson in his west Seattle home, downstairs in his Rattan bedecked recreation room with the solid Mahogany bar, bamboo basket weave wallpaper bordered with heavy rope giving it a nautical flair, and otherwise decorated with the loot of a myriad of South Sea voyages. Charlie's grandson revered him…wanted to be just like him…wanted to be a marine engineer. Charlie looked at his grandson…waxed poignant and introspective, and with the sting of union misconduct still fresh in mind, wondered aloud if he had been wrong about the socialization of the Merchant Marine and the unions.

Today the American President Line, the big ticket San Francisco based, Pacific Ocean serving American operator in 1940, which had reacquired the American Mail Line in 1954, is still a large and viable company. Today it goes by the moniker of APL and is owned by an Asian firm based out of Singapore. Sea-Land was absorbed by Maersk of Copenhagen, Denmark.

America used to build a lot of ships, and that is gone also. During WWII when America decided to cut the crap and put a real effort into it for a few years, American shipyards built over 2700 Liberty ships. They were manned by capable and well-trained American sailors like Charles Parker. This was considered to be one of the primary reasons why we won the war. On top of that, the American yards churned out over five hundred Victory ships, and a combined total of nearly two thousand C1s, C2s, C3s, C4s and T2s. Long addicted to government contracts, the few remaining shipyards today idle along on life support. The rumor in the ship repair business is that the government won't "let" them go out of business. That is the current state of affairs there, a sad commentary.

It was charged by some that the sea-going unions had priced themselves out of existence. Others might say they were too inflexible. Of course others like to blame the corporations, and

naturally the government weighs in as well. In any event, the net result was that a lot of American jobs went overseas.

This would have been bad enough if it was in fact the first time this had happened, but, as it were, it was not. America had grown a large and prosperous Merchant Marine by the decades preceding the American Civil War. This was in the age of sail, and it was the American Clipper Ships that figured so prominently, the American sailor being among the finest in the world in that era. The American Merchant Marine had achieved this by enterprise, daring, and grit—and little else. By contrast, the governments of Europe sought to help their merchant marines' by subsidies, politics and military interventions.

Britain gained the early upper hand in the new steamship trade, and subsidized the Cunard Line. America tried to do the same. This created imbalance and corporations that were doomed to fail. Referring to the fledgling American steamship lines in the era just before the American Civil War, John Spears wrote in his *Story of the American Merchant Marine* (1910): "It is fact beyond dispute that subsidies to a few favored lines greatly injured all other shipping trading to the same ports" and "In the United States the paying of subsidies to the few lines simply killed private enterprise on the North Atlantic."

The Civil War proved ruinous to the American Merchant Marine, and Britain took advantage to gain a firm upper hand with iron steamships utilizing the more efficient screw propeller. Americans stuck to their sail ships, and lost the Atlantic trade to the Europeans for the rest of the nineteenth century.

In WWI America formed the Emergency Fleet Corporation, and again tried to form a Merchant Marine, a government Merchant Marine. But, along came Robert Dollar who made good with private enterprise, which worked well throughout the 1920s. Then, we have socialism of the Merchant Marine in the 1930s along with Roosevelt's takeover of the nation's largest steamship line. By the end of the twentieth century we had almost no Merchant Marine. Perhaps we are slow learners.

The Legacy

The Age of the Steamship is Gone, and the Age of Aviation Upon Us.

The age of the passenger steamer is gone. The airliner has taken its place. Instead of the Alaska Steamship Company, we have Alaska Airlines taking passengers and freight to and from Alaska. A cruise liner is nothing more than a resort hotel. The giant oil tankers are still with us, and the container ships, but most have foreign crews. There is no longer the American fleet of the mid twentieth century. There is a giant American airline industry, however. And this is the direction that Christian Parker, great-grandson of both Benjamin Poole Parker and Adolf Nils Loken was to take.

The airplanes are not as romantic as the steamships; gone are the leisurely voyages up and down the coast, snug in your cabin, and your evening meal in the dining salon. But, now we get there quick in our bus that plies the skies. These days we just want to get there as soon as possible for the most part.

The Richard D. Kuyuper Airborne Observatory. A survey vessel of the late twentieth century. It flew high and took pictures of the stars. Chris did regular maintenance to the engines on this jet when he was in the service. NASA photo

Young Christian wanted to be just like his grandfather and become a Marine Engineer. He wanted to go to the Marine Engineer school run by the union. But young Chris decided to become a dad at an early age and plans changed. He joined the Air Force as a jet engine mechanic, thinking that for some reason all ships would some day be gas turbine powered. Well, Chris was obviously wrong, but American shipping was dying anyway.

Instead of the romance of the sea, Chris looked to the skies. Aviation was to be his calling. Aviation is, after all, the successor to the maritime world of the past. And just as his grandfathers were into the nuts-and-bolts side of steamships, Chris was into the nuts-and-bolts side of airplanes.

Surprising as it may seem to some, there are quite a few similarities between ships and airplanes. For one thing, some airlines refer to their aircraft as "ships," such as Southwest Airlines, which would refer to one of its aircraft in internal documents as "ship N342SW." Most refer to their airframes as "hulls." The way aircraft airframes are built is much like that of the hulls of wooden sailing ships, or the early riveted iron ships, only done with aluminum sheet metal. The way passengers and freight are processed on airline flights is much the same as in the steamship line and railroad days. Both use turbines in their engines, the airplane with the gas turbine and the ship with the steam turbine. Large aircraft used to have "Engineers"

that flew with them but they have been pretty much eliminated by computers, and the people who would be engine room crew stay on the ground in the airline world. In the United States aircraft maintenance people were called Airframe and Powerplant Mechanics, and are now called Aircraft Maintenance Technicians, but in European countries, Canada, and Australia, they are known as Aircraft Maintenance Engineers, or AME's.

The airline world enjoyed its heyday in the 1950s & 60s. It was ultra cool to work for an airline, and the pay was great. Then came the 70s and the gas crunch and the Carter administration. In the 80s, airline deregulation tried to prevent the cycle of what had happened to the shipping industry. But it was going to be a long road to hoe.

Christian's government service in the 1980s was in the U.S. Air Force. While in the service Chris got to work on the Richard D. Kuyuper Aerial Observatory, an airborne research vessel, predecessor to the Hubble Space Telescope.

Unfortunately coinciding with airline deregulation, at the close of the Cold War, and after Desert Storm, the military "laid off" a lot of its skilled technical workers, creating a glut in the market in the early 1990s. This was coupled with a recession that affected the airlines greatly.

After the Air Force, Chris worked for a year as an airline "longshoreman" in an air-freight warehouse at Sea-Tac international airport.

The way this works at the air "port," is that there is a warehouse adjacent to the parking ramp, right off a taxi way. The situation is a throwback to the old steamship port days. Cargo is bulk loaded, just as in the old days. Pallets with various commodities stacked on them and tied down with nets are carefully loaded into the cargo airliners. Just like in an old movie involving New York longshoremen, the boss of the freight house where Chris worked was a screaming Prima Dona. The forklifts scurried around the warehouse at a furious pace, often tilting over on two wheels in no-holds-barred bravado. It was a hive of activity. Young men actually like these circumstances.

Ironically, the freight is delivered to the warehouse by truck, which is often a 40′ shipping container, which is then unloaded, and the freight built up into a pallet package to be loaded onto an aircraft. Seems like the airline freight world needs to catch up. There are, however, "cans" which are mini containers used in air freight. But the system relies on a lot of secondary loading and unloading. Unlike the maritime longshoremen, whose unions had garnered them huge wages, the aviation air freight jobs hover closer to the minimum wage threshold.

Chris went from making a dollar an hour more than minimum wage in the freight warehouse, to two dollars an hour more than minimum wage as an aircraft mechanic at BfGoodrich Aerospace, MRO division, in 1994. Goodrich was a third-party independent aircraft maintenance provider, a product of airline deregulation.

Not counting a brief stint at United Airlines, Chris worked at BfGoodrich Aerospace, later Goodrich Aviation Technical Services, for twelve years, the majority of which was ultimately spent on the Southwest B737 unit. He spent most of these years performing heavy D checks to Boeing 737-200 and 737-300/500 aircraft as Flight Control Master Mechanic. The details of this can be found in *The Care and Maintenance of Heavy Jets,* also by the author. Though Chris started at a low wage, his pay tripled over the following twelve years. This was entirely due to market forces, as no union was ever present. In addition to work performance and advancement, the increases followed the market, strong when business was good and demand for mechanic labor was high, slow when business wasn't.

In August of 2007 Chris took a flightline position with Boeing to work on the new 787 Dreamliner. This struggling-to-get-off-the-ground program was to prove to be the frustration of a lifetime, and inspired Chris to write the book *The Care and Maintenance of Heavy Jets.* The book was a plea to the U.S. aviation industry to shape up, or suffer the fate of the U.S. Maritime industry.

During the downhill slide of the American Merchant Marine occurring in the decades following World War II through to the 1980s,

the congress of the United States was controlled by Democrats, like the Kennedy's, and the AFL-CIO unions were all-powerful. If they did not cause the demise, they surely did not prevent it from occurring, either.

True, passenger steamship traffic died off in the 1950s due to the rise of air travel, but the airplane doesn't explain the loss of the container shipping and the tankers.

As America slips ever more into socialism, one industry after another is rendered unable to compete on the world stage, all in the name of "fairness" and "decent job conditions" as defined by the left, who, incidentally, embrace illegal alien labor. Socialism acts as a cancer that slowly kills its host. When there is no job, however, conditions are the least tolerable—according to many.

When the heads of corporations lie and cheat, and labor organizations lie and cheat, guess what? We both lose, especially if the government takes over the whole mess. The answer has to lie somewhere in our American roots, the values of the founding fathers.

At present, the traditional model of the large corporate structure working with an AFL-CIO type union does not work well.

Conversely, a traditional large corporate structure working without a union does not work especially well either. The large corporation without a union tends toward the baser nature, tends toward the nature of an uncaring monarch.

The answer must lie somewhere in between, or, somewhere "outside" of that box. The answer must lie in creating free markets at the labor level, governed by democratic bodies like the chamber of commerce of a town. This was early America. In *The Story of the American Merchant Marine,* Spears gives examples of how this even worked on sailing merchant ships, and resulted in an American Merchant Marine that was second to none at one time.

The proposed solution here alluded to is presented in *The Care and Maintenance of Heavy Jets.*

Will the fate of the U.S. aviation industry be similar to that of the U.S. Merchant Marine?

Bibliography

Armbuster, Kurt E. *Orphan Road* Pullman, Washington: Washington State University Press, 1999.

Best, Gerald M. *Ships and Narrow Gauge Rails* Berkeley, California: Howell-North Books, 1964.

Bixby, William. *Track of the Bear* New York: David McKay Company, Inc., 1965.

Canney, Donald L. *U.S. Coast Guard and Revenue Cutters, 1790-1935* Annapolis, Maryland: Naval Institute Press, 1995.

Eells, Rev. Myron. *The Twana, Chemakum, and Klallam Indians of Washington Territory* Washington, District of Columbia: Smithsonian Institution, 1889.

Hawkins, N. *Maxims and Instructions for The Boiler Room* New York, New York: Theo, Audel & Co., Publishers, 1902.

Hawkins, N. *New Catechism of The Steam Engine* New York, New York: Theo, Audel & Co., Publishers, 1903.

Haugland, Marylou McMahon. *A History of Alaska Steamship Company* Seattle, Washington: University of Washington Press, 1968.

Hines, J.S. *Pacific Marine Review* San Francisco, California: 1918.

Howden, J. R. *The Boys' Book of Steamships* New York, New York: Frederick A. Stokes Company, Publishers, 1911.

McDonald, Lucile Saunders. *Alaska Steam: a pictorial history of the Alaska Steamship Company* Anchorage, Alaska: Alaska Geographic Society, 1984.

Newell, Gordon. *Pacific Coastal Liners* Seattle, Washington: The Superior Publishing Company, 1959.

Newell, Gordon. *Pacific Lumber Ships* Seattle, Washington: The Superior Publishing Company, 1960.

Newell, Gordon. *The H.W. McCurdy Marine History of the Pacific Northwest* Seattle, Washington: The Superior Publishing Company, 1966.

Osbourne, Alan. *Modern Marine Engineer's Manual* New York, New York: Cornell Maritime Press, 1941.

Parker, Rev. Theodore. *Genealogy and Biographical notes of John Parker of Lexington* Worcester, Massachusetts: Press of Charles Hamilton, 1893.

Sale, Roger. *Seattle, Past to Present* Seattle, Washington: University of Washington Press, 1976.

Spears, John R. *The Story of the American Merchant Marine* New York, New York: The MacMillan Company, 1910.

Strobridge, Truman R. and Noble, Dennis L. *Alaska and the U.S. Revenue Cutter Service 1867-1915* Annapolis, Maryland: Naval Institute Press, 1999.

Talbot, Frederick A. *Steamship Conquest of the World* Philadelphia, Pennsylvania: J.B. Lippincott Company, 1913.

Tate, E. Mowbray. *Transpacific Steam* Cranbury, New Jersey: Rosemount Publishing and Printing Corporation, 1986.

U.S. Department of Commerce. Coast and Geodetic Survey. *Annual Report of the Superintendent of the Coast and Geodetic Survey.* Washington, DC. Government Printing Office, 1908-1932.

Waterhouse, Frank. *Pacific Ports Annual* Seattle, Washington: Pacific Ports, Inc., 1919.

Index